A TRAILS BO

HISTORICAL WISCONSIN GETAWAYS

TOURING THE BADGER STATE'S PAST

SHARYN ALDEN

Trails Books
Black Earth, Wisconsin

Library of Congress Catalog Card Number: 2001088634
ISBN: 0-915024-93-4

Editor: Stan Stoga
Cover Design: John Huston
Cover Photo: Larry Michael
Design: Kathie Campbell
Production: Heather Larson and Carol Lynn Benoit

Printed in the United States of America.

06 05 04 03 02 01   6 5 4 3 2 1

Trails Books, a division of Trails Media Group, Inc.
P.O. Box 317 • Black Earth, WI 53515
(800) 236-8088 • e-mail: info@wistrails.com
www.trailsbooks.com

Lake Superior

MINNESOTA

Duluth
Bayfield
Superior ➓
Ashland ②

MICHIGAN

④⑤ 45   41

Hayward 53

51

➌

Eagle River

2

Rhinelander

Washington
Island

41

WISCONSIN

8

Hudson   Chippewa
          Falls

Marinette

Eau Claire

Wausau

Sturgeon Bay

Pepin

45   ➒

❶

Alma

Stevens Point

Green Bay

❸

41

90

Tomah

39

Oshkosh

Manitowoc

La Crosse

Fond du Lac

❷

Sheboygan

Viroqua

Kohler

43

❹   61

Baraboo

Wisconsin Dells

IOWA

151   41

Cedarburg

Spring Green

❽

❶❷ ❶❶

Prairie du Chien

Dodgeville

❻

Madison   94

Milwaukee

Cassville

Mineral Point
Platteville   Janesville
              New Glarus

Eagle

❼

Racine

43   94

Dubuque

Lake Geneva

Kenosha

ILLINOIS

90

Chicago

Michigan

Lake Michigan

A driver behind the wheel of his Wisconsin-made Kissel around 1910.

CONTENTS

Zulime Garland, the wife of Wisconsin novelist Hamlin Garland, shares a picture album with her daughters.

INTRODUCTION

I N TRAVELING THE LENGTH and breath of Wisconsin visiting locations for this book, I came to realize that historical travel is more than museums and monuments and mausoleums. It's easy to take for granted or forget a building, statute, or artifact, but it's harder to ignore the people whose memory these objects conjure up and who were once so closely connected with them. And it's particularly hard to avoid thinking about the living people one has encountered on such historically related trips.

This book was designed not only to retrace the history of 13 distinct areas of the state, it was also put together as a collection of stories about people from the past, as well as a few touching and terrific stories from those who are currently stewards of historical destinations. I've met many of those people in my journeys, and I've shared some of their historical insights in this book.

Experience has told me historical buildings may not impress the folks back home, but people you've met along the way, or people "you've met from the past," may give you additional memories to lean on.

That's why this book was created, to guide you to some of Wisconsin's most interesting historical treasures, along with some of the personal histories of those who helped shape the state.

Historical Wisconsin Getaways was not written with the intent of including all of the state's historical spots. To do justice to every part of the state which is historically interesting, would take many years of research. I have tried to include as many of the state's most popular and well-known historical areas, as possible. I've also included some of its lesser known treasures and artifacts. If I've inadvertently left out your favorite historical stopping point, I hope you'll use this book to find new places to discover.

This book is intended for those of you, like me, who are curious travelers and naturally gravitate to historical inns, restaurants, museums, and lodges.

When you head to a new destination, do you ache to uncover its real identity, to peer into its past and find out who, how, and why the community was settled long ago? If you're a traveler who loves to know more about the history of a city or destination, the stories that were part of the landscape long before Interstate highways, neon signs and fast food chains came along and altered the landscape, then this book is for you.

Before I began my year and a half combing the state in pursuit of some of Wisconsin's most intriguing historical spots that would make wonderful weekend destinations, I knew that the task would be daunting. After all, Wisconsin has a rich historical legacy that it takes pride in and keeps alive; the state is fortunate to have numerous resources at hand for preserving its past, both on a statewide and local level. I also knew that the past, at least for Wisconsinites, means more than museums and reenactments and historical markers.

But I was pleasantly surprised to find that other places not generally thought of as being "historic" have fascinating stories to tell about their past. Some of Wisconsin's most interesting inns and lodges are a case in point. The American Club, a resort known primarily for its elegant appointments and world-class golf, has a rich history that is well documented and preserved. The main building, for example, once served as the rooming house for Kohler Company employees. Today's guests are served elegant meals in a room that 100 years ago was the main dining hall for the company's immigrant laborers.

You may know that Spider Lake Lodge near Hayward is an old fishing lodge, but you may not know that it was built by Al Capone's auto mechanic, with the help of a local Indian craftsman, from the area's enormous pines. In its heyday as a fishing resort, in the 1920s and 1930s, big bands played in the dining room, and well-heeled travelers from Chicago often stayed for weeks on end.

Chances are you won't hear this and dozens of other tales about Spider Lake Lodge, unless you're offered verbal history by one of the owners, or you happen upon the wonderful scrapbooks in the dining room documenting the lodge's distinctive past as one of the North Woods' great fishing camps.

There are other places, like the Victorian, Scandinavian-flavored, Harbor House Inn, in Gills Rock, in Door County, that are so connected to the commercial fishing history at the tip of the peninsula, it's well worth your time to seek out owners David and Else Weborg. I'm sure they'll fill you in on the area's rich and vibrant past, and the Weborg family's century-long role in shaping its history.

Historical Wisconsin Getaways should be used as a starting point on your excursions, but you'll learn much more about these historical areas by talking to the local "keepers of the keys." These are people who not only have firsthand knowledge of key events of the past but also the individuals who preserve and foster Wisconsin's rich history. These are the folks who will make your journeys throughout the state more rewarding and enjoyable. I want to thank my family, Siri, Nissa, and Sim for their patience and understanding when I was writing or exploring, and didn't have as many hours in the day as I would like. I also want to thank Bob Granflatten at the Wisconsin State Historical Society for providing interesting historical information and photos about some of Wisconsin's unique destinations.

CHAPTER 1

DOOR COUNTY

TOURIST MECCA WITH A SENSE OF HISTORY

Pat Bonner, on Beaver Island, with the Eclipse thresher that his father purchased in the 1870s.

DOOR COUNTY, more than anything else, is evocative. It calls forth former lives, imagined and real, and it does this in a most benign way: by having more pleasant, century-old architecture than just about anywhere in Wisconsin. Is that Jay Gatsby there on the sweeping porch of a lakeside Victorian? If it isn't, perhaps it should be.

While the old public and retail buildings provide a sense of history, visitors who admire quaint architecture can find it in most any of Door County's residential districts. Admittedly, homes and resorts have continued to be built down through the years, giving rise to the notion that urban sprawl is taking over the landscape. But visitors looking for a tranquil past will be relieved to know that there are no franchised eateries north of Sturgeon Bay (which has a McDonald's), and there aren't many tract houses. The results are structures with a 19th- or early 20th-century craftsperson's idea of what looked good in wood.

First-time visitors are surprised by the county's remoteness. Some 230 miles north of Chicago and 330 miles east of the Twin Cities, the pinky-shaped peninsula juts far into Lake Michigan, less than an hour northeast of the city of Green Bay. The year-round destination deserves the attention of a three-day weekend, at the very least.

Once there, seeing much of the Midwest's answer to Cape Cod is a breeze:

Highway 42 services the picturesque, touristy villages on the west, or bay, side of the peninsula, while Highway 57 connects towns on the quieter east, or lake, side. The highways travel together north out of Sturgeon Bay, the county seat, then quickly separate, allowing visitors to decide whether to take in Door history in clockwise or counterclockwise fashion. (This chapter assumes travelers will drive the peninsula clockwise, returning to Sturgeon Bay on the lake or "quiet" side of the peninsula.)

Speaking of history, travelers approaching Door County from the south will retrace the route of the area's major ethnic groups. In the 19th and early 20th centuries, immigrants of Belgian, Icelandic, Norwegian, Pomeranian German, and Swedish heritage, among others, arrived in Chicago and Milwaukee before making the overland journey north, where land was not only available but amenable to growing crops ranging from corn and hay to apples and cherries. Come to think of it, visitors today driving in from the west may be retracing a path taken by Door County's very first residents.

EARLY DOOR DWELLERS

This area must have been livable for quite some time—Menominee Indians, the state's oldest residents, drifted in from the north and west more than 10,000 years ago. Unlike today's travelers, who concentrate on the peninsula, the Menominee were most attracted to Green Bay, which separates the west shore of Door County from the mainland. The bay was thick with fish and the waters were warmer and much easier to traverse than potentially stormy Lake Michigan. Besides rich catches of grayling, pike, sturgeon, and more, the Menominee harvested wild rice from the shores of several local streams. It is believed that the Menominee were named "people of the wild rice" for their dependency on it.

The first European to navigate Lake Michigan in the vicinity of what is now Door County was Jean Nicolet. The hardy Frenchman came in search of the Northwest Passage to Asia and took note of the richness of the area, particularly of the furs worn by the Menominee. French fur traders showed up twenty years later, and so did Roman Catholic missionaries. The Menominee were served by a mission as early as 1672.

Then the English came and the French departed, with a fort on Green Bay coming into British hands in 1761. The Menominee would remain the area's primary residents for 75 more years, until the creation of the Wisconsin Territory in 1836, a signal that the area was ripe for settlement by people looking for new opportunities. By 1848, the year Wisconsin became a state, political unrest was sweeping across Europe and the notion was growing that much of the good, cheap land in the eastern U.S. was being swallowed up. European immigrants began to flock to Wisconsin and the Door area. It's no surprise that many of Door's new residents were Scandinavian, attracted by the climate and geography that resembled their native land.

Apple-picking in Door County.

ORCHARDS ON THE GROW, SHIPPING ON THE RISE

At about the same time, in 1858, Joseph Zettel established the first commercial orchard on the peninsula. Of Swiss descent, Zettel found a favorable growing climate that produced good yields. His effort took place just north of where Highways 42 and 57 split. The first commercial red cherry crop was harvested in 1896. Soon, the county enjoyed a national reputation for the quality and quantity of its fruit. The University of Wisconsin has operated a research station here since 1922 in order to aid fruit growers.

Central and northern Door reminded folks of Norway or Sweden, Sturgeon Bay took on the bustle of both an agricultural center and a port, and southern Door became a replica of the Belgian countryside. That changed abruptly in 1871 when a torrid fire swept much of southern Door, destroying European-style farms and villages and killing 150 people.

Simultaneously, bigger and bigger boats were plying the Great Lakes. Initially, they carried Wisconsin timber east and returned with all sorts of manufactured goods. From 1885, lumber had to compete with iron ore for passage east and south on steamers. Some of these boats were constructed in Sturgeon Bay, where a 6,600-foot ship canal connected the bay and the lake beginning in 1891.

Lake traffic made for big changes in Door County. Lighthouses were built, many of them intended for steering ships safely through Porte des Morts (Door of Death), the treacherous, storm-tossed route separating Green Bay and Lake Michigan. Shipwrecks line the bottom around Washington Island to this day, making for fascinating underwater exploration. Some come from a fishing industry that employed many northern Door County residents in the early part of the last century.

Today, orchards are much more in evidence than is the fishing business. Wisconsin ranks fifth in the production of tart cherries, with almost all of them grown in Door County. Some 15 million pounds of cherries are produced here. There is meaningful farming and industry, too. But tourism has provided the sense of well-being that took hold in the 20th century and looks to remain important in the future.

Door County boasts of 250-plus miles of coastline—more miles than any other county in the country. It has 10 mostly well-preserved lighthouses, also a U.S. county record, and a trio of large shipbuilders. Such romantic stuff, together with the sense that the place is a refuge, has lured writers and artists, many of whom hole up and create in the peace and quiet.

A WEEKEND IN HISTORIC DOOR

With its profusion of historic inns, museums, and primarily Scandinavian heritage, Door County is a great place to spend a weekend. There's plenty to see and do for all ages and budgets. For those who want to immerse themselves in a historical getaway, the peninsula has historic bed-and-breakfast inns, museums, and antique shops.

History buffs who are crunched for time should consider visiting the middle portion of the county, consisting of Sturgeon Bay, Egg Harbor, and Fish Creek, all on Highway 42. Those who want to explore the northern tip of the peninsula should allow an hour's drive from Sturgeon Bay to the tiny village of Gills Rock. The midpoint between Sturgeon Bay and Gills Rock is Sister Bay, where Highways 42 and 57 rejoin. Southern Door County, south of Sturgeon Bay, is overwhelmingly devoted to orchards and dairy farming, with a proliferation of campsites on the bay side.

No matter where people visit in Door County, they're only a few minutes' drive from great views of scenes that people have been enjoying for years. Following either 42 or 57, wanderers may see old stone fences, wooded islands offshore, century-old barns, cherry orchards, meadows painted with wildflow-

A well-worn Door County commercial fishing boat lying at anchor.

ers and, occasionally, at water's edge, large wooden crosses. The latter are remnants of the explorations of La Salle, Nicolet, and Joliet.

History buffs—and just about everyone else visiting Door County, for that matter—need to make lodging reservations, especially in the summer. Most inns, lodges, motels, and cottages require a minimum two-night stay on summer weekends and often through the annual Fall Festival in early October. For help in finding accommodations, contact the Door County Chamber of Commerce at (920) 743-4456, or visit the official Web site at doorcountyvacations.com.

STURGEON BAY

A logical and logistically correct place to begin your historical weekend is in Sturgeon Bay, the Door County seat and a busy city of about 9,500 residents. Just 45 miles northeast of Green Bay, the town has its own brand of charm but offers many big-city conveniences. Sturgeon Bay's strategic location at the base of the peninsula, an hour east of Green Bay, has earned a reputation as being "the friendliest small town in Wisconsin" by readers of Wisconsin Trails magazine.

Halfway up the peninsula, between Green Bay on the north and Lake Michigan on the south, and well within the safe confines of the bay, the town was destined to prosper when it was founded in 1835. This destiny was fulfilled in the 1850s after the opening of the canal linking the lake and the bay. An abundance of local oak led to the growth of shipbuilding and repairs. Today, the city still is home to a thriving shipbuilding industry, which continues to produce some of the finest vessels in the country.

Shipbuilding has been important to the local economy since the mid-19th century. The Sturgeon Bay shipyards built its first ship in the mid-1850s. By 1900, shipbuilding was big business. By World War I, Bay Shipbuilding was the largest operation of its kind, churning out tugboats used in the war.

For a fascinating insight into this industry, a mix of science, craftsmanship, and art, wander down to the shipbuilding docks to peer into the world of Peterson Builders, Inc., Bay Shipbuilding, or the Palmer Johnson operation.

For many, Door County begins in Sturgeon Bay; for others it's a place they pass to get to where the "real Door County," the one with the charming water's-edge villages, begins. Visitors who spend time in the city will want to stroll Third Avenue in the downtown area to take in the restored and/or very well maintained old retail buildings. They evoke an era when steam-powered boats and horse-powered wagons were the chief conveyances for large numbers of people. You can begin your historical tour of Sturgeon Bay by visiting its fine museums, which will give you a broad introduction to the Door's rich history. If you want to step back into bygone days on a more intimate basis, there are also a number of old mansions and inns, now transformed into bed-and-breakfast inns and lodges, where you spend a night surrounded by the luxuries of the past, as well as by the most modern conveniences.

The Door County Maritime Museum, 120 N. Madison Avenue, (920) 743-5958, is devoted to shipbuilding history starting in the early part of the 20th century. Visitors who appreciate precision and authenticity in miniature will enjoy the many model ships on display, plus the chance to operate a real submarine periscope. Similar to its sister museum in Gills Rock, but each museum highlights nautical history in different parts of the peninsula. Gift shop. Open year round, seven days of the week (hours fluctuate by season).

The Door County Historical Museum, 18 N. 4th Avenue, (920) 743-5809, was named the "best small museum in the Midwest" by the Chicago Tribune. The museum features area heritage. Old photos of cherry picking and processing are particularly fascinating, as is the visitor's ability to walk through a historic Sturgeon Bay cityscape. Look, too, for a pioneer-era firehouse and displays of local wildlife. Kids and adults alike will enjoy themselves here. Open early May through late October; small donation is recommended.

For a change of pace, you may want to visit the Door Peninsula Winery, a few miles north of Sturgeon Bay in Carlsville. The winery is housed in a historic old school. There are tours of the cool cellars and free wine tasting. Call (920) 743-7431 or (800) 551-5049.

LODGING

The Barbican, 132 N. Second Avenue, (920) 743-4854. The sumptuous setting includes arbors and a garden along the historic waterfront area. Three homes with connecting walks. Fireplaces, whirlpools, many amenities, lots of romantic touches.

The Black Walnut Guest House, 454 N. 7th Avenue, (920) 743-8892, also could be called the house of nine gables. This charming 1899 guest house makes a delightful refuge.

The Chanticleer Guest House, 4072 Cherry Road, (920) 746-0334. On 70 acres, the 1915 house and barn have been revamped to include amenities such as fireplaces, refrigerators, and double whirlpools. Eight special suites and two cabins.

Colonial Gardens Bed & Breakfast, 344 N. 3rd Avenue, (920) 746-9192. This white-pillared, 1877 colonial features five bedrooms and views of the water. Each suite has its own private entrance, fireplace, and double whirlpool; a full breakfast is delivered to the room.

The Gray Goose Bed & Breakfast, 4258 Bay Shore Drive, (920) 743-9100. There are four guest rooms in this lovely landmark 1862 home, along with a large

Although the Door County fish boil would seem to have a long tradition, its modern version is a fairly recent development.

porch on which to stretch and relax after a scrumptious homemade breakfast.

The Inn at Cedar Crossing, 336 Louisiana Street, (920) 743-4200. Canopy beds, double whirlpools, fireplaces, and antiques fill each of the nine guest rooms in this historical in-town inn. Also known for the restaurant, which serves fine regional cuisine.

The Scofield House, 908 Michigan Street, (920) 743-7727 or toll-free, (888) 463-0204. Many publications have gushed about this three-story, turreted Victorian, which dates from 1902. The library has free movies, there's a fine gourmet breakfast, and those who can't get enough of antiques are in the right place.

This historic barn, south of Egg Harbor, houses the Cornerstone Suites inn and an antiques center.

White Lace Inn, 16 N. 5th Avenue, (920) 743-1105 or (877) 948-5223, with 18 rooms and suites, is in an older residential neighborhood. Featured in national magazines, this outstanding inn is comprised of four historic homes, connected by showy gardens. Canopy beds, fireplaces, fine linens, down comforters. Web site is www.whitelaceinn.com.

DINING

Door County Coffee & Tea, 5773 Highway 42, (920) 743-8930. Delicious early-morning fare and lunches, accompanied by more than 50 rich coffees, plus lattes, cappuccinos, and freshly baked pies and pastries. Open daily from about 9 a.m. to 5 p.m.

Inn at Cedar Crossing, 336 Louisiana Street, (920) 743-4249. Victorian atmosphere with fireside dining. Regional cuisine, lunch specials, superb desserts, and baked items. Open daily for breakfast, lunch, and dinner.

EGG HARBOR

The most asked question about Egg Harbor is—you guessed it—how the town acquired its name. The story goes that Pierce Roulette, a French fur trader, was sailing to Mackinac Island in 1825. Roulette ordered the crew to pull into one of the coves near what is now Egg Harbor for a lunch break. The fellows in the lead boat decided they wouldn't follow orders, so the crew of Roulette's boat retaliated by throwing eggs, provisions each of the boats happened to be carrying.

The town's natural harbor once was used by the Winnebago Indians, as well as traders and militia, who recognized the coves as natural stopping spots. These days, many visitors drive into this quaint village and are fascinated by the revitalized downtown and its ice cream-colored shops.

On a bluff overlooking the churning waters of Green Bay, Egg Harbor, 17 miles above Sturgeon Bay on Highway 42, is the first resortlike community on the bay side. It has long been linked with some of the best water views in Door County.

While in the area, you should plan a trip to the Birch Creek Music Performance Center, on County E three miles east of Egg Harbor, (920) 868-3763. It's a nationally renowned music academy featuring evening concerts (attention, big band fans) in a 100-year-old barn at Birch Creek. Performances usually are mid-June to late August.

LODGING

The Alpine Inn & Cottages, southwest of town along the bay, (920) 868-3000. This old inn has been going strong for several decades. Heated pool, private beach, 27-hole golf course.

Cornerstone Suites, south of Egg Harbor at 6960 Highway 42, (920) 868-3005 or (888) 495-3005, is one of the more unusual and enchanting places in which a visitor will ever stay. Travelers see this huge red barn and silo on the right side of the road as they travel north. Many stop for the collection of antiques on the first floor. But there are also suites (each has more than 1,000 feet

The Cupola House is a restored 1871 mansion in Egg Harbor that now is home to gift shops and boutiques.

of living space) available in this glorious 19th-century barn. The facility reminds some of the south of France.

DINING

Hof Restaurant, at the Alpine Inn, (920) 868-3000. Popular spot and lounge, features live entertainment in the summer.

Shipwrecked Restaurant, 7791 Egg Harbor, (920) 868-2767 or (888) 868-2767. Favorite spot in the midst of downtown. Hand-brewed beer, lunch and dinner specials. Open year-round.

Trio, 4655 County E, (920) 868-2090. Classic European country dishes with Mediterranean feel. Cassoulets, stews, pasta.

FISH CREEK

Visitors following Highway 42 north from Egg Harbor will wind around majestic limestone bluffs, then plummet 200 feet into the tiny village of Fish Creek. It's a brief but lovely drive—a mere six miles. Sure, Fish Creek is crowded with coffeehouses, art galleries, restaurants, and trendy shops. But this is also a hub of cultural activity and some historical significance.

The performing arts community is the soul of this picturesque coastal town. Look beyond the boutiques (The Whistling Swan is a favorite) and book seats early for the Peninsula Players, the oldest professional summer theater in America.

This venerable live theater, located south of Fish Creek on Highway 42, is a nice piece of 20th-century history. It has been presenting approximately five different productions each summer since 1935, making it a popular destination not only for playgoers but for actors and actresses as well.

Names like Harvey Korman, Stacy Keach, and Jean Sincere, are posted regularly on the marquee, as are less familiar names whose faces we've all seen on network dramas and sitcoms. Equally fun is the chance to pass a familiar person on the streets of the village and wonder if he or she will be taking center stage that same evening.

Productions down through the years have included "Wuthering Heights," "Harvey," "On Golden Pond," "Always, Patsy Kline," and "The Odd Couple." Among many character actors, look for 84-year-old Robert Thompson, who has been in at least one production here every year since 1938!

For more information, telephone (920) 868-3287, or head for the Web site, www.peninsulaplayers.com.

In 1854, Asa Thorp, Fish Creek's founder, built the first pier on Green Bay north of the city of Green Bay. By 1900, the village was a lumber and fishing center and a booming area that has become a resort center. Small wonder the place is such a rich source of historic architecture.

Fish Creek's oldest unchanged home is Noble House, constructed in 1875 where Main Street crosses Highway 42. The traditional, two-story frame home is on state and national historical registries and is open as part of a walking tour in warm-weather months. So are 20 other buildings. For a schedule, visit the Tourist Information Center, just north of Fish Creek Beach on the east side of Highway 42.

The Orchard Country Winery and Cider Mill south of Fish Creek.

To get an idea of what Door County was like one hundred years ago, stay a night and take in a fish boil at the White Gull Inn, a historic guest house often called one of Wisconsin's finest. Three blocks west of Highway 42, (920) 868-3517, the White Gull is the oldest inn on the peninsula (built in 1896). It is so popular in winter that many people reserve its renovated rooms months in advance. The inn brims with original antiques and is within walking distance of shops and the harbor.

No trip to Door County would be complete without a fish boil, and the White Gull has been offering one for years; it's one of the best on the peninsula. Outdoors, massive black cauldrons, atop flames reaching skyward, are used to cook a combination of fresh whitefish and potatoes. The meal, offered on Fridays as is the custom, is traditionally followed by cherry pie, filled with cherries from none other than Door County. The inn also offers a varied menu all week long, including fresh whitefish, shrimp-and-artichoke Romano, grilled lobster, and honey-glazed Atlantic salmon. Breakfast and lunch are also served. Web site is www.whitegullinn.com.

OTHER SITES AND ATTRACTIONS

Eagle Bluff Lighthouse. Built in 1868, the lighthouse is on the National Register of Historic Places. Once inside Peninsula State Park, stretching between Fish Creek and Ephraim, look for lighthouse directions in the park office. And the 3,400-acre park itself is most impressive, offering good cross-country skiing and on-the-ice views of frozen Green Bay. The land rises 180 feet above the lake at Eagle Bluff. Tubers and sledders take to the park's Hill 17 for sledding to their heart's content.

Peninsula Art School, 3906 County F, near Highway 42, (920) 868-3455. Not historical, but located in a wondrous and architecturally interesting building that, since 1999, has held year-round art classes. The building also houses the Paul Sills Community Theater, (920) 854-5072, that performs what is called "story theater" (winter only).

LODGING

Thorp House Inn and Cottages, 4135 Bluff Lane, (920) 868-2444. The inspiration for the romantic LaVyrle Spencer book Bittersweet, the inn and cottages are listed on the National Register of Historic Places. Cottages with fireplaces, five antique-filled guest rooms.

The Whistling Swan Inn, 4192 Main Street, (920) 868-3442. Unparalleled elegance in the heart of town. The structure was built in 1887 and transported across frozen Green Bay in 1907.

DINING

The Cookery, Highway 42 (Main Street), (920) 868-3634. This is where to go for a big menu and lots of value. Everything from pancakes to whitefish. A popular longtime landmark in the heart of town. Open for breakfast, lunch, and dinner from April through October, with limited winter hours.

EPHRAIM

Five miles north of Fish Creek on Highway 42, the road bends and Eagle Harbor in the town of Ephraim comes into splendid view. For a weekend getaway, Ephraim (a Biblical name meaning faithful) lets visitors absorb the heart and soul of the county.

History buffs will note that the charm of the landscape comes from whitewashed buildings resembling a Cape Cod village. The Moravians, who settled in the area in the mid-1800s, dictated that the village be whitewashed. While the decree has not always been followed, the tradition has stuck. Verticals break up the landscape as the road curves around the bay. Sailboat masts and the Moravian Church steeple come into view. The village has been around since 1853, and it's justifiably proud of its roots. A good place to absorb more flavor is the Anderson Dock and Museum.

Eagle Harbor, in the center of town, is a magnificent bay that is usually adorned with sailboat masts swaying in the wind. Other spires on the landscape include the steeple of the Moravian Church, built in 1857 and the oldest church in the county on the right, looking at the village from the harbor. The Bethany Lutheran Church spire is sharply visible on the left of this postcard scene.

The quaint Ephraim Village Hall.

Another must-see attraction is the Anderson Barn & Store, Highway 42, down the bluff, on the water's edge. Travelers in the 1800s headed to Door County by steamer and put in at the Anderson Dock. The area still has a lost-in-time feel about it. The store, put up in 1858 by Aslag Anderson, is one of the original Scandinavian buildings in the town. Now on the National Register of Historic Places, the site has memorabilia on display. The weathered barn next door is a photographer's delight. It was built in 1870 and restored in 1990.

For more information about the town, contact the Ephraim Information Center at (920) 854-4989.

LODGING

Eagle Harbor Inn, Highway 42, (920) 854-2121. Some say this is one of the best inns on the peninsula. The small, nine-room establishment brims with antiques and hospitality. One- or two-bedroom whirlpool suites feature two-way fireplaces, full kitchen, and private deck.

The Ephraim Inn, Highway 42, (920) 854-4515. The showy inn across from the main water sports area wraps itself around the setting in a white-washed horseshoe, sporting a belvedere tower at its center. The charming bed and breakfast has 16 rooms with canopy beds and private baths and is open during the warmer months.

The French Country Inn, 3052 Spruce Lane, a short walk from the village center, (920) 854-4001. Genteel, Old World atmosphere. This beautifully decorated 1911 summer home has been transformed into a bed and breakfast with garden views. The inn features seven summer guest rooms and four guest rooms in winter. If you visit in winter, ask about the winter special—the entire inn may be rented for your group.

The Hillside Hotel, Highway 42 (look for the white fence across from the harbor), (920) 854-2417. This is a bed and breakfast with strong historical roots. Originally built as a rooming house, the 12-room inn, featuring feath-erbeds and hearty breakfasts, also has two separate cottages. Among the most photographed and painted attractions in the village, this renovated 1890 inn provides the best harbor-watching in the area. Take a cup of tea and sit in one of the inn's rocking chairs on the one hundred-foot veranda. Inside, indige-nous antiques include the lovingly cared-for collection of vintage sailboat memorabilia, and primitive antiques. After a while it's hard to believe you're in the 21st century. Karen and David McNeil run this antique-filled inn and delight in sharing local stories and information.

DINING

The Second Story, Highway 42 in the Ephraim Shore Motel, (920) 854-2371. Before you refuse to chase down a good meal at a motel, consider this: Perhaps the best cherry pie in the county is served here. This is no-nonsense, no-frills fare with reasonable prices, and the Eagle Harbor views, from the sec-ond story, are exceptional. Groups may find some seating not conducive to conversation—on one side of the table facing the harbor.

Wilson's Restaurant and Ice Cream, Highway 42, (920) 854-2041. This institution has been going strong since 1906, when it first opened its doors. The biggest draw here is the setting overlooking Eagle Harbor, and fast-food fare including juicy burgers and hand-dipped ice cream. The best place to enjoy the views is the outdoor dining area on the side porch.

A warning is in order if you haven't been here on a hot summer night. It seems like everyone in the county gravitates to Wilson's for ice cream. The place is jammed, lines are long, and tempers frazzled, but hey, this is less crowded than, say, Provincetown on Cape Cod in August.

SISTER BAY

What do visitors remember most about Sister Bay? Probably the goats munching the thatched roof of Al Johnson's Swedish Restaurant. This is another Door County institution, and for that reason, the place is packed for breakfast, lunch, and dinner. Now cross the street to another downtown marvel. Permanent residents of this old lumber-shipping town number 700, the largest town in northern Door, and their library is a surprise. Tall windows look out on a white sand beach, in the midst of a waterfront park. Sailboats from a nearby marina ply these waters. Resting is easy, reading is hard. Three miles north of Ephraim, this is where Highways 42 and 57 rejoin.

LODGING

The Inn on Maple, 414 Maple Drive, (920) 854-5107. Listed on the National Register of Historic Places, this six-bedroom inn is filled with antique furnishings. Open all year.

The Wooden Heart Inn, 11086 Highway 42, (920) 854-9097; Web site is www.woodenheart.com. This new log home in a secluded, woodsy setting has a huge fireplace and rooms filled with antiques.

DINING

Whether your historical trek through Door County includes doing some heavy-duty research or is a whirlwind tour to catch a few sites, **Al Johnson's Swedish Restaurant**, Highway 42 (702 Bay Shore Drive), (920) 854-2626, is a must-see. And the place could be considered historical. The log building housing the restaurant was constructed in Norway, then carefully shipped to Sister Bay and reconstructed at its current location in 1949. But the real treat are live goats chomping on the thatched roof in warmer weather. With a waitstaff outfitted in native Swedish dress, this is the place to sample Swedish cuisine, including pancakes, meatballs, and fruit soup. Standard American fare is also available. And it's open year-round, for breakfast, lunch, and dinner. Before or after dining, you'll need to take a few more minutes to visit Johnson's Swedish Butik, a nearby shop that features all sorts of merchandise from Sweden.

Sister Bay Bowl and Supper Club, 504 Bay Shore Drive, (920) 854-2841. This longtime bowling alley—still going strong—has a reputation for pizza, burgers, and fries. It also draws fans with a Friday night fish fry. Open all year.

Pipkais, a unique shop for gifts and hand-painted art, is housed in one of Sister Bay's charming old houses.

ELLISON BAY

Driving farther north from Sister Bay along Highway 42, you'll keep close to the waters of Green Bay and be able to peer at the islands below. Here traffic has thinned out, and the gentle rural charm of long ago still permeates the area. One authentic vestige of days gone by that you shouldn't miss is the Pioneer Store on Highway 42. It's an anachronism that operates in low gear. This traditional general store and grocery has wide wooden counters, antiques galore, barrels of bulk items, and a pot-bellied stove. It's still going strong after one hundred years.

A visitor contemplates the waters of Green Bay inside Jens Jensen's secluded Cliff House, built in the walls of the lakeshore cliffs on The Clearing's property.

Another not-to-be-missed attraction for history enthusiasts is The Clearing, 12171 Garrett Bay Road, (920) 854-4088, high above the waters of Green Bay. This "School of Discovery in the Arts, Nature and Humanities" was founded in 1935 by landscape designer and conservationist Jens Jensen. It emulates Danish folk art schools, where students gain self-discovery through solitude. When you "clear your mind" (thus The Clearing name) you are apt to appreciate and learn. Not the easiest place to find, the school's lovely, rambling old buildings are secluded within 128 acres of woodland, but visitors are welcome on weekends. Call ahead for visiting hours.

It's doubtful you will be able to take classes as a weekend visitor—most classes run on a weekly basis, and students are in residence during this time frame. However, put The Clearing on your list for spending time. The architecture, trails, and setting make for a wonderful side trip. Walking the sawdust trails and hearing the calls of the abundance of birds is akin to walking through an aviary.

Buildings on the property include the main lodge, which was built in 1930, then rebuilt eight years later after a fire destroyed the original structure. Especially intriguing is the Cliff House, Jensen's own retreat when he wanted to get away from it all. It's past the old school house. A rustic trail, atop enormous boulders, leads to a worn door covering an opening to a cave in the rocks. Looking like a storage shed, it's actually a place for those profoundly interested in clearing the mind in a spare environment.

A bed, a simple table, two chairs, a broom, and two kerosene lamps are all there is. Views of the waves lashing the rocks below are spellbinding. Sitting inside a primitive cliffside dwelling makes a visitor wonder how long Jensen stayed here at one time.

Unwind the piece of birch bark curled in a stone crook above the cove's plain bed to find this handwritten note: "Here is beauty and solitude, where one can recapture the serenity of yesteryear. Here lies the spirit against the crowded influence of our developer society." Despite The Clearing's efforts to retain the past, it does make concessions to the modern world—its Web site is www.theclearing.org.

LODGING

Grand View Motel, Highway 42, (920) 854-5150 or (800) 258-8208. A popular place because of its spectacular water views from the bluffside location. Continental breakfast, 26 rooms and 2 suites, reasonable rates.

Hotel Disgarden Bed & Breakfast, Highway 42, (920) 854-9888. This beautifully restored 1902 hotel features a lodge interior with handcrafted furniture. Seven bedrooms.

DINING

Viking Restaurant, Highway 42, just north of the Pioneer Store, (920) 854-2998. For many Door County regulars, when they think fish boils, they think of the Viking. This is the first restaurant on the peninsula to serve the concoction, and it still draws crowds when it hosts its daily fish boils, April through October. The restaurant is open most of the year for breakfast, lunch, and dinner.

GILLS ROCK

Bluffs, bays, raw beauty—all are part of Gills Rock. At the northern tip of the peninsula, five miles up the road from Ellison Bay, this picturesque fishing village remains a tranquil, laid-back settlement. It's a perfect place for absorbing the flavor of the "old" Door County, much the way the peninsula used to be before tourism became a major revenue producer. Gills Rock, with its commercial fishing industry, survives nicely and is a good place to visit.

The Gills Rock area appeals because it's "far from the madding crowd." Consequently, it remains one of the peninsula's best-kept secrets. Nevertheless, like other favorite offbeat destinations, the word is slowly getting out, and Gills Rock is changing.

Up to 1997 or so, cars were seldom heard rumbling by on Highway 42, the main artery through the village. Now, at the summer peak, the village draws a steady stream of traffic, albeit far less than Egg Harbor, Fish Creek, Ephraim, and Sister Bay to the south.

The town was originally named Hedgehog Harbor by Washington Island fisherman and boat builder Amos Lovejoy. The name came about in 1855 when Lovejoy harbored his sloop over the winter in the town. The area's hedgehogs, or porcupines, knew a good thing when they saw it. They flocked to the sloop and had a field day chewing holes in the hull. Needless to say, the sloop sank when Lovejoy launched it in the spring. In 1870 the small fishing village and harbor were renamed in honor of Elias Gill, a local lumberman.

A favorite pastime here involves hanging around the fishing docks for a glimpse of commercial fishermen at work. The atmosphere is an artful blend of Mediterranean seacoast village and the rugged, hardy nature of a Scandinavian outpost. In the evening, when the boats come in with the catch, the pillars, posts, and pilings along the water's edge are festooned with white specks as sea gulls wait for fish scraps.

Door County's nautical heritage is on display at the newly refurbished Door County Maritime Museum on Highway 42, (920) 743-5958. Visitors learn about the peninsula's shipbuilding heritage and the area's variety of boats from the early 1920s. This is a must-stop for history buffs fascinated with nautical memorabilia. One of more intriguing glimpses into the past is an inside tour of *The Hope*, a commercial fishing boat built in 1930. Its name was chosen as a glimmer of optimism during the Great Depression. *The Hope* was used as a commercial fishing vessel until 1992. The museum, not to be confused with the institution with the same name in Sturgeon Bay, is open Memorial Day through mid-October.

LODGING

When the blue, lilac-trimmed **Harbor House Inn**, across from the Weborg Wharf on Highway 42, comes into view, history enthusiasts and even everyday travelers know they've reached a major northern Door landmark. Else and Dave Weborg opened their Scandinavian bed-and-breakfast inn in 1987. The historic 1904 home, which has been in the Weborg family (built by Willie and

Looking at some of the artifacts in the Door County Maritime Museum at Gills Rock. The museum has a branch in Sturgeon Bay.

Olga Weborg and open to travelers who arrived by schooners from Chicago) since its inception, has seen many transformations.

The Harbor House Inn has a fairy-tale sort of story behind it, as many old and interesting places do. Else was vacationing in the area from her native Viborg, Denmark, and she eventually met Dave Weborg. The result is that the girl from Viborg married a Weborg, and they eventually came to manage a Scandinavian country retreat overlooking one of the more colorful harbor bluffs on Green Bay.

Weary travelers can drop their bags and let go of the world for a while in the beautifully transformed Jenny Lind room with its stunning stained glass window. Over the years, David and Else have added several wings and hideouts where guests can choose to stay, in addition to the inn's original Victorian rooms. There are many amenities on the property, including an all-season indoor whirlpool, sauna, bike rentals, a charming gazebo, and a comfy great room where guests serve their own continental breakfast.

The Harbor House Inn has added a lighthouse where guests can stay.

On a recent visit, one guest told another that the reason she had chosen Gills Rock was because "We wanted to go as far north as we could go." One of Oprah Winfrey's staff members recently visited. She asked David what there was to do in the area. "Nothing is our specialty," he told her. That pretty much sums up Gills Rock, but what a wonderful nothing it is.

A March 1969 copy of the National Geographic lying among the magazines in the great room confirmed matters, with the cover pronouncing

"Wisconsin's Door Peninsula—A Kingdom So Delicious." The story nicely conveyed the flavor of the area, including this wise observation: "The wonderful thing about Door County," said Irving Miller, dockmaster at the town of Fish Creek, "is the perfect combination of wilderness and civilization. Each makes its presence known, but neither one crowds the other." The nice part about reading that today? The situation is pretty much the same—particularly on the northern edge of the peninsula.

Accommodations at the Harbor House Inn include the original 1904 inn, a new Scandinavian country wing, and a lighthouse built in 1998. There's also the troll cottage, a tiny dwelling that was originally a carriage house, with plenty of rustic charm, complete with Franklin fireplace, schooner ceiling hatch, and an antique nautical interior. The Danish cottage, new in 1992, is a spacious place with a full kitchen, cabana, fireplace, and gas grill. The inn is open May through October. Call (920) 854-5196 for reservations.

Maple Grove Motel of Gills Rock, 809 Highway 42, (920) 854-2587. You'll see the sign on the right side of the highway while driving toward the Northport Ferry docks. The Maple Grove is a no-nonsense sort of place caught in a time warp reminiscent of the 1940s and 1950s. The motel was built right after World War II. What's the draw? Reasonable rates and a beautiful maple grove—the property's four original maples, now harboring the landscape with their massive trunks and branches. Annie Drastata, who bought the motel in 1999, is only its second owner. Expect clean, comfortable rooms, a no-frills place with a lovely setting, just slightly off the beaten path. Open May 1 to October 31.

The Shoreline Resort, 12747 Highway 42, (920) 854-2606, www.theshorelineresort.com, is one of the best sunset viewing spots on the peninsula. The Shoreline, advertised as "the northernmost resort on the Door County Peninsula," is a venerable institution in these parts. There are waterfront views from every room in the motel and a marina for renting or docking boats. The popular restaurant serves breakfast, lunch, and dinner, but is best known for its delicious dinners featuring steak and prime rib. Expect long waits on a summer Saturday night. Even with a reservation you may wait an hour before being seated. Request a waterfront table at sunset and you won't be disappointed.

WASHINGTON ISLAND

Washington Island, the largest of Door County's islands, is historically significant for several reasons, not the least of which is that it was settled by Icelandic pioneers in the early 1800s, the first and possibly largest influx of these people in our nation's history. The rugged island, named after George Washington, continues to be home to the largest Icelandic settlement in the country. About 600 residents live here year-round; many still have ties to Iceland. The Icelandic heritage lives on in the small population of Icelandic horses, most visible at Field Wood Farm, where visitors can embark on trail rides or take riding instruction.

For those looking for beauty and serenity in a peaceful, weatherbeaten seaside environment, Washington Island makes a perfect weekend getaway. Its lack of a slick, overly polished exterior gives the island a raw and primitive feel. Even though it's only a 30-minute ferry ride from the mainland, the island has an isolated, secluded air that eludes many of Door County's hot spots. Whether renting an old cottage or staying in a more modern lodge, visitors find this a place that makes them feel they've stepped back in time.

A Scandinavian-designed building with a thatched roof on Washington Island.

The island offers a variety of things to do, including biking (more than 100 miles of paved roads), hiking, swimming (count on chilly water until mid-August), horseback riding, boating, and cross-country skiing and snowmobiling. Many art galleries show the work of local artists from early summer through early fall.

The feeling of splendid isolation one finds here is reinforced by the island's sparseness of large motorized vehicles. Many visitors riding the ferry to the island come with bikes and camping gear, but not cars or trucks. Travelers who can get along without a car on the island should consider renting a bike or moped during their stay. Either is available at the ferry dock. Cabs can be hired from Vi's Taxi, (920) 847-2283 or (920) 493-2388.

For more information, call the Washington Island Chamber of Commerce at (920) 847-2179.

OTHER SITES AND ATTRACTIONS

For a Lawrence of Arabia sandy knoll experience visit **Jackson Harbor Ridges**, a 90-acre State of Wisconsin Scientific Reserve that is a fragile ecosystem comprised of dunes and boreal forest unlike any other spot in Door County. Another great "dunescape" is Sand Dunes Public Beach, along South Shore Drive, southeast of Detroit Harbor.

Field Wood Farms, one half-mile west of Main Road on West Harbor Road, (920) 847-2490. The Icelandic ponies are descendants of the original horses brought to the island. Trail rides, horse-drawn wagon rides, and riding instruction are available.

Sievers School of Fiber Arts, Jackson Harbor Road, (920) 847-2264. The vanishing school of folk art is alive and well here. Take a class (if you have more than a weekend) or come by for a visit or to purchase fiber arts and supplies. Classes, held in a 100-year-old barn and two newer studios, include those on woodcarving, spinning, papermaking, quilting, and basketry.

LODGING

Deer Run Golf Course & Resort, Main and Michigan Roads, (920) 847-2017. A nine-hole golf course, a pub, and a grill can be found at this attractive country inn.

Findlay's Holiday Inn, Detroit Harbor, (920) 847-2526. Norwegian-style ambiance and a dining room overlooking the harbor. Not affiliated with the motel chain.

Sunset Resort, West Harbor, (920) 847-2531. On the waterfront, the small lodge has rooms overlooking the water, a sandy beach, and a tennis court. The restaurant is a favorite local hangout for breakfast.

DINING

(Don't expect posh restaurants to pop up unexpectedly. The few places on the island serve down-home fare that doesn't command a lot of lingering.)

The Albatross, Lobdell and Main Road, (920) 847-2203. Open in the warmer months, this is a popular drive-in with hearty burgers as the main draw.

Papa Tino's, in town, (920) 847-2785, used to be known as the Island Café.

Sunset Resort, Old West Harbor Road, (920) 847-2531. This breakfast-only spot, a favorite with locals, is worth a trip for the authentic Icelandic pancakes.

SHOPPING

Mann's Mercantile Shops, Main Road, (920) 847-2030. This place has been an island institution for more than a hundred years. The collection of Scandinavian items, plus grocery store/general store goods, makes an interesting stop. Bike rentals are available.

FERRY SERVICE

Island Clipper, Highway 42, Gills Rock, (920) 854-2972. The fancier, more pampered way to get to the island. The ferry has a narrated tour, lunch, and includes the Tour Train, a "tiny-town" sort of choo-choo that meets passengers at the island dock and escorts them to the island's highlights. Bike or moped rentals available.

Washington Island Ferry Line, Northport Pier, Highway 42 and Death's Door, (920) 847-2546 or (800) 223-2094. Operates year-round with daily car ferry service. Daily schedule tapers off mid-October. Bike and moped rentals at the dock.

ROCK ISLAND STATE PARK

Rock Island State Park, with 900 beautiful acres to explore, is a must for visitors who want to experience some secluded northern waters. It's also rich in history, due to Chester H. Thordarson, a Milwaukee inventor who held more than one hundred patents, including one for the first million-volt transformer. Chet paid a mere $5,725 for the private island in 1910. He spent the next 55 years planning to build a feudal estate that was to rival those owned by the wealthiest crowns of Europe.

The mansion never came to fruition, but a magnificent limestone boat-house, containing the great Viking Hall and constructed from island stone, is a gem and is open to the public from the end of May through mid-October. The estate is listed on the National Register of Historic Places. Other limestone arches and oddities, which give the island a Stonehenge look, are part of the allure. While Thordarson was contemplating building his masterful designs, he was consumed by the study of the island's rich biological heritage. Because of this the University of Wisconsin gave Thordarson an honorary Master of Arts degree in 1929. Later, the state purchased the entire island, including Thordarson's library. It has been called one of the world's best collections of Scandinavian literature.

In addition to Thordarson's 30-acre development, the island is fascinating for its rich Native American history. Natives lived on the south shore from 600 B.C. until the end of the 1600s. At that time, the Potawatomi came to the island from Michigan. French traders inhabited the island off and on until the

In Rock Island State Park, the original stone water tower built by Chester Thordarson stands on the walking trail bearing his name.

mid-1700s. Artifacts and remnants from French and early Native American settlements have been discovered here and are visible in some locations. The grand Viking Hall contains exhibits that include Indian artifacts dating from 1678 and a potpourri of photos and memorabilia relating to Thordarson.

The Thordarson estate also features a massive limestone boathouse listed on the National Register of Historic Places.

From the 1700s through the time Thordarson bought the island, the land was primarily used by fishermen who set up shanties along the shoreline. The foundation of one of the fishing villages is still visible.

Chester Thordarson's Boathouse on Rock Island.

Since there's no place to stay on Rock Island, visitors may opt for one of the campsites. This is the most isolated state park in Wisconsin, and the state's most northeastern point. Getting to Rock Island means two ferry rides from the mainland—one to Washington Island, then another aboard the Karfi (it means seaworthy ship for coastal voyages) to Rock Island. And don't forget that you'll need to traverse Washington Island to get from one ferry dock to the other.

And carefully plan your return time from Rock Island to the mainland via

Washington Island. For one thing, the Karfi between the two islands runs from late May through mid-October, and usually the last return ferry of the day departs around 3:30 p.m. Day visitors who miss the last ferry of the day will have to find a private boat to take them back, or they'll have to spend the night on the island. I mention this because I missed the boat the first time I visited. Fortunately, I found a park ranger who, by coincidence, was taking a boat to Washington Island and was generous enough to give me a ride. This incident turned out fine, but don't count on finding gratuitous help around the corner if you miss the boat.

No cars or bikes are allowed on Rock Island. So what's the draw? History, nature, and wilderness are the prime reasons to go. Hikers come to explore the trails, swimmers come to take in spectacular beaches with a bevy of seaside boulders that add bold emphasis to the shore's raw beauty. Kayakers furrow the waters around the island. Hikers follow paths like the Thordarson trail. It takes three hours, but other, shorter loops are equally well marked.

Campers come by the droves, more with each passing year. The campsites amid pristine scenery add up to why Rock Island is often called one of the best places to camp in the state. For camping reservations, call (920) 847-2235.

One reason the island appeals to campers and hikers is that there are no bears or raccoons to contend with. The island does have a profusion of poison ivy (usually marked with ground signs) and a not-so-small population of non-poisonous snakes.

Another isolated but compelling site, which appeals to history buffs as a well as nature lovers, is Potawatomi Light. Dating from 1836, it's the oldest lighthouse in Wisconsin. Situated at the northernmost point of the island, it's about a two-hour trek from the Thordarson estate. Ask the park ranger for tours or take the stairs down the dolomite cliffs to the water's edge.

DOOR COUNTY AT A GLANCE

MUSEUMS

Door County Historical Museum: Learn about the area's cultural heritage, including the cherry growing business, Sturgeon Bay.

Door County Maritime Museum: Shipbuilding and commercial fishing history. Walk through The Hope, 1930 commercial fishing boat. Gills Rock.

HISTORICAL SITES AND ATTRACTIONS

Anderson Barn & Store at Anderson Dock: Store built by Aslag Anderson in 1858 is on the National Register of Historic Places. Weathered barn next door was built in 1870. Overlooking the waters of Green Bay at Ephraim.

The Clearing: A school of discovery in the arts, nature and humanities, founded

Cana Island Lighthouse, built in 1870.

by Danish landscape designer Jens Jensen in the 1930s. Ellison Bay.

Commercial fishing docks at Gills Rock: For more than 150 years the docks have been the mainstay of the community.

Eagle Bluff Lighthouse: 1868 lighthouse is on the National Register of Historic Places. Peninsula State Park.

Jackson Harbor Maritime Museum: Remnants of the island's fishing industry. Washington Island.

Moravian Church: Built in 1857, the white-steepled church in Ephraim is the oldest in the county.

Noble House in Fish Creek: The oldest unchanged home in Fish Creek—walking tours in summer.

Peninsula Players: The oldest professional summer theater in the U.S. Fish Creek.

The Pioneer Store: Early 20th-century grocery and general store still brimming with atmosphere and wares. Ellison Bay.

Potawatomi Lighthouse: On Rock Island—1836, the oldest lighthouse in Wisconsin.

Sievers School of Fiber Arts: Located in an 1895 schoolhouse. Washington Island.

Thordarson Estate: Massive boathouse listed on National Register of Historic Places. Rock Island.

OTHER HISTORICAL SHOPS

Al Johnson's Swedish Restaurant: Log building constructed in Sweden, then reconstructed in Sister Bay in 1949.

Cana Island and Range Lights & Lighthouse: 1870 lighthouse, built on a windy point, is a good place for exploring the surrounding grounds. Baileys Harbor.

Canal Station Lighthouse: Built in 1899. Sturgeon Bay.

Cupola House: Restored 1871 mansion now houses gift shops and boutiques. Egg Harbor.

Harbor House Inn: 1904 Scandinavian home—the property has been expanded to include new buildings linked to the heritage of the original home. Gills Rock.

Mink River Estuary at Rowleys Bay near Wagon Trail Resort: Note the circa 1600 cross marking early exploration of French explorers.

Peterson Builders, Inc., Bay Shipbuilding and the **Palmer Johnson shipbuilding operations**: Tours offered. Sturgeon Bay.

White Gull Inn: 1897 inn and restaurant; it's the oldest inn on the peninsula. Fish Creek.

HISTORICAL EVENTS AND FESTIVALS

MAY

Lighthouse Walk, throughout the county.

JUNE

Historic Walking Tours, Ephraim.

Historic Walks, Fish Creek.

Fyr Bal Festival, traditional fire festival
on the waters of Eagle Harbor, Ephraim.

Maritime Days, Washington Island.

JULY

Old-Fashioned 4th of July, Potawatomi State Park.

AUGUST

Scandinavian Festival, Washington Island.

10th Annual Wooden Boat Show, Door County.

Old Barns Tour, Ephraim.

DECEMBER

Door County Christmas, Sturgeon Bay.

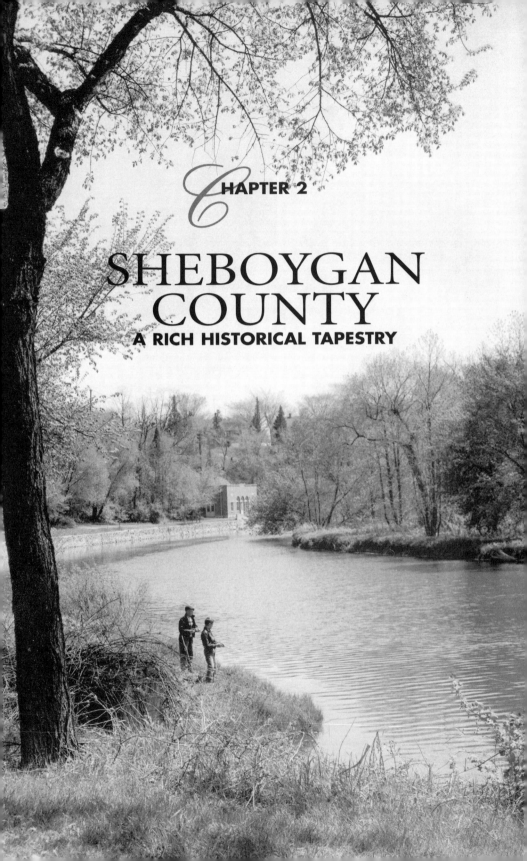

CHAPTER 2

SHEBOYGAN COUNTY
A RICH HISTORICAL TAPESTRY

The All Saints Chapel on County P in Elkhart Lake.

HERE'S AN IDEA—maybe the reason some people are so resistant to history is that it seems so, well . . . old. If that's the case, plan a weekend around Elkhart Lake in Sheboygan County, a village small enough that it doesn't have a real stoplight. Yet this resort hamlet of 1,019 yields some of the liveliest recent history you're apt to find in the entire state. In the process, it's a great place to begin a historic exploration of east-central Wisconsin.

As a visitor might expect, there are well-kept and refurbished old houses, a nice old depot, and a couple of bars in the vicinity of deep and clean Elkhart Lake (a lake so clear that, with its gravel bottom, it's among the most potable in the state). What isn't expected is that the town of Elkhart Lake looked the other way during Prohibition and especially after World War II, when a number of rendezvous here offered undisguised gambling. Not until local, state, and federal authorities conspired against resort owners did slot machines disappear from the local establishments.

At about the same time, around 1950, young World War II veterans from Chicago were looking for a place to race their newly imported sports cars. They talked village fathers into staging races on highways circling the lake. This went on for a couple of years before highway officials decided that closing roads so that Illinois drivers could exceed the speed limit was not a good idea.

Enter Cliff Tufte, owner of a gravel pit south of town. Tufte formed a corporation, sold stock to the locals, and laid down a four-mile, 14-turn road racing course on the northern edge of the Kettle Moraine State Forest. The ribbon of asphalt, called Road America, opened in 1954 and has played host to drivers, celebrities, and fans of sports car and motorcycle road racing ever since. The deep-throated roar of engines audible throughout the area on summer weekends is the sound of some serious horsepower and nearly 50 years of big-time racing.

Unfortunately, the sound of trains is more subdued these days, so Elkhart Lake residents have turned their railroad depot into a shrine devoted to train memorabilia. Located at the corner of Rhine and Lake Streets, the Depot Museum is on the National Register of Historic Places. Call (920) 876-2922 to find out about the times when you can view its original furnishings, clippings, photos, and other items. You can also call this number to reach the Elkhart Lake Chamber of Commerce and Tourism Commission. The commission also offers a free map that guides tourists to preserved homes, lake resorts, bed-and-breakfast facilities, and other attractions.

Visitors will find Elkhart Lake 150 miles north of Chicago, 60 miles north of Milwaukee, 97 miles northeast of Madison, and 300 miles east-southeast of Minneapolis-St. Paul. And they needn't exceed the speed limit (55 mph on two-lane roads) to cover the area's sites in two days spent here. That's because all the destinations on this weekend tour are located in spacious but easily accessible Sheboygan County.

SHEBOYGAN

With approximately 50,000 residents, Sheboygan is the largest city in the east-central area. To reach the city from Elkhart Lake, head south on Highway 67 to Plymouth, then east on four-lane Highway 23, a trip that should take about 20 minutes.

Who wouldn't want to visit a city named as the "Best Place to Raise a Family" by Reader's Digest in 1997? Sheboygan, whose name comes from an Ojibwa word that means "the sound like the wind on the rushing waters," is not only a great place to but also a superb nook along the Lake Michigan shore for soaking up history and visiting extraordinary recreational spots.

Self-billed as the "Bratwurst Capital of the World," the city grew from a group of smaller communities that had sprung up along the Sheboygan River, a few miles away. Logging and trapping were dominant industries on the river, but when Sheboygan was officially settled in 1844, some pioneers had other ideas. They built a substantial pier out into Lake Michigan that allowed schooners to transport goods to and from the area, as well as to bring in a workforce of German, Dutch, and English immigrants.

The Dutch settled in Cedar Grove and Oostburg, south of Sheboygan.

Many had arrived in New York in the early 1840s from the province of Zeeland, only to head westward in search of cheap, fertile land. Around this time, one group of about 300 immigrants was headed from Holland to their new homes when they met with disaster. Five miles off the Wisconsin shoreline, the steamship Phoenix caught fire and more than 200 lives were lost.

The German migration was so strong that, by 1890, some 20,000 Germans were calling Sheboygan home. Many of the townships in Sheboygan County are still predominantly populated by descendants of these folks. They include Germans from Russia, from Hanover, Hessian Germans, German-speaking Austrians, and a number of Slovenians.

Today the city maintains strong ties to its ethnic roots. Yet visitors should know there are many new additions to the area that should not be missed. If you come in summer, for instance, there is bound to be something going on along the Sheboygan lakefront, a favorite gathering point for all ages.

Downtown Sheboygan's century-old buildings have been renovated and restored to their original elegance and are now finding new life. An old ironworks building, for example, is home to a courtyard art gallery. A former carriage factory houses a mix of businesses. To see this charming area, head to the Harbor Centre. While there, hop onto the Midwest's only battery-operated trolley, a replica that transports pedestrians between the Harbor Centre and the Riverfront and Marina. The trolley moves around town from late May through early September.

OTHER SITES AND ATTRACTIONS

The **Sheboygan County Historical Museum** is housed in the former home of Judge David Taylor, who lived there in the 1850s. On the grounds are other nineteenth-century buildings that well represent Sheboygan County's varied past, including the Weinhold Family Homestead, a barn, and a cheese factory. The complex has recently grown by 20,000 square feet. Exhibits include those on Native American history, maritime activities, the circus, and medical developments. Located on Sheboygan's west side at 3110 Erie Street; (920) 458-1103.

Indian Mound Park, 9th Street and Panther Avenue, contains 18 rare Indian burial mounds, products of the Woodland Indians from about 500–750 A.D. The natives also were called the Effigy Mound People, since the mounds they created were shaped like animals, reptiles, and birds. The five deer mounds and two panther mounds here are rare and perfectly preserved. There also are conical and linear mounds, one of which, Mound 19, shows an exposed burial with artifacts. History buffs who find pre-Columbian times fascinating should make a point of visiting.

John Michael Kohler Arts Center, 608 New York Avenue, (920) 458-6144,

To take a break from your trip into the past, visit Kettle Moraine State Park, a few miles southwest of Sheboygan.

is housed in the 1882 home of the founder of the plumbing firm that bears his name; the center features 11 art galleries and performance space for stage presentations. Usually open every day.

Lakefront Promenade on Broughton Drive is a ribbon of waterfront connecting the boat launch and the North Breakwater. It's a good place for meandering and contemplating the breakers.

Family, friends, and neighbors gather to celebrate a plentiful harvest around 1895.

Another in-city historical site is the intersection of **Center Avenue and North Water Street**. It was here, in 1918, that the Lindemann Brothers Circus gave its first performance. The circus prospered during the 1920s, adopting the name Seils-Sterling and acquiring many motorized vehicles. Before folding the following year, the circus played in 10 states for 29 weeks in 1937. In 1965, the three Lindemann brothers were enshrined in the Circus Hall of Fame in Sarasota, Florida.

Also on Broughton Drive, in Deland Park, is a reconstruction of the *Lottie Cooper*, a schooner that sank in an unimaginable storm off Sheboygan Harbor in 1894. When the local marina was built, the shipwreck was discovered on the bottom of the lake. The lakefront is now the scene of the Polar Bear Swim, which is more tradition than history. It takes place here on New Year's Day morning. Most of the "bears" don't stay in the icy lake Michigan water, which hovers around 35 degrees, for very long, but they are brave or foolhardy souls. Part of the draw is the postswim party at Sheboygan's Municipal Armory. Bratwurst sausages rule supreme, along with spine-tingling stories of the big lake's raw challenge. The armory is at 516 Broughton Drive.

Riverfront Boardwalk, Riverfront Drive. Walk the walk and take in the old commercial fishing shanties, now transformed into retail establishments.

Bratwursts have been around the Sheboygan area as long as anyone can remember. Most of the credit for the popular sausage is given to the many German immigrants who brought recipes with them, then concocted their specialties in smokehouses behind homes and farms. There probably are as many bratwurst recipes as there are people in Sheboygan, but most recipes, which are held dear and secret, fall into categories of having German, Polish, or Italian origins.

Many of the area's finest bratwurst cooks come together during August **Bratwurst Day**. That's when more than 100,000 people jam the streets in the spirit of bratwurst (and beer) mania. To be historically accurate, the sausage was a regional food until a company north of town, Johnsonville, began to distribute its products to Milwaukee, Chicago, and beyond in the latter years of the 20th century. Nowadays, folks coast to coast know the taste of bratwurst, which usually involves pork but can also be veal-based.

LODGING

Brownstone Inn, 1227 N. 7th Street, (920) 451-0644 or (877) 279-6786, an elegant 1907 brownstone, has lots of amenities, including four-poster beds, fireplaces, whirlpools, porches, and Lake Michigan a few blocks away.

English Manor Bed & Breakfast, 632 Michigan Avenue, (920) 208-1952, is within walking distance of Lake Michigan. This lovely 1908 English Tudor features five rooms and plenty of pampering, including afternoon tea, a gourmet breakfast, and even a billiards room.

Gramma Lori's Bed & Breakfast, W1681 Garton Road, (920) 565-3853 or (800) 595-1009, is down-home lodging with a flair. The 1875 farmhouse features three guest rooms and two big bonuses: Visitors can shop for antiques in 100,000 square feet of space in the property's barn, or sip Wisconsin wines in the farm's cellar.

SHEBOYGAN FALLS

Heading inland from Sheboygan, you'll find a rich variety of attractions that played an important part in Wisconsin history. One suggested stop is Sheboygan Falls. Drive west five miles on Highway 23, then turn left, or south, on Highway 32. Sheboygan Falls is the magnet that brought settlers to the area to begin with. It has two historic districts and a riverwalk for viewing the falls' whirling waters. The city (population around 6,000) won the 1995 "Great American Main Street Award," designating it as having one of the top five downtowns in the country. For more information, check with the Chamber of

Commerce, (920) 467-6206; also visit the Web site at www.sheboyganfalls.org.

A not-to-be-missed historic site is the Cole Historic House, 518 Water Street, (920) 467-4667, a Greek Revival home built in 1837 by the Rochester Lumber Company as a boarding house for employees. When it was purchased by Charles Cole in 1860, he had a wall constructed down the middle of the house, dividing it so his two sons could live side by side in a two-family "mirror" home. The two-family living unit concept was virtually unknown at the time. In 1985, the Cole House was purchased by people who intended to replace it with a parking lot. Local preservationists were successful in getting the owners to deed the property to Sheboygan County Landmarks, Ltd. The oldest building in Sheboygan County, the Cole House has been restored and is part of a group of five Greek Revival buildings on the National Historic Register. Open Tuesday through Saturday, 9 a.m. to 4 p.m. It is also the home of the Sheboygan County Historical Research Center.

LODGING

Rochester Inn, 504 Water Street, (920) 467-3123, is a handsome 1848 inn that has six bedrooms adorned with Queen Anne furnishings. Try to book a room in one of the two-level suites featuring an intimate first-floor sitting room with a staircase leading to a cozy, romantic bedroom.

KOHLER

This village, just west of Sheboygan and Interstate 43, is of importance in the industrial history of the state. It is the home of the Kohler Co., a major supplier of bath and plumbing supplies to the new- and existing-home markets.

Founder John Michael Kohler, an immigrant from Austria, came here and prospered in the 19th century. When Walter J. Kohler, third son of the founder (and 27th governor of Wisconsin from 1919 to 1931) dedicated The American Club, across the street from the Kohler Co., on June 23, 1918, he noted, "The worker deserves not only wages but roses as well." The club was an amenity-filled rooming house where immigrants were taught how to succeed in their new land. The name, The American Club, was picked because Walter thought it personified the high standard of living offered to those working in their adopted country.

Kohler didn't stop there. He hoped The American Club would inspire great love of this country. Profoundly interested in the Americanization of its residents, he promoted an educational atmosphere. Rooms were converted to classrooms and immigrants were taught to speak, read, and write English. An American flag hung at the end of the dining hall and while residents ate hearty food, Sousa marches played on the Victrola.

An early bathroom at the Kohler Co.

Visitors from all over are drawn to this red brick, Tudor-style, three-story retreat, which looks more like a manor house in the English countryside than a rambling oasis in Wisconsin. Now a grand resort, The American Club uses Kohler fixtures and more to showcase its many baths, among other things.

The cozy Lincoln Room is a great place to get a feel for what the Kohler Company meant to the immigrants who worked here. Just outside these walls, which used to enclose a card room for early residents, is a long corridor with two walls of old photos. It is fascinating to see the yellowed letters from immigrants who once lived here, expressing gratitude to the club for the chance to live out the American dream.

Exterior of The American Club in Kohler.

Above the leaded glass panels on the French doors leading to the main dining hall, with its Wisconsin theme tapestries and oak paneling, are etched some words that express Walter J. Kohler Sr.'s philosophy. The quote by John Ruskin reads: "Life without labor is guilt, labor without art is brutality."

A peek at the Immigrant Restaurant and Winery, where the bowling alley once existed, reveals a romantic cubbyhole in the Holland room (restaurants here represent the decor of several countries). But for sheer drama and getaway pleasure, visitors can't get enough of the Greenhouse Cafe. This is a marvelous spot to enjoy scones, coffee, and ice cream. Diners are surrounded by superb stained-glass treasures from an old retirement hospital in Lancastershire, England.

A nearby place not to miss is Waelder Haus ("house in the woods"), which is a short drive from the inn. Governor Kohler's sister, Marie, had this grand Austrian house built in 1931 to serve as a meeting place for the Girl Scouts of Kohler Village. Beyond being an intriguing meeting place (the chandelier sports Girl Scout merit badges of the 1930s), this Black Forest museum is now a showplace of Austrian art and architecture.

Greenhouse Café in The American Club.

The three-story house, with its red-fir interior walls, is reminiscent of the Bregenzerwald, a mountain valley in Vorarlberg province on Austria's western border. But it represents something else: The ancestral home of the Kohlers, where the dream of emigrating to America began.

Pamper yourself in Kohler at The American Club—Conde Nast Traveler readers call it "one of the 500 best places to stay in the world." The American Club, listed on the National Register of Historic Places and the Midwest's only AAA five-diamond resort hotel, has been a favorite compound for those seeking serious pampering since the early 1980s. That is when the historic 1918 structure was transformed from its early identity as a rare slice of Americana— a piece of history deeply embedded in the Kohler Company story.

The Kohler dynasty had firm views about how workers should be treated. They could be anything but independent. The village of Kohler was constructed for employees and their families, and until perhaps 1960, a homeowner could not sell the family place to just anyone—he or she had to seek company permission. Kohler suffered labor problems before and after World War II that resulted in wrenching strikes and loss of life. Finally, if you doubt Kohler influence, ask a local about the Interstate 43 interchange that was put in and then removed!

Nevertheless, visitors from all over the world are drawn here because of the variety of recreational pursuits. The two 18-hole golf courses at Blackwolf Run have received numerous awards, including Golf Magazine's "Gold Medal Award," ranking it one of the best golf resorts in America for the past six years. In 1998, Herb Kohler opened another course, Whistling Straits, which is his tribute to ancient courses he played on in Ireland. Located in Haven, about 10 miles northeast of Kohler, the course offers spectacular views of Lake Michigan along two miles of shoreline. Whistling Straits was complemented two years later by the Irish course, with a layout every bit as challenging as its predecessor.

Down the road from Blackwolf Run is River Wildlife, a rustic, 500-acre wilderness preserve which looks like a scene from the movie "A River Runs Through It." It is an easy place to lose stress and enjoy being outdoors. Go canoeing, ride horses, shoot trap, hunt, or hike the 20 miles of meandering trails. After an outing, take in the comfort of a log cabin at a bend in the Sheboygan River. Enjoy brook trout and other savory selections in the lodge's restaurant, or rest a while near the huge fieldstone fireplace.

A short drive from the inn is the Sports Core, a large complex where visitors can walk the indoor trail, swim in the pool, enjoy the spa, play racquetball, play tennis inside or out (children have their own court and summer day camp program), or work out and take fitness classes.

Visitors to The American Club's resort hotel will be enchanted by its out-of-the-ordinary amenities and the pampering they receive. There are stunning accents such as fine heirloom-style furniture from Baker and McGuire (both are Kohler companies), Waterford crystal chandeliers, padded silk walls, stained glass, tapestries, vast bouquets of fresh flowers, and of course, luxurious baths showcasing the latest Kohler designs.

History enthusiasts will be especially satisfied with the hotel's appointments. Every one of the 184 guest rooms in the main wing is named for a famous American: Alexander Graham Bell, Juliet Ward Howe, Houdini, etc. The additional 52 in the nearby Carriage House have whirlpool baths. Those after intense luxury should choose a Carriage House suite with Habitat Masterbath. Adjust the dials so you alternate soothing steam, gentle rain, warm sun, or summer breeze.

The American Club packages include room selections ranging from Standard to Superior, with special accommodations in the Carriage House as

The lodge at Blackwolf Run, Kohler.

well as the Wisconsin, Governor's, and Presidential suites. Almost all amenities at the resort are included in the price. Fifty percent-off deals usually include the following: Getaway on Thanksgiving, Easter, Mother's Day, Memorial Day, Father's Day, Labor Day, or Columbus Day. Call the inn at (800) 344-2838 for more information.

DINING

The American Club provides a wealth of dining experiences that include the first four restaurants listed below. Diners are welcome whether or not they are overnight guests. The phone number for all four is (920) 457-8888.

Blackwolf Run Restaurant, 111 W. Riverside Drive, (920) 457-4448, is a suitably cozy old log clubhouse on a golf course. Hearty lunch and dinner daily, with breakfasts available during golf season.

The Greenhouse (see above for more information).

The Horse & Plow provides an early 20th-century pub atmosphere, with hearty and traditional choices.

The Immigrant Restaurant is a charming re-creation of various ethnic style restaurants, connecting with one another. It's hard to choose one over another, all done with style and interesting artifacts. International cuisine and fine wines. Reservations are required.

Whistling Straits, N 8501 County LS, Sheboygan, (920) 565-8888, features all your favorite fare with an emphasis on Irish specialties.

The Wisconsin Room exudes elegant Old World charm, including beautiful appointments, floral arrangements, and impeccable selections. A special entree is featured each night. Breakfast, dinner, and Sunday brunch served. Reservations required.

GREENBUSH

How times change. Nowadays, the drive between Kohler and Fond du Lac takes less than an hour. But in the 19th century it required an overnight stay, which is why Sylvanus Wade, a transplanted New Englander, built a hotel six miles west of Plymouth between 1847 and 1851. The Wade House, just off Highway 23, has been faithfully restored so that it's easy imagine its early visitors discussing Civil War issues or the country's westward expansion. To compare the 21st-century luxury of The American Club to the 19th-century Wade House, drive a mere 18 miles west.

The structure was brought back to life in the early 1950s, thanks to the efforts of Ruth De Young Kohler, who received financial support from the Kohler Foundation. The property was then deeded to the State Historical Society of Wisconsin in 1953.

Frequent visitors are always struck by how easy it is to slip back into time once on this property. Today, they start out watching a multimedia program called "An Apron Full of Stars," then board a horse-drawn wagon that brings guests to the imposing white inn. Costumed guides are well-versed on life at Wade House back in the mid-1800s, due to interesting and insightful information found in Wade's business ledgers and documents.

The Wade House in Greenbush has been restored to its former condition as a nineteenth-century stagecoach stop.

A trip here would not be complete without a visit to the Wesley Jung Carriage Museum on the property. This outstanding collection of antique carriages was preserved by Wesley W. Jung, grandson of Jacob Jung Jr., who was the son of Wisconsin carriage maker Jacob Jung. The Jung Carriage Company of Sheboygan was launched in 1855 and lasted until 1917, when it could no longer compete with the automobile. What an amazing collection of antique vehicles this is! There are more than a hundred hand- and horse-drawn vehicles, enough to study over several visits.

In addition to the carriage museum and Wade House, the historic site also includes a smokehouse, the Robinson House (home of Wade's daughter and her husband), and a blacksmith shop. Thanks to the Kohler Trust for Preservation, work has begun on the reconstruction and restoration of the Robinson-Herrling Sawmill, millpond, and mill dam. When finished, the project will resemble the mill that once stood here by the Mullet River.

The entire complex is open daily beginning in early May through end of October. Many special events take place throughout the season, including the largest Civil War encampment and battle reenactment in the state. Admission is charged. For more information, call (920) 526-3271; send e-mail to wade-hous@danet.net; Web site: www.shsw.wisc.edu/sites/wade.

PLYMOUTH

About six miles east of Greenbush, just off Highway 23, in the midst of the state's eastern cheese industry and home to the first Cheese Exchange, sits the small town of Plymouth. The nice part about visiting Plymouth, with a population of about 7,000, is that it can easily be explored by walking. In fact, that is the best way to see this historical and architectural treasure. Take the Historical Walking Tour for a look at 50 buildings. None is far from the Visitor Center, where you can obtain information about the tour. The center is itself of architectural interest.

The town's profusion of interesting old bed-and-breakfast inns is a bonus for the weekend traveler seeking historical getaways. In fact, visitors could spend several weekends here trying all the charming historical homes now doubling as places to stay. Plymouth is a few minutes northeast of the enchanting Kettle Moraine State Forest, a wondrous all-season souvenir of ancient glacial activity. Several countryside inns in and around the Kettle Moraine welcome visitors. Some are listed below.

In addition to offering historical inns, Plymouth's history is synonymous with agriculture. Travelers can't miss that point if they enter from the west side of town. There stands Antoinette, a half-ton, 20-foot-long likeness of what people in these parts have been sharing the land with for many decades—the Holstein cow. For more information, contact the Plymouth Center, (920) 893-0079. The center is inside a historical building that also is home to a museum.

LODGING

52 Stafford Irish Guest House, 52 Stafford Street, (920) 893-0552. If you really want to cozy up in a historic spot and not go anywhere all weekend, this is the place. Nineteen guest rooms, sumptuous food, and a well-stocked bar.

Hillwind Farm Bed & Breakfast Inn, N 4922 Hillwind Road, (920) 892-2199, is set in a romantic Victorian farmhouse (think mini-mansion) brimming with antiques, canopy beds, fireplaces, special soaps, chocolates, and loads of other creature comforts. It's set in a beautiful location, eight miles from the Kettle Moraine Forest.

Spring Tulip Cottage, N 4502 County S, (920) 892-2101, provides an escape route to northern Europe via the Kettle Moraine. The inn's name says it

In the mid-1920s, dirt roads in Wisconsin were often the only way of getting from one place to the next.

all. This richly decorated, fully equipped Dutch cottage is laden with accessories that include quilts, lace, and art. Check out the spiral staircase leading to the loft and bedroom above.

Yankee Hill Inn Bed & Breakfast, 405 Collins Street, (920) 892-2222. This is one of those places where everyone who loves history should stay at least once. On the National Register of Historic Places, the inn, set in a residential area, combines two beautifully restored homes. The oldest B & B in the county, this 12-room inn oozes 19th-century charm.

DINING

52 Stafford Irish Guest House, 52 Stafford Street, (920) 893-0552. This is an absolute must for anyone who loves terrific atmosphere and good food. Listed on the National Register of Historic Places, this charming spot, also an inn, features Irish entrees, as well as more local fare.

SHEBOYGAN COUNTY AT A GLANCE

MUSEUMS

Elkhart Lake Depot Museum: A collection of community history housed in the town's century-old train depot. Elkhart Lake.

Henschel's Museum of Indian History: Indian artifacts dating to 8,000 B.C. Elkhart Lake.

Sheboygan County Historical Museum: Featured exhibits include early circus memorabilia, agriculture, and industry of the area. Sheboygan.

HISTORICAL SITES AND ATTRACTIONS

The American Club: Listed on the Register of Historic Places, the original 1919 building was once a rooming house for the Kohler Company's immigrant workers. Now a grand resort, it's beautifully appointed and richly etched with historical touches. Several restaurants, golf courses. Kohler.

Cole Historic Home: A rare Greek Revival turned into a two-family "side-by-side" home in 1860. On the National Historic Register, it's the oldest building in Sheboygan County. Sheboygan Falls.

Heritage School: Visitors experience what a school classroom was like at this restored 1876 school. Sheboygan.

Indian Mound Park: 18 rare Indian burial mounds, created by the Woodland Indians from about 500–750 A.D. Sheboygan.

John Michael Kohler Arts Center: The impressive 1882 home of the founder of the famous plumbing firm, now features art galleries and performance space. Sheboygan.

Wade House & Jung Carriage Museum: Once a stagecoach stop, this 19th-century New England-type structure is operated as a historical site by the State

Historical Society of Wisconsin. Costumed guides and tours of antique carriages at the Jung Carriage Museum. Greenbush.

The Wreck of the *Lottie Cooper*: The 1894 schooner, which sank in a blustery storm off Sheboygan Harbor, is now on display in Deland Park in Sheboygan.

A room in the Robinson House, on the grounds of the Wade House.

OTHER HISTORICAL STOPS

Harbor Centre: Restored 19th-century grand buildings now house restaurants, apartments, retail stores. Downtown Sheboygan.

Old Plank Road Trail: Seventeen miles of historical trail between Sheboygan's lakefront and Greenbush connect with the Ice Age National Trail in the Kettle Moraine. Walk, run, bike, or snowmobile.

Riverfront Boardwalk: Old commercial fishing shanties have been transformed into shops. Riverfront Drive, Sheboygan.

Road America: A four-mile, 14-turn road racing course on the northern edge of the Kettle Moraine State Forest has been hosting road races since 1954. Elkhart Lake.

HISTORICAL EVENTS AND FESTIVALS

Museum Family Adventure Day: Yearly summer event features outdoor historical experiences and learning opportunities for all ages. On the grounds of the Sheboygan County Historical Museum.

JUNE

Sheboygan County Draft Horse Exposition, Greenbush.

JULY

Sheboygan County Historical Museum Adventure Days, Sheboygan.

Vintage International Challenge, classic-car races, Elkhart Lake.

Wade House Birthday Celebration, Greenbush.

Wade House Historic Trade School, Greenbush.

AUGUST

Bratwurst Day, Sheboygan.

Centennial Muzzle-Loader Encampment, Sheboygan.

SEPTEMBER

Wade House Civil War Weekend, Greenbush.

OCTOBER

Heritage and Arts Festival, Plymouth.

NOVEMBER

Sheboygan County Historical Museum's Holiday Memories, Sheboygan.

Wade House Yankee Harvest Dinner, Greenbush.

DECEMBER

Sheboygan County Historical Museum's Holiday Memories, Sheboygan.

Wade House 1860 Christmas Wedding, Greenbush.

CHAPTER 3

THE
GREAT
RIVER
ROAD

NORTH FROM
LA CROSSE

The *K. M. Hutchinson,* filled with weekend revelers, sits for its portrait at an Oshkosh dock in 1901.

THE UPPER Mississippi River stretches 1,100 miles, from Lake Itasca, Minnesota, to Cairo, Illinois. A highway into history, the big river has transported countless Native American, French, English, and American adventurers. In the 19th century, paddle wheelers by the hundreds moved passengers and freight; immortal writers such as Mark Twain recorded it all.

Railroads caused the river to diminish in importance in the late 19th and early 20th centuries. But judicious dredging and damming, performed in particular by federal work crews during the Great Depression of the 1930s, brought the river back into its own. In one recent year, some 40 billion tons of grain, coal, cement, and other products moved among the locks and dams in the nine-foot channel, which can accommodate barges as long as 300 feet.

When examining a Wisconsin map, one thing becomes evident: Driving the Great River Road is an ambitious undertaking on any two-day weekend. Happily, La Crosse and Interstate 90 provide a nice midpoint between two manageable segments of the trip, allowing travelers to visit southwestern Wisconsin one weekend and far western Wisconsin another. This chapter covers the first segment and Chapter 4 the second. Officially, La Crosse is 286 miles northwest of Chicago, 201 miles west of Milwaukee, 136 miles west of Madison, and 155 miles southeast of the Twin Cities.

The Great River Road is a combination of several highways. It parallels the Mississippi River along two-thirds of Wisconsin's western flank. The northern segment we'll be following here is Highway 35 from La Crosse and up to Prescott. This small town, situated where the St. Croix River joins the Mississippi, is where the Great River Road leaves Wisconsin and enters Minnesota. From Prescott, it's a mere 15 miles north to Hudson, Interstate 94, and the Twin Cities' eastern suburbs.

Stretches of the highway both north and south of La Crosse have been praised for their beauty. The 30 miles between Alma and Maiden Rock and the 60 miles between La Crosse and Prairie du Chien are not only some of the most beautiful in Wisconsin, they're often talked about as being two of the most beautiful drives in the country. Motor carefully on these immensely scenic two-lane thoroughfares and watch for "paddle wheel" signs, which point to historic sites, along the way.

The valleys in the area north of La Crosse hide streams and rivers that feed the mighty Mississippi. Early French visitors called such narrow valleys coulees, a designation that survives to this day. Glaciers failed to reach this area, so the bluffs separating the coulees have been untouched but for wind and weather for quite some time. Views from these imposing outcrops have been compared to the Palisades of the Hudson or the hills along the Rhine.

Yet for all its beauty, the terrain can be unyielding. No one knew this better than writer Hamlin Garland, born in a log cabin in West Salem, just east of La Crosse. Garland attended a seminary and then went east to train as a teacher. Returning to the Midwest, he saw how hard and shabby were the lives of his parents and other inhabitants of the coulee region. Garland immortalized their struggles in Main-Travelled Roads, a collection of short stories published in 1891. These generally grim, realistic tales, along with his other fictional accounts, influenced everyone from Sherwood Anderson to William Faulkner. Garland won the Pulitzer Prize in 1922 and died in 1940.

A spunkier view of pioneering days was held by Laura Ingalls Wilder, another writer who was born in this region and at about the same time as Garland. Her novels, most notably Little House on the Prairie, depicted the hard times of farming but were generally more uplifting than the prose of Garland. Wilder drew on memories from her years growing up near Pepin (and in other parts of the Midwest in which she lived) to show what life was like just east of the frontier, where land was being farmed for the first time. Both writers have worldwide reputations.

While the Great River Road is as placid a stretch as a traveler might find, the Mississippi River itself has been known to rile. Farmers and residents of several states continue to recover economically from severe flooding that took place in 1993. And experienced sailors know enough to get off a wide area of the river known as Lake Pepin, 40 miles south of Prescott, when storms approach.

LA CROSSE

Along the scenic bluffs of the Mississippi is one of the state's most intriguing sites. La Crosse, population 51,000, is a city historically tied to the big river. In 1680, Father Louis Hennepin and several other Frenchmen were among the earliest people to travel here. During the next 150 years, many French trappers and traders followed. River exploration flourished after 1823, when sternwheel paddleboats began their maneuvering, making good mileage for their time—some 800 miles in 20 days!

At the confluence of three rivers, La Crosse was a natural to develop into a thriving commercial port.

Riverfront land, at Front and State Streets (now Barrons Island or Pettibone Park), has always been fertile. Consequently, the Winnebago settled here in the 18th century before ceding the area to the federal government. The first white settler, Nathan Myrick, built a log cabin and a trading post on the site in 1841, and it became a public boat landing 10 years later. Indians always considered this neutral ground. In fact, different tribes competed in athletic events on a prairie east of here. Their most notable game was lacrosse, from which the city derived its name.

The name stuck and is even more appropriate when the location is considered. It's at the cross or confluence of three rivers: the La Crosse, the Black, and the Mississippi. Interestingly, Indian legend says that when three rivers come together, the area will be protected from big winds. So far, that forecast has come true. No tornado has ever touched Riverside Park, where the three rivers meet.

Visitors fall in love with this long and narrow city that stretches along the willowy river bluffs because of its natural beauty. And the historically inclined traveler is drawn by the area's intriguing legends and colorful characters. William F. Cody, or Buffalo Bill, was one of those larger-than-life folks. He staged his traveling Wild West Show in the area many times at the La Crosse Opera House.

History here shows up in some unusual places. The site of the Valley View Mall, on Highway 16, once was a thriving Indian village. The Oneota, ancestors of the Winnebagos and the Ioways, chose this place to live around 1000 A.D. It offered several advantages: farming, fishing, hunting, transportation, and defense. There was a stockade, with as many as one hundred residents. Archeologists and students from the University of Wisconsin–La Crosse excavated here in 1978, prior to the mall's construction.

Life in the engine room of a Mississippi steamship was anything but glamorous.

When travelers see a site named after a Native American, they usually assume its history dates back several centuries. Red Cloud Park, where St. Andrew Street meets the La Crosse River, remains an exception. It was named after Mitchell Red Cloud, a U.S. Army corporal who fought in the Korean War. Red Cloud was posthumously awarded the Medal of Honor for single-handedly holding off an enemy attack with machine gun fire in 1950 until his death.

Before departing La Crosse in either direction, head east on Main Street to Granddad Bluff. The view to the west over La Crosse, the river, its several islands, and on into Minnesota, is worth the brief side trip.

For more information, contact the La Crosse Convention & Visitors Bureau by calling (800) 658-9424 or (608) 782-2366.

The arrival of a boat laden with passengers and cargo was an exciting event in towns along the Mississippi.

OTHER SITES AND ATTRACTIONS

The Hixon House, 429 N. 7th Street, (608) 782-1980, a lovely mansion built for lumber baron Gideon Hixon, is a favorite with devotees of Victorian and Italianate architecture. The palatial house, brimming with architectural details, is usually open from Memorial Day through Labor Day. Admission fee.

The Pump House Regional Arts Center, 119 King Street, (608) 785-1434, is a must-see for those who love old buildings—this one is a 19th-century Romanesque Revival structure. The city's first water pumping station, it has been transformed into an arts center. There are galleries, plays, and musical performances.

Riverboat Tours. Riverside Park is the mooring site for the not-to-be missed American Queen, the largest paddle wheeler in the world. Also frequenting these docks are the famous Delta Queen and Mississippi Queen.

Riverside Museum and Riverside Park, (608) 782-1980, is something visitors can't miss, with its huge replica of Hiawatha watching over the docks of the popular La Crosse Queen Riverboat cruises. The La Crosse Convention & Visitors Bureau is here, as is the Riverside Museum. The latter recounts local riverboat history.

Crown Prince Ludwig and Princess Therese knew how to party. They married outdoors in Bavaria in 1810 amid a fall harvest celebration. The "Trachtenfest," or yearly festival of the harvest, was such a hit, it has continued throughout Europe to this day. La Crosse's "Oktoberfest USA," (608) 784-FEST, is among the oldest such celebrations in this country. The waterfront is awash in brats, beer, music, and other Wisconsin favorite foods and pastimes. The party takes place adjacent to Riverside Park at Copeland Park.

LODGING

Four Gables Bed & Breakfast, W5648 Highway 14/61, (608) 788-7958, is a Queen Anne–style structure with loads of Old World ambiance; it's on the National Register of Historic Places. Think turrets, a sweeping porch, and antiques. A quarter of a mile from the La Crosse city limits.

Great River Cruises, 2700 Del Ray, (608) 248-2854. Houseboats—why not? This is for travelers who want their own inn on the water. La Crosse is one area of the country where houseboat rentals are big business and where visitors can absorb the area's historical flavor by going with the flow of the big river. Many houseboats have full amenities, almost like home. This is one of several area rental companies.

DINING

The Freight House, 107 Vine Street, (608) 784-6211, is located in a 1880s brick storage building that once housed freight for the Chicago, Milwaukee & St. Paul Railroad. On the National Register of Historic Places, the structure is considered the city's premier steak and seafood restaurant.

The draw at **Piggy's Steakhouse,** 328 S. Front Street, (608) 784-4877, is succulent barbecued beef and pork ribs and other smoke-enticed offerings, including, of course, steaks. Other reasons travelers make pigs of themselves are the attractive atmosphere (note the old-fashioned back bar) and piggy decor.

SHOPPING

The Antique Center of La Crosse, 110 S. 3rd Street, (608) 782-6533, is in a 1890s building that holds three floors of finds, ranging from serious antiques to memorabilia to odds and ends. More than 50 dealers display their goods.

The La Crosse Clock Company, 125 S. 2nd Street, (608) 782-8200, appeals to people regardless of whether or they're clock collectors. Everyone will have a new appreciation for clocks when you visit this interesting shop with great finds for sale.

TREMPEALEAU

To begin the drive on the northern section of the Great River Road, head out of La Crosse to Trempealeau, a distance of just over 20 miles. A portion of the trip features some of the only multilane highway to be found on the Great River Road. But it also has traffic lights, on- and off-ramps, and franchises—"modern conveniences" that people who visit the area to get away from it all might find out of character for this stretch of the Mississippi. From I-90, drivers should head north on Highway 53 for about eight miles, then turn left on Highway 35. In a few minutes, they'll find themselves in Trempealeau.

Nicholas Perrot, according to French and natives alike, was a dark, handsome, and intelligent fellow. After constructing a fort at Prairie du Chien in the summer of 1685, he moved north to spend the winter near the present-day village of Trempealeau. Perrot chose to stay the cold months here because bear, buffalo, cougar, deer, elk, and lynx were plentiful. Four years later, Perrot claimed the entire region west of the Great Lakes in the name of his king, Louis XIV.

The Sioux were common here, and another Frenchman, Godefroy du Linctot, built a fort in 1731 at "the mountain whose foot is bathed by water," or "la montagne qui trempe a l'eau." The mountain, of course, is now called Mount Trempealeau. As for the fort, its ruins were rediscovered in 1887. The area is now Perrot State Park, with 1,400 acres nestled among 500-foot bluffs where the Trempealeau and Mississippi Rivers meet. In addition to sweeping views here, check out the burial mounds. The park is at W26247 Sullivan Road, west of Highway 35.

The tiny hamlet of Trempealeau, recognized by the National Register of Historic Places, was founded in 1851 and was known at the time as Reed's Landing. The village serviced river traffic beginning in 1857, witnessed the arrival of the railroad in 1871, and survived a two-block fire in 1888. Today, there are several beautiful lakes and wildlife areas in the region, plus a main street with numerous historic buildings, as well as Mississippi River Lock and Dam No. 6.

The big draw in town, for those looking to soak up the past, is the Trempealeau Hotel, a historic 1871 structure that features eight rooms with river views. You can't beat the prices—about $35 a night—at this endearing place. The shared-bath arrangement comes with few amenities (no TV or phone), but who can resist a stay amid the bluffs where French explorers once held court? The hotel is located at 150 Main Street, (608) 534-6898.

OTHER SITES AND ATTRACTIONS

Perrot State Park, (608) 534-6409, is a wonderful 1,400-acre park filled with Indian mounds, wildflowers, bluffs, campsites, and cross-country skiing.

Along the Mississippi, a train stops at the tiny Buena Vista station near Alma, in 1889.

Brady's Bluff, a 520-foot precipice, offers magnificent climbing trails.

Trempealeau National Wildlife Refuge, (608) 539-2311, has marshes, forests, and abundant wildlife within its 5,600-acre confines.

For more information, contact the Trempealeau Chamber of Commerce, (608) 534-6780. Visit the Web site at www.trempealeau.net or send e-mail to chamber@trempealeau.net.

DINING

Ed Sullivan's, 25498 Sullivan Road, (608) 534-7775, bears no relation to the late entertainer, but this supper club features a rollicking Irish atmosphere and offers succulent prime rib, seafood, and a nicely presented salad bar.

Trempealeau Hotel, 150 Main Street, (608) 534-6898, serves blackened fish, steaks, chicken, pasta, seafood. Mexican, Italian, and American dishes, along with vegetarian offerings. Open for lunch and dinner.

The rooms of some Mississippi River steamboats could be quite elegant.

FOUNTAIN CITY

Fountain City, 20 miles north of Trempealeau, is named for the many springs that flow down the sandstone bluffs. The town was originally named Holmes Landing, after the town's first settler, Thomas Holmes, who arrived in 1839. A rugged individualist, Holmes married a Sioux woman and thrived in the wilderness until he moved on when it became "overcrowded." Today, the village of 938 residents has a European feel to it. Thanks to some of the original settlers, you'll see Swiss-style homes and an identity that has water as its centerpiece, an ambiance often found in small European fishing villages. Once here, travelers understand why immigrants liked this place enough to settle here. Fountain City's Eagle Bluff, at 550 feet, is the highest spot along the Mississippi in Wisconsin.

OTHER SITES AND ATTRACTIONS

The Cat-Tail, 32 S. Main Street, (608) 687-8674, has gifts and crafts for the cat owner and lover. A block from the river, this small shop is brimming with whimsical creations.

Elmer's Auto and Toy Museum, W903 Elmers Road, contains a nice collection of old toys, including windups and Japanese metal playthings. Open from later spring until late fall. Admission charge.

The House with a Rock in It, 404 N. Shore Drive (Highway 35). No, this isn't the House on the Rock. Rather, it's an ordinary dwelling that was the target of a giant boulder that crashed down from one of the bluffs. The rock ended up in one of the rooms and has been there ever since. Open irregularly.

ALMA

Alma, 17 miles north of Fountain City, is billed as a "mirror of the past, vision of the future." It's a great destination for the history lover who fancies architecture—the entire village is listed on the National Register of Historic Places. It was founded by Swiss immigrants in the 1850s. You'll know you've reached Alma when you see craggy "twelve-mile bluff" as you head into town; this large rock formation was used as a landmark when riverboats navigated this stretch of the Mississippi.

A tiny, quiet place, halfway between La Crosse and Prescott, Alma is home to two- and three-story mostly brick buildings that invite travelers to wander the streets and catch the feeling of long ago. Several antique shops line Main Street, as do galleries showcasing innovative art. So inviting is the town that weekend travelers book a room in one of the small inns or funky hotels, then use the village as home base for touring other spots along the Great River Road.

OTHER SITES AND ATTRACTIONS

Buena Vista Park provides a good viewing spot for migrating tundra swans; thousands of these graceful birds can be seen in the spring and fall. The park is set above Alma, off County E, 500 feet above the river. Look for signs.

Lock and Dam No. 4 is a busy hub for river sightseeing and fishing. Anglers haul in plenty of northern pike, catfish, walleye, and bass. You can't miss this large dam; it's across the street from Alma's town center.

Reick's Park is another fine swan-gazing spot, but this one has an observation platform staffed during peak viewing times in the spring and fall. Three miles north of Alma. Look for signs.

LODGING

The Gallery House Bed & Breakfast, 215 N. Main Street, (608) 685-4975, as the name implies, is laden with art and antiques. Built in 1861 overlooking the Mississippi, it's a relaxing spot to perch and view river activities from the terraced garden and decks. There's a collectibles shop on the premises.

An overhead view of Alma around 1900.

The Laue House, (608) 685-4923, is an Italianate-style inn built by one of the town's German founders. Don't be surprised if you call and a friendly recorded voice says, "If it's a room you want, just tell me when." Look for sign on the south side of town.

The Tritsch House Bed & Breakfast, 601 S. 2nd Street, (608) 685-4090, is a 1901 Queen Anne–style Victorian home offering authentic brass beds and lots of old-fashioned ambiance.

DINING

The Alma Hotel, 202 N. Main Street, (608) 685-3380, offers traditional down-home fare all day long but specializes in huge and tasty dinners; the pies are out of this world. And it's all served by a friendly waitstaff in historic surroundings.

PEPIN

Lake Pepin, actually part of the river that is 22 miles long and 2.5 miles wide, is the centerpiece of this beautiful retreat. The lakeshore scenery is so showy and idyllic that William Cullen Bryant once said that a Lake Pepin visit should be mandatory for every poet and painter in the country. Indeed, the Pepin area is a popular spot for summer visitors who usually come away knowing more about Laura Ingalls Wilder, who was born here in a log cabin, than do most librarians or schoolteachers.

The *War Eagle*, named for the mascot of Wisconsin's Eighth Regiment in the Civil War, sits at the dock.

A pair of brothers, French fur trappers named Pepin, are responsible for the name of the lake and the village (the latter has 873 citizens and is 16 miles northwest of Alma). Founded in 1846 and briefly a steamboat boomtown, the site was familiar to Mark Twain and to wealthy Chicago socialites who summered on the lake. All of which poses a question: Is Pepin a true lake or merely a large, wide spot in an already expansive river? Geologists say the lake was formed naturally where the smaller, steeper Chippewa River met the Mississippi. The small river brought in more glacial debris than the big river could carry away; the resulting delta provided a natural dam and the water backed up in the gorge of the Mississippi.

OTHER SITES AND ATTRACTIONS

Lake Pepin Players, Second Street and Great River Road, (800) 823-3577 or (715) 442-3109. Fine professional theater, launched in 1995. Performances often feature nationally known actors. June through October.

Laura Ingalls Wilder Wayside Park, seven miles northwest of Pepin on County CC. Marked by a simple cabin (a replica), the 1867 birthplace of the author of the *Little House* books features a picnic area and historical information about the site.

Pepin Historical Museum (also known as the Laura Ingalls Wilder Museum), (715) 442-3011. Interesting memorabilia pertaining to the author's life. Usually open May through October.

Pepin Depot Museum, vivid red with a green roof, houses a modest collection of railroad and steamboat historical items. Both museums are in the village.

For more information, please call (715) 442-3011, check out the Web site, www. pepinwisconsin.com or e-mail the Pepin Area Community Club at pepinwis@win.bright.net.

LODGING

A Summer Place, 106 Main Street, (715) 442-2132. If the name conjures memories of Sandra Dee and Troy Donahue embracing in the movie, "A Summer Place," this B & B is for you. It's a bit of New England on the shores of Lake Pepin. The romantic spot features superlative views, featherbeds, and double whirlpools. There's a gift shop in the 100-year-old barn behind the main building.

DINING

Harbor View Cafe, First and Main Streets, (715) 442-3893. A favorite hangout for knock-your-socks-off gourmet items, including grilled salmon and Chilean sea bass. The menu's cuisine changes daily. Serves breakfast, lunch, and dinner. Expect long waits, but worth the time. This restaurant is considered one of the state's finest dining spots. Usually open March through November (often closed in April).

STOCKHOLM

Travelers who drive seven miles further north will be in one of Wisconsin's smallest towns (the population hovers around one hundred inhabitants)—Stockholm. A few years before 1850 (the exact date is questionable), Erik Peterssen arrived in the area from his hometown, Varmland, Sweden. Peterssen was on his way to California to seek his fortune. Apparently, the lure of lumberjacking in the rugged Lake Pepin area was stronger than gold, and Peterssen decided to found a settlement along the lakeshore. By 1853 he had arranged for his brother, Anders, and 200 Swedes from Varmland to join him. More than half of the immigrants died of cholera on their journey, but those who survived joined Peterssen to found Stockholm. While Wisconsin had other Swedish settlements, this was the first in western Wisconsin.

Life along Lake Pepin in the 19th century can still be felt in this tiny hamlet. Radiating from the town's center at Highway 35 and Spring Street, visitors see a few architectural treasures, including Victorian homes and century-old buildings, now doubling as shops and restaurants. Lake Pepin is a block west of the downtown. It offers travelers and locals alike the opportunities to view the gorgeous river scenery or wade in the clear water.

Life for boat crews on the Mississippi was marked by long periods of inactivity.

The main attraction today, though, one that brings curious visitors to this charming community, is shopping. Stockholm is a tourist destination that belies its size. Renovated storefronts hold antiques, quilts, art, baskets, handpainted silk, even some Mississippi pearls.

Amish Country, at the town's main intersection, specializes in Amish-made art and household accessories. The huge building, once a general store, is a perfect place to display large pieces of art, including quilts. Artisans are so prevalent in the area they've been holding an annual art fair in summer since the 1970s. Visitors in July can stock up on treasures—like the five-foot didgeridoo (a primitive Australian musical instrument) for sale here by a musician and artisan.

LODGING

(Accommodations are very limited in the area, so if you're planning to stay during art fair days in July, book well in advance.)

Great River B & B, (800) 657-4756 or (715) 442-5656, provides more than just a "room." What you get is a multiroom cottage furnished with 19th-century antiques and available for only one party. Built in 1869, the stucco structure is the oldest house in town. Guests actually rent access to the entire 45-acre property. For more information, visit the Web site at www.bbinternet.com/greatriver.

About 6 miles upriver from Stockholm is **Maiden Rock**, a mere speck of a town set along a bend in Lake Pepin. One of the best reasons to visit is the lovely panoramic view of the lake and valleys from the Harrisburg Inn, (715) 448-4500, www.harrisburginn.com, a great place to unwind.

PRESCOTT

In 1851, trapper Philander Prescott officially named the 10-year-old riverfront outpost. He built himself a cabin and decided to stay a while. Not only did he name the place, he held claim to some 1,200 acres. One of the earliest towns in western Wisconsin, Prescott is 31 miles above Maiden Rock and at the confluence of the Mississippi and St. Croix Rivers, a fact important to its settlement. Immigrants found they could access the area by navigating the river and setting up stakes along the border of Minnesota and Wisconsin.

Prescott is touted as "Wisconsin's Most Westerly City." The scenery is a showstopper as visitors drive toward it. After Bay City, at the top of Lake Pepin, the winding road's vantage points offer spots where oohing and ahhing are de rigueur.

Today, Prescott, just 30 minutes from downtown St. Paul, is an enjoyable place to take in a variety of antiques and gift shops, or watch the bridge open over untroubled waters. Very few spots on the St. Croix have crossing access, so here, when the drawbridge opens, onlookers show up.

For more information, contact the Prescott Area Chamber of Commerce (in an interesting building offering exhibits and local history), at 237 Broad Street N., (715) 262-3284 or (888) 262-1090.

LODGING

The Arbor Inn, 434 N. Court Street, (715) 262-4522; the Web site is at arborinn.com. Open year-round, this 1902 mission-style, bed-and-breakfast inn features glorious views of the St. Croix River. Quilts and country-style furnishings are nice touches. Good resting and relaxing on the comfortable porches.

DINING

Steamboat Inn, Highway 10, (715) 262-5858. Superb views, good lunch and dinner offerings, including seafood, salads, and chicken entrees. At the bridge as travelers cross into Minnesota. Hours are limited during the winter.

The Virginian, Highway 10 East, (715) 425-5600. This is another in the long line of North Woods–style supper clubs that have been going strong for decades. The Virginian has been a Prescott-area institution since the 1950s. Steaks reign supreme.

A GLANCE AT THE GREAT RIVER ROAD (NORTH OF LA CROSSE)

MUSEUMS

Elmer's Auto and Toy Museum: A diverse collection of old windup and Japanese metal toys. Fountain City.

Laura Ingalls Wilder Wayside Park: The 1867 cabin marks the birthplace of the author of the *Little House* books. Pepin.

Pepin Depot Museum: Historical collection of railroad and riverboat exhibits. Pepin.

Pepin Historical Museum: Also knows as the Laura Ingalls Wilder Museum, the museum has gathered together memorabilia pertaining to the author's life. Pepin.

Riverside Museum: Riverboat memorabilia. On the grounds of Riverside Park in La Crosse.

Swedish Institute: Artifacts relating to settlement of Stockholm. At the old Post Office in Stockholm.

HISTORIC SITES AND ATTRACTIONS

Barrons Island or Pettibone Park: Riverfront land at Front and State Streets in La Crosse was settled by the Winnebago Indians in the 18th century before being ceded to the federal government.

Perrot State Park: Once the site of a 1731 fort built by Frenchman Godefroy du Linctot. Ruins of the fort were uncovered in 1887. The area, now a recreational spot, is nestled among 500-foot bluffs. Ancient Indian burial mounds within the park's 1,400 acres. Near Trempealeau.

OTHER HISTORIC STOPS

Alma: Founded by Swiss immigrants in the 1850s, the entire village is on the National Register of Historic Places.

Antique Center of La Crosse: This 1890s building holds three floors of antiques, memorabilia, and odds and ends. La Crosse.

Hixon House: Lavish Italianate mansion open for tours Memorial Day through Labor Day. La Crosse.

Holmes Landing Cafe: Named for the first settler, Thomas Holmes, who arrived in 1839, the cafe serves diverse entrees including Cajun-stuffed quail and catfish. Fountain City.

The Martindale House Bed & Breakfast: A fashionable 1850s Italianate home, complete with cupola and widow's walk, is listed on the National Historic Register. La Crosse.

Riverboat tours: Get a feeling of what life was like when the great paddle wheelers plied the waters of the Mississippi. Today's giants, the American Queen, Delta Queen, and Mississippi Queen, moor at Riverside Park. La Crosse.

Riverside Museum and Riverside Park: Local riverboat history, legends and lore. La Crosse.

Trempealeau Hotel: Small 1871 hotel has river views and offers plenty of history. Trempealeau.

HISTORICAL EVENTS AND FESTIVALS

JULY

Founders Day, West Salem.

SEPTEMBER

Laura Ingalls Wilder Days, Pepin.

OCTOBER

Oktoberfest, La Crosse.

DECEMBER

Country Christmas, Pepin.
Country Christmas, Trempealeau.

CHAPTER 4

THE GREAT RIVER ROAD

SOUTH FROM LA CROSSE

The Cass Street Bridge, known locally as the "Big Blue Bridge," spans the Mississippi in downtown La Crosse.

THE SOUTHERN SEGMENT OF THE Great River Road is at least as scenic and historic as, if somewhat less gentrified than, the northern route. The towns tend to be smaller and less artsy, but the area has seen its share of characters and events contributing to what the state is today. Carved amid bluffs and the great Mississippi, the route begins in La Crosse as Highway 35 and snakes its way down for 60 miles to Prairie du Chien. There it follows a succession of twisting and hilly state and county roads until rejoining 35 near Potosi, finally entering Illinois at East Dubuque.

WEST SALEM

Before beginning on the trip you may want to take a quick jaunt over to West Salem, a few miles east of La Crosse just off I-90. The community is known as the home of Hamlin Garland, a fine writer who went on to earn a Pulitzer Prize in 1922 for his book *A Son of the Middle Border*. His home, at 375 Garland Street, is now a National Historic Landmark. Tours are available between May and September.

Also worthy of a visit is the Palmer Gullickson Octagon House, 358 N. Leonard Street. Once the home of Dr. Mary Lottridge, one of the first woman physicians in the country, this place is a beauty. It's usually open only in summer.

For a change of pace and a chance to view the operation of a dairy farm, give the Wolfway Farm a try. The farm, one of the state's "Century Farms," is located midway on the 21-mile La Crosse River Bike Trail, which hooks up with the Great River Bike Trail in La Crosse and the Elroy-Sparta Bike Trail in Sparta.

You know you've entered another universe once you reach lightly traveled County Road B leading to the farm. Run by Dianne and Dave Wolf (the Wolf family homesteaded the farm in the 1850s), the farm has about 150 Holsteins. The modern dairy barn is a short walk from the oversized 1920 farmhouse. While the operation may use modern milking techniques, there are enough vestiges of how things used to be that you'll forget you're in the 21st century.

Dianne opened a portion of the grand old clapboard farmhouse as a bed and breakfast over a decade ago. "The B & B has brought the world to me," she says. Two antique-filled bedrooms are set aside for guests, each with its own queen-sized bed and bath. A studio apartment downstairs has two double beds. My room had acorn-carved walnut furniture and a handmade Dresden plate-patterned quilt on the bed. There are several quilts in the farmhouse, all pieced by Dianne.

The whole experience boils down to a big farmhouse, friendly folks, and a hearty breakfast cooked by Dianne. Wolfway Farm is open April 1 through November 1; call (608) 486-2686 for information.

GENOA

After that bit of diversion, it's time to hit the Great River Road. Your first stop is tiny Genoa, 17 miles south of La Crosse and 11 miles north of DeSoto, the location of Lock and Dam No. 8. The facility, created following federal legislation in 1935, is a good example of the 26 locks and dams constructed to improve navigation between Minneapolis and the mouth of the Missouri River. Watercraft enter a 110-foot-wide chamber and are lifted 11 feet from the lower to the upper pool. The dam cost $6.7 million when new and affected 18,591 acres of land.

DESOTO

One of the most vicious and well-known confrontations on the frontier ended 2.5 miles north of here in 1832. Black Hawk, a Fox-Sauk war leader, balked at ceding land to miners and farmers in south-central Wisconsin. He gathered like-minded natives and refused to move permanently west of the Mississippi.

From present-day Rock County, the 60-year-old Black Hawk led a protracted retreat north and west. With starving and wounded Indians in his wake, Black Hawk reached the Mississippi, only to be confronted by a gunboat on the river and troops on shore. The Battle of Bad Axe, fought August 1–2,

1832, on the banks of the Bad Axe River, was a rout. Indians were shot, drowned, even scalped by soldiers. Black Hawk escaped but was captured a short while later.

In contrast, Chief Win-No-Shik, a notable leader of the Winnebago, lived and prospered as head of a village in the same geographical area in the 1820s. He was known for his courtesy and dignity, and he was made head chief of the entire tribe when it was moved to what would become the state of Iowa.

FERRYVILLE

Ferryville has a nice observation deck that juts into the Mississippi. Eight miles south of DeSoto, this hamlet of 154 persons no longer has a ferry but is a nice place to stop for fuel, a snack, or a look around.

LODGING

Mississippi Humble Bush, Highway 35 (Main Street), (608) 734-3022. Built in 1908, the Bush displays fir woodwork and family antiques.

LYNXVILLE

Once Wisconsin became a territory in 1837, settlers began to cut timber with a vengeance. Ten years later there were more than 30 sawmills on the Wisconsin, Chippewa, and St. Croix River systems. During the long, cold winters, loggers felled and stacked white pine logs on the frozen rivers. Spring thaw flushed the logs toward the Mississippi River. Logs were caught, sorted, scaled, and rafted at a site 1.2 miles south of here.

Between 1837 and 1901, more than 40 million board feet of logs floated down the Mississippi to sawmills. The largest log raft on the Mississippi was assembled at Lynxville, eight miles south of Ferryville, in 1896. It was 260 feet wide and 1,550 feet long, containing 2.25 million board feet of lumber. The last rafting of lumber on the Great River took place in 1915.

PRAIRIE DU CHIEN

Wisconsin's European history virtually begins here, where the mighty Wisconsin River meets the even mightier Mississippi. It was at the present site of Prairie du Chien on June 17, 1673, that explorer Louis Joliet and Father Jacques Marquette entered the Mississippi River. They were directed to the Mississippi by Indians, who guided them through the Fox-Wisconsin waterway from Green Bay on Lake Michigan. Once past Green Bay, the adventurers saw more than 2,000 miles of country never seen by Europeans.

Even earlier, this area was shaped by glacial activity. The vast melting action formed a wide floodplain here, beneath the bluffs. The first settlers were

Guides at Villa Louis dressed in period costumes.

members of the Fox tribe, led by a man named Alim, or Dog. English-speaking Jonathan Carver named the site Dog Plain in 1766, but the locals preferred the French version, Prairie du Chien.

Three important treaties were negotiated with the Indians here in 1825, 1829, and 1830. The 1825 meeting established territorial boundaries for each participating tribe. Meanwhile, men such as fur trader Hercules Dousman were getting rich off the local bounty. Dousman built what became known as Villa Louis, his palatial home, in 1843. Now owned by the state, the mansion has been authentically maintained and is a popular place to visit.

A young visitor to Villa Louis admires a nineteenth-century doll.

The railroad reached Prairie du Chien, which today has a population of 2,380, from Milwaukee in 1857. Commerce took on a new dimension shortly after steamboats replaced keelboats on the river. Bridges spanning the Mississippi were built in earnest after the Civil War; by 1887, fifteen different spans were being used.

Drivers headed south out of Prairie du Chien will want to follow the Great River Road sunburst signs along county roads to Cassville. This route will pass Wyalusing State Park, with frequent river glimpses.

OTHER SITES AND ATTRACTIONS

Prairie du Chien Museum at Fort Crawford, 717 S. Beaumont Road, (608) 326-6960. This national historic landmark once was a military hospital. On display are old-time physician's instruments. Small admission charge.

Villa Louis, 521 N. Villa Louis Road, (608) 326-2721. Operated by the

State Historical Society of Wisconsin, the former Dousman home was constructed while Indians still roamed nearby. It sits majestically on a hill and is a wonderful example of a Victorian country estate. Admission charge.

A view of Villa Louis soon after it was built in 1870.

LODGING

Neumann House Bed and Breakfast, 121 N. Michigan Street, (608) 326-8104 or (888) 340-9971. Five bedrooms and a full breakfast await visitors to this Victorian home. The Web site is www.prairie-du-chien.com, while the e-mail address is lneumann@mhtc.net.

DINING

The Barn, County K, (608) 326-4941, offers food and beverages in an appropriately rustic atmosphere three miles north of town.

Jeffers Black Angus Supper Club, Highway 18/35/60, (608) 326-2222. Two miles south and across from the airport, this is another quality Wisconsin supper club.

CASSVILLE

Cassville hoped, in 1836, to become the capital of the new Wisconsin Territory, which at the time also embraced all of Iowa and Minnesota. While it lost out to a swampy site to the east that would become Madison, the village of 1,144 some 32 miles south of Prairie du Chien, boasts a number of well-preserved historic sturctures.

OTHER SITES AND ATTRACTIONS

Denniston House, 117 E. Front Street, on the waterfront, is part of a village walking tour. Now an apartment building, the home was offered free to legislators in 1836 if they would establish themselves in Cassville.

Nelson Dewey State Park, (608) 725-5374, is adjacent. Visitors can ride bikes, take in a panoramic view from a river bluff, or camp within a brief walk to the river. Admission charge.

River steamboats played an essential role in the state's economic growth.

Stonefield, two miles north of Cassville on Highway 133, (608) 725-5210, is owned and operated by the State Historical Society of Wisconsin. It is a wonderfully re-created turn-of-the-century village where costumed guides help visitors experience a bygone era. There's a museum here, with old-time implements and machinery. Look, too, for the estate of Wisconsin's first governor, Nelson Dewey. His reconstructed home and limestone outbuildings are delightful. Admission charge.

LODGING

The Geiger House, 401 Denniston Street, (608) 725-5419 or (800) 725-5439. This 1855 Greek Revival home near the Mississippi has a library, an antique piano, and a parlor with a Victrola. The Web site is www.geiger house.com, and the e-mail address is geigerhs@pcii.net.

River View Bed and Breakfast, 117 W. Front Street, (608) 725-5895, was built in 1856 as a boarding house. River views can be had from bedroom windows. The Web site is www.riverviewbb.com.

For more information, contact Cassville Tourism at 608) 725-5855 or visit the Web site at cassville.org.

POTOSI AND TENNYSON

The villages of Potosi and Tennyson are midway between Cassville and the Illinois-Wisconsin line. The towns are a mile apart, a mile from the Mississippi, and have present-day populations of 654 and 378, respectively. Unlike most sites along the Great River Road, Potosi and Tennyson did not depend on the Mississippi for their mutual economic well-being.

Rather, Potosi looked to the St. John Mine to sustain it. The mine, ironically, caused Potosi to be visited frequently between 1836 and 1846. Across the street, miners lived in "badger" huts while employed digging out lead. The mine closed in 1870 as richer deposits were found elsewhere.

Many of the miners, who may have showed up as early as 1820, enjoyed Potosi Brewing Company beer. The brewery was in production for 120 years before closing in 1972. Happily, the historic building is being carefully restored at the moment.

These days, people show up because this is the catfish capital of Wisconsin. Restaurants serve the sweet, tender river fish on a regular basis. By the way, there are no intersections in Potosi. Since the main street runs parallel to a sizable bluff, all other streets head off in the opposite direction without actually crossing Highway 133.

For more information, telephone (608) 763-2261, visit the Web site at www.pcii.net/~harryh/index.html or send e-mail to harryh@pcii.net.

OTHER SITES AND ATTRACTIONS

Passage Through Time Museum, N. Main Street, Potosi. Housed in the former Potosi State Bank building, this museum has a nice doll collection, plus memorabilia from the old brewery. Admission charge.

St. Andrew Church, County O, Tennyson, was built in 1875. The ornately carved altar in the big brick church is original.

St. John Mine, Highway 133, (608) 763-2121. Tours are available here. Admission charge.

DINING

Frieman's Supper Club, the Legion Bar, and the Yacht Club, Potosi, all serve catfish at one time or another during the week.

A GLANCE AT THE GREAT RIVER ROAD (SOUTH OF LA CROSSE)

MUSEUMS

Passage Through Time Museum: Collection of dolls and memorabilia from the old brewery. In the former Potosi State Bank building. Potosi.

Prairie du Chien Museum at Fort Crawford: This museum, once a military

The confluence of the Wisconsin and the Mississippi, south of Prairie du Chein.

hospital, exhibits include old time physicians' instruments. Prairie du Chien.

HISTORICAL SITES AND ATTRACTIONS

Battle of Bad Axe: A vicious chapter in history was fought here in 1832 when Black Hawk, a Fox-Sauk warrior balked at ceding land to farmers and miners. North of DeSoto.

Lynxville: Between 1837 and 1901, more than 40 million board feet of logs floated down the Mississippi to sawmills. The largest log raft was assembled at Lynxville, eight miles south of Ferryville.

St. John Mine: Tour the 1800s lead mine. Potosi.

Stonefield: Operated by the State Historical Society of Wisconsin, it's a wonderfully re-created turn-of-the-century village where costumed guides help visitors experience a bygone era. Cassville.

Villa Louis: Hercules Dousman built this palatial home in 1843. The mansion is now operated as a historical site by the State Historical Society of Wisconsin. Prairie du Chien.

OTHER HISTORICAL SITES

First American flag brought into Wisconsin: At Prairie du Chien in 1805. Lieutenant Zebulon Pike of the U.S. Army stepped ashore during an exploration to locate sites to build forts, and brought with him the first American flag to appear in the state.

Geiger House: This 1855 home, now a bed-and-breakfast establishment, is a wonderful example of Greek Revival architecture, and one of the oldest existing homes in Cassville.

Hamlin Garland Home: Home of the author Hamlin Garland who won a Pulitzer Prize for his novel *A Son of the Middle Border*. A National Historic Landmark. West Salem.

Lock and Dam No. 8: The facility was created in 1935. It's a good example of the 26 locks and dams that were constructed to improve navigation between Minneapolis and the mouth of the Missouri River. Genoa.

Mississippi River's discovery by Jacques Marquette and Louis Joliet: On June 17, 1673, the explorers, guided by Indians through the Fox-Wisconsin waterway, discovered the Mississippi River. At the site of Prairie du Chien.

Nelson Dewey State Park: Tour the home of Nelson Dewey, Wisconsin's first governor, in nearby Stonefield Historic site and enjoy panoramic views of the Mississippi River. Cassville.

Palmer Gullickson Octagon House: Nineteenth-century home was once the residence of Dr. Mary Lottridge, one of the first women physicians in the country. West Salem.

Wyalusing State Park: At the confluence of the Mississippi and Wisconsin

Rivers, it's one of the state's oldest parks, established in 1917. The area has a rich geographical and cultural history. Wyalusing is a Munsee-Delaware Indian word for "home of the warrior." Rivers cut into this area over a 400-million year period, leaving behind towering bluffs of limestone, shale, and sandstone. The earliest known natives appeared here around 1000 B.C., followed by Hopewell Indians and Effigy Mound builders. Indian burial mounds are prevalent in the park. Ten minutes from Prairie du Chien, near Bagley.

HISTORICAL EVENTS AND FESTIVALS

JUNE

Prairie Villa Rendezvous, St. Feriole Island, Prairie du Chien.

JULY

Steamboat Visit, Prairie due Chien (and in following months).
The Ties That Bind: Aprons, Stonefield Historic Site, Cassville.

AUGUST

In the Good Old Summertime, Stonefield Historic Site, Cassville.

SEPTEMBER

Carriage Classic, Villa Louis, Prairie du Chien.

NOVEMBER

Victorian Christmas, Villa Louis, Prairie du Chien (also December).

CHAPTER 5

CENTRAL WISCONSIN
PATHWAY TO THE PAST

The many unusual rock formations of the Wisconsin Dells were created millions of years ago by rivers carving a path through layers of sandstone.

WHILE TRAVELING THROUGH the central part of the state, the casual visitor can't help but be struck by the rich diversity of the region's historic sites. One can easily see how they symbolize the history of the entire state and made it what it is today. The beginnings of tourism in the state, for example, can be traced to the efforts of H. H. Bennett in the 19th century to photograph the Wisconsin Dells. Wisconsin's standing as an agricultural giant can be seen in its long history as one of the world's leading cranberry-growing regions. The history of the state's other significant industries—lumber and papermaking—can be seen in various sites around Wisconsin's central region.

Running through the region, binding all its various communities and people together, is the Wisconsin River. For more than 150 years, the river has powered paper mills, sawmills, and generators and has served as a commercial pathway, vacation destination, and wildlife refuge.

The journey in this chapter covers a lot of territory and a rich collection of historic sites, but that's the nature of the region. While there is a lot of driving, there are also more than enough changes of terrain and quirks of history to interest anyone.

TOMAH

We'll begin the tour in Tomah, a small town northwest of Wisconsin Dells that has, oddly enough, a bigger city feel. Yet it's only six and one-half square miles in size and home to about 8,000 people. Those who migrated here sought solace from the big-city hustle and bustle, but they wanted some of the amenities of a metropolitan area. For history-oriented weekenders, it's a good place to begin a mid-state visit.

Why the name? In 1856, early settlers, Robert E. and Robert A. Gillett, father and son, climbed onto high ground, surveyed the land, and seized the opportunity to name their new home. They had heard of Chief Tomah, a popular negotiator, who built a council house where the Menominee and Winnebago tribes met to iron out concerns. The Gilletts were quick to emulate Chief Tomah's spirit and his purported fairness and idealism, so they named the land after the Native American legend.

Today, Tomah's location is a good reason to stop and scout the town. Back in the mid-1850s, the location also was important, due to the fact that it was a halfway point between Milwaukee and Minneapolis. It also didn't hurt that Tomah was on the itinerary of the great Chicago, Milwaukee and St. Paul Railroad, which was built in 1858.

You can't talk about Tomah without mentioning cranberries. In fact, the town calls itself the "gateway to cranberry country," as well as to Wisconsin's Amish culture. Both are prevalent in the area, and both draw visitors for the cultural and historical atmosphere.

About cranberries: The cranberry season is celebrated each year in September. Wisconsin in recent years has been the largest cranberry producing state in the country, with the largest cranberry-processing station in the world. The area where cranberries are screened and processed is a few miles east of Tomah, off Highway 21. More cranberry trivia—there are 2,000-plus acres of cranberry marshes in the Tomah area.

Here's one more reason why historical weekend travelers should gravitate to Tomah: the profusion of antique shops in and around the area. If you want convenience, visit the Tomah Antique Mall described below in the Shopping section.

For more information on the area or for information on self-guided tours of area cranberry marshes, contact the Greater Tomah Area Chamber of Commerce/Convention and Visitor Bureau, (608) 372-2166 or (800) 94-TOMAH (948-6624), visit the chamber at 805 Superior Avenue, or check the Web site at www.tomahwisconsin.com.

OTHER SITES AND ATTRACTIONS

Amish Country. Most of the area's Amish people live south and west of

Tomah. Since the Amish are quiet, unworldly folks, respect their privacy if you decide to take a tour of area back roads. Do ask permission before snapping their photos and don't speed along roads dotted with buggies, bicyclists, and pedestrians. "Gateway to Cranberry Country Adventure Guide Driving Tours," a guide to the area Amish communities, is available at the Greater Tomah Area Chamber of Commerce, 805 Superior Avenue.

Cranberry Expo Museum and Gift Shop, County EW, east of Warrens, (608) 378-4878; Web site is cranberry.expo.com. If your interest in history extends to cranberries, this is your cup of tea. This museum showcases and preserves cranberry culture and machinery.

Little Red Schoolhouse, Superior Avenue. Yes, Virginia, there really were little red schoolhouses in Wisconsin's pioneer days. This one is usually open for your curiosity between mid-May and Labor Day. In Gillett Park (named for the father-son team who named the town Tomah).

Tomah Area Historical Society Museum, 1112 S. Superior Avenue, (800) 94-TOMAH. Displays of Tomah native Frank King's syndicated comic strip, "Gasoline Alley." Also, industrial history regarding lumber, railroads, and cranberries. Usually open mid-May through late October. Call for days and hours.
LODGING
Lark Inn, 229 N. Superior Avenue, Highway 12, (608) 372-5981. Country charm includes colorful quilts and comforters, a gazebo, suites, historic log cabins, antiques, and homemade cookies and muffins.
DINING
Burnstad's European Village & Cafe, Highways 12/16 East, (608) 372-4040. The European-style cafe features fine food throughout the day. Salads, soups, sandwiches, entrees. Cranberry country chicken is a chicken sandwich served on toasted sourdough Craisin (raisinlike dried cranberry) bread, and there are freshly made banana cream and other pies. Who can resist the revolving window of luscious, mile-high pies, breads, and pastries?

Crockers Supper Club, off Highway 16 in Sparta, 15 miles west of Tomah, (608) 269-2406. A satisfying supper club with good choices, including steak and seafood.
SHOPPING
Antique Mall of Tomah, Cranberry Country Mall, (608) 372-7853. A big place to shop for antiques and collectibles—more than 60 dealers.

Burnstad's European Village, Highway 12/16 East, (608) 372-3277. In 1944, Edna and Chester Burnstad started a grocery half a mile from the current operation. The Burnstads are still in the grocery business, employing nearly 450 people in several Wisconsin towns, including the one next to their Tomah

Wisconsin has long been a top cranberry-producing state; here, the harvest is in full swing near Cranmoor in Wood County.

shopping emporium. Some 16 shops vie for attention here. Upscale shops offer sterling collections of clothing, jewelry, floral displays, and kitchen creations. Live piano tunes (with somewhat syrupy melodies) accompany shoppers as they stroll along the indoor brick path.

WISCONSIN DELLS

The drive from Tomah to the Dells takes about 45 minutes on the interstates, but a more scenic trip involves a couple of state highways. Hop on Highway 131 and take it south for about 25 miles to Highway 33, then take that through Reedsburg. A quick left on Highway 23 will have you knee-deep in Dells attractions, but with a real appreciation of a part of Wisconsin the latest glaciers never reached.

Some 15,000 years ago, following the last Ice Age glacier, melted water gouged out canyons, glens, "dells," and fantastic rock formations in the Wisconsin Dells area. The place has been colored with natural beauty ever since. The ground also has been deemed sacred for Native Americans who lived here over several generations. The Ho-Chunk (formerly known as Winnebago) were the first to settle.

In the 1860s, word of the splendid, ancient rock formations began to spread, drawing tourists to the area for the first time. Lure of the Dells' peculiar rock outcroppings and unusual beauty captivated more and more tourists. It was only natural that a plethora of businesses would spring up to accommodate the growing number of curious travelers.

By the looks of today's tourist trade, this year-round playground would amaze the 19th-century inhabitants, particularly between May and October. They would be shocked to see how tourism has expanded the once sleepy town adjacent to a backwater bend on the Wisconsin River.

Today, more than three million people a year visit the 15 miles of scenic inspiration dotting the Upper and Lower Dells of the Wisconsin River. Even though there has been controversy over the commercialism of the area, there is plenty to see and do if a visitor's goal is to concentrate on the vintage Dells. Every year more hotels, restaurants, and attractions open, but there remains a sense of the old Dells—travelers just have to look harder for it. The following listing of inns, restaurants, and sights and attractions should provide more of a look at the Dells of long ago.

The best way to see the Dells is by one of the cruise boats that ply the waters of the Upper and Lower Dells. Not much has changed in the cruise business since the area began drawing 19th-century travelers. The Upper Dells is my favorite ride. The two-hour narrated tour on blue-and-white boats built in

H. H. Bennett surveys his beloved Dells for another appealing site to capture on film.

the 1950s floats past rock formations carved 500 million years ago from Cambrian sandstone. Many formations have odd shapes and the game on board is to find the Indian chief, piano, or other likenesses in the rocks.

Once you reach Witches Gulch, an area discovered by photographer H. H. Bennett in the 1870s when he climbed a frozen waterfall to snap an image, you'll disembark to explore the landscape. (More about Bennett and his studio, now a museum, later.) A boardwalk heads into a cool, eerily spectacular canyon. There is also a one-hour Lower Dells tour, which flows past many memorable rock formations; a guide fills visitors in on local history.

In 1888, the Wisconsin River near the Dells was less populated but still a magnet for people seeking summertime fun.

People who have spent some time in Wisconsin tend to take one of the most popular tourist attractions in the United States for granted. It's glitzy, gaudy, and bigger than life, but it's also where many families find more to do, no matter what their ages, than anywhere else in the state. Drivers headed Dells-ward are bombarded with billboards advertising hundreds of attractions tightly clumped together in the main city section, but also spread over 10,000 acres.

If someone were to arrive for the first time in the U.S. from a foreign country, and their first stop were the Dells, the culture shock could be severe. Some other recreational areas, like Disney World, are obviously based on fantasy. At the Dells, almost everything is a fantasy, but the foreign visitor might find it hard to differentiate what's real and what's not. That is due to the fact that many of the local businesses go along with the Dells mystique. Even though that gas station resembles a gas station, it is also ready with souvenirs, maps, and memorabilia that perpetuate the fantasy.

H. H. Bennett was there when the side-wheeler *Alexander Mitchell* waited to take passengers on an excursion through the Dells in the mid-1880s.

Before the Dells mushroomed into a major tourist attraction, it was inhabited by lumberjacks, loggers, and Native Americans. It wasn't too many years ago that "real Indians" could be seen selling their wares and occasionally allowing their pictures to be taken next to a wooden cigar-store Indian.

But the times, they have been a-changin' the Dells. The area has been transformed from a woodsy, natural sort of place to one full of slick, touristy operations. Now the atmosphere is more high-tech (see Tommy Bartlett's Robot World) and full of quick thrills (Noah's Ark Waterpark), just the sort of atmosphere that instills a sense of wonder in kids today.

But can the Dells provide some bona fide links to Wisconsin's past? The answer is yes, and it's in the form of the H. H. Bennett Studio and History Center, 215 Broadway, (608) 253-3523, opened in 2000. It's all history and no hype.

Henry Hamilton Bennett was an extraordinary 19th-century photographer whose pictures of places he loved helped popularize Wisconsin Dells as a tourist destination. During the "golden age of landscape photography," from

Two girls admire the Wisconsin River from a rock canopy in the Dells in this H. H. Bennett photo.

after the Civil War to the late 1890s, Bennett was making a name for himself by producing provocative portraits of the land and its people. From an eight-room brick building on Broadway, in what was then Kilbourn City (its name was changed to Wisconsin Dells in 1931), Bennett created stirring photographs that continue to haunt and captivate the viewer. His favorite subjects were the area's Ho-Chunk Indians, ice palaces, and Midwest city life.

Considering the artistic nature of his work, it's hard to imagine he was so prolific. Yet his energy was legendary. By 1887, he was selling a staggering number of stereoscoptic images, about 30,000 per month. Studio portraits and an adjacent souvenir shop helped pay the bills for his alleged first love, landscape photography. Bennett said, "You don't have to pose nature and it's less trouble to please."

Not only did Bennett have an exceptional eye for capturing the beauty and personality of people and places, he was also a technical innovator. The field of photography is indebted to him for his trailblazing invention of a stop-action shutter that allowed subjects to be caught in mid-motion. Among some of his other inventions are various types of cameras, print frames, print washers, and customized mounting apparatus.

His technical and creative artistry have been heralded throughout the world, and his work is seen in collections at the New York Museum of Modern Art, at the Getty Center in Los Angeles, and the Smithsonian Institution in Washington, D.C. Bennett's studio is part of the State Historical Society of Wisconsin.

Bennett died in 1908, but the beauty he captured on glass plate negatives hasn't been lost. Since his death, four generations of family members have preserved his 8,000 negatives. Prints continue to be made from them.

Oliver and Jean Dyer Reese (Bennett's granddaughter) initiated the project of the H. H. Bennett Museum and Historic Studio with a $1 million gift of the studio and its historic collections of photographs, equipment, and memorabilia. The restoration of the site, as well the raising of an additional $2.9 million, was finalized. At completion, the property was deeded to the State Historical Society of Wisconsin to operate as its ninth official historical site.

Visitors will see a re-creation of the world as Bennett saw it. More than 6,000 square feet of exhibits trace Bennett's career and the impact he had on places he photographed, including the Dells. This historic studio is not to be missed. For those intrigued by history and photography it's a must, but it's also a remarkable place to visit for those interested in peering into the life of an artist and his work. Call for more information.

For more information on the area, contact the Wisconsin Dells Visitors & Convention Bureau, 701 Superior Street, (608) 254-8088 or (800) 22-DELLS.

OTHER SITES AND ATTRACTIONS

Dells Army Ducks, (608) 254-6080; Web site is www.dellsducks.com. Get an up-close and personal look at the waterways and scenic trails when you take a ride on these amphibious World War II landing craft. Some 75 of the awkward but sturdy hulks have been brought out of retirement so visitors could enjoy a one-hour journey along eight miles of wilderness paths and sandbars. Some say it's the only way to explore the offbeat areas of the Dells.

Mirror Lake, a few miles southwest of the Dells, has long been a tranquil alternative to its fast-paced neighbor.

Dells Auto Museum, 591 Wisconsin Dells Parkway, (608) 254-2008. Alerting all antiques lovers. This spot has old cars (plenty of convertibles) spanning the first 85 years of the 20th century, plus dolls and toys.

Dells Boat Tours, (608) 254-8555. Contact them to make reservations for both Upper and Lower Dells boat tours.

Indian Ceremonial at Stand Rock, for ticket information, (608) 253-7444. The mystical ceremony has been keeping visitors captivated since 1929. Traditional Ho-Chunk Nation songs, chanting, dancing, and music in a natural outdoor amphitheater.

Noah's Ark, south on Highway 12/23, (608) 254-6351. The largest water complex in the U.S., this water-filled theme park covers 65 acres. This is a gigantic operation for those who want water fun and activities presented dozens of different ways. Open Memorial Day weekend through Labor Day. All-day passes get you all the water activities.

Ripley's Believe it or Not, 115 Broadway, (608) 253-7556. A wide assortment of odd and unbelievable stuff, including supposed curses by King Tut himself. Look for the only building around with part of an airplane (simulating a crash) hanging out the front. Open May through October.

LODGING

Hawk's View Bed & Breakfast, E11344 Pocahontas Circle, (608) 254-2979. Good place to eagle-watch and enjoy the views of the Lower Dells. Chalet features three guest rooms and private cottage.

Historic Bennett House, 825 Oak Street, (608) 254-2500. The 1863 former home of H. H. Bennett. The lovely structure, surrounded by a white picket fence, features three guest rooms, antiques, and fireside breakfasts.

Seth Peterson Cottage, Mirror Lake State Park, (608) 254-6551 (book far in advance). If you're a fan of Frank Lloyd Wright's architecture, this place is for you. The one-bedroom, completely furnished cottage offering sensational views was designed by Wright, and is the only Wright-designed home known to be available for rent.

Thunder Valley Inn, W15344 Waubeek Road, (608) 254-4145; Web site is www.thundervalleyinn.com. This Scandinavian working farm features 10 bedrooms, authentic Scandinavian food, a woodsy setting, farm animals, even old-fashioned "threshing suppers" (for more information about its restaurant, see Dining below).

DINING

The Cheese Factory, 521 Wisconsin Dells Parkway, (608) 253-6065. An old-fashioned soda fountain, cappuccino bar, and The Secret Garden (restaurant in downtown Dells) are reasons to visit the place that calls itself "one step closer to heaven." International vegetarian choices, plus Dairy State favorites like thick and creamy milkshakes.

Del-Bar Supper Club, 800 Wisconsin Dells Parkway, (608) 253-1861. Since 1943, this Dells institution, designed by a Frank Lloyd Wright-trained architect, has been going strong. Killer steaks and seafood. Open daily for dinner.

Fischer's Supper Club, 441 Wisconsin Dells Parkway, (608) 253-7531. Opened in 1949, this family-owned, old-style supper club has about anything you can imagine. The menu is long and well-tested: orange roughy, chicken Florentine, Wiener schnitzel, prime rib, fresh salmon, lamb chops, pike ... you get the picture. Open year-round for dinner.

Ishnala, S2011 Ishnala Road, (608) 253-1771. The Mirror Lake property with the pines poking through the roof started up in the 1950s. Ever since, they've been serving up steaks, ribs, seafood, and other entrees in this pretty wooded setting.

Thunder Valley Inn, W15344 Waubeek Road, (608) 254-4145. This working farm with Old World charm features great breakfast fare including Norwegian pancakes with lingonberries, country dinners with many home-grown foods, and seasonal Saturday night, fiddle-driven, hoedown jamborees.

Wally's House of Embers, 935 Wisconsin Dells Parkway, (608) 253-6411. Salmon, Austrian dishes, barbecued ribs, pasta, seafood, and a mean special occasion Sunday brunch make Wally's a popular dining spot.

SHOPPING

Broadway is Wisconsin Dells' Main Street. Go up and down this avenue of kitsch and the few side streets to check out the profusion of gift shops, souvenir shops, and a sprinkling of merchants catering to antiques.

Wisconsin Dells Antique Mall (two locations), 720 Oak Street, (608) 254-2422. Same owner, larger space, the second location is at 2270 S. Highway 12, (608) 356-7600. Many dealers, lots of collectibles.

FESTIVALS

Flake Out Festival. The third week of January brings in huge crowds as snow sculpting, ice carving, sleigh rides, and hot-air balloon rides punctuate the winter's skies. Contact Wisconsin Dells Visitor & Convention Bureau. (800) 22-DELLS.

Great Wisconsin Dells Balloon Rally. The weekend after Memorial Day, about one hundred hot-air balloons wrap the landscape in every imaginable color. Liftoff takes place in a field near I-90/94 and Highway 12.

DEVIL'S LAKE

After a visiting the Dells, you're faced with a dilemma. Should you head south to Devil's Lake and from there on to Baraboo? Or will it be north, and the many attractions of Stevens Point and Wausau? Or maybe both? No matter—we'll cover both jaunts and you make the final choice. You can't go wrong with either.

First Devil's Lake, mainly because it's only a 17-mile drive south from the Dells. Take Highway 12 south and pass through Lake Delton and West Baraboo to the high bluffs encircling the big lake. Turn left on Highway 33, which will take you into the North Range of the park and into the Lower Narrows Gap or North Shore entrance. You can also enter this land of Indian mounds, Devil's Doorway, Balanced Rock, Elephant Cave, and soaring turkey vultures with six-foot-wide wingspreads, by the South Shore entrance.

But the North Shore is the more scenic way to enter this treasure trove of natural wonders. The drive meanders through heavily canopied birches, aspens, maples, and oaks. Intermittent light filters through the umbrella of intertwining branches and leaves. Ads for Devil's Lake in the mid-1800s hyped the area as an "enchanted summer land." It was also heralded as a perfect spot for "tired brain workers, a place to rest and get strong." The advice still is good.

Any time of the year, Devil's Lake provides an oasis for those seeking tranquil beauty.

At park headquarters, visitors can buy park passes from an attendant in a rambling stone building put up by Civil Conservation Corp workers in 1939. Walking through the cleared woods toward the lake, travelers will see why all this has been compared to the beauty of New York's Adirondacks.

Aficionados of historical weekends will love Devil's Lake because evidence of its long past has been well documented. Tourists and scientists alike have been studying and enjoying Devil's Lake for well over a century. Based on radiocarbon dating, it is believed that Native Americans lived here for 500 generations. Twelve miles southwest of Devil's Lake, a rock shelter contributes to evidence that this area is one of the oldest known settlements in the Midwest.

Among the earliest settlers were the Effigy Mound Builders. About a thousand years ago, they built mounds in the form of animal shapes for burials and important festivals. Today the mystery continues as to why the mounds were built and why they took on animal shapes. This is one of the only sites in the country where you will see their work. Look for Mound Builders' creations in the form of a lynx near the Nature Center, a bear on the lake's north shore, and a bird mound on the southeastern corner of the lake.

The story of the formation of Devil's Lake starts a million years ago. According to geologists, rivers drained into seas, which in turn covered this area. Over the next hundreds of thousands of years, a series of seas withdrew, then invaded the area again. Finally, about 15,000 years ago, the Wisconsin Glacier plowed through, defining the area even further. The result of centuries of ongoing geological activity is the splendid Baraboo Valley. This picturesque landscape is marked by gorges and massive bluffs 500 feet high. They ring Devil's Lake, a sparkling, spring-fed body of water 50 feet deep and about a mile long.

In the late 1880s Rand McNally's *Tourist Guide to the North-West* called Devil's Lake "a tremendous gorge, hemmed in on all sides by frowning rocks, of prodigious size, piled up in every conceivable form." The glowing report went on to conclude that Devil's Lake "is one of the loveliest sheets of water in the whole world."

When the railroad was completed in 1873, the mountainous setting was a draw for visitors from all over the world. In its heyday, 18 trains a day, nine in each direction, pulled through here. To accommodate the swell, several hotels were built. One of the most popular, the Minniwauken House, later known as Cliff House, played host to thousands of guests between 1866 and the early 1900s. Today, more than a million visitors a year enjoy the park, but they come by car, camper, or bike, and if they stay overnight, they pitch a tent in one of many campgrounds.

In the early 1900s, when the railroad cut back on scheduled arrivals and departures, the drop-in traffic had a direct effect on the hotels. Eventually, the hotels closed (there are no hotels on the lake any longer), the trains stopped coming, and in 1911, private land surrounding the lake became Devil's Lake State Park.

Think again if you believe tourism declined when the hotels closed. Tourists kept coming in droves, to camp and for day trips. The area also was being regularly visited by scientists whose outdoor classrooms studied the park's "weird beauty." The University of Wisconsin, the University of Chicago,

Parfrey's Glen, a few miles east of Devil's Lake; the area has long been a haven for campers, climbers, and other nature lovers.

and Northwestern University all had geology camps here at one time. Today, more than one hundred colleges and universities sponsor geology field trips to one of the Midwest's most unusual places.

The Circus World Museum in Baraboo preserves the magical memories of the American circus.

Perhaps the most frequently asked question about Devil's Lake is one no one can answer for certain. There are many theories as to how the lake was named. When the first white settlers arrived, in the 1840s, they called it Spirit Lake. A few years later, the name was changed to Devil's Lake. Indian legends said the lake was tainted with evil once the white man arrived.

Another Indian legend says a giant, devilish meteor struck the area, carving out great gap between the bluffs. The most interesting legend describes a fierce battle between water spirits, who lived deep in the lake's underwater caves, and giant thunderbirds, which flew over the lake. (Watch the vultures gliding over the bluffs and you will see how legends get started.)

The war over the water supposedly lasted for days. Huge boulders, still visible today, tumbled from the rugged cliffs. Most of the water spirits were killed, but the legend says not all were destroyed. Some, they say, still live in the depths of the lake.

Then there is the romantic legend about Minnewawa, an Indian princess who fell in love with Pierre, a French hunter. A tragic love triangle developed when Windago, a young Indian brave, became wildly jealous of the pair. To decide who would marry Minnewawa, the men fought each other to both of their deaths. Minnewawa was so distraught she took her own life. This would allow her to join Pierre in the spirit world. Today, legend says if you look at the lake on a moonlit night, you might see the spirits of the lovers floating over the water.

Many families still picnic along the lakeshore's grassy knolls. Doing nothing but gazing at the mountainous setting is still a good activity, judging from the number of blanketed spots held down by coolers and picnic baskets. The restless can sit on a boulder and fish for brown trout, walleye, northern pike, bass, and panfish. Children enjoy watching tiny minnows and other fish swim close to the water's edge.

Or walk to the North Shore's Chateau, a large log-and-stone structure that serves as a mini-market, gift store, and boat-rental facility. Here visitors can rent sailboats, sailboards, canoes, and small rowboats. No inner tubes are for rent, although the concession area often sells inflatable water toys. A majority of visitors, young and old, bring inner tubes (bring an air pump or have it filled at a gas station near the park) or rafts and spend hours bobbing on the peaceful waters among the majestic bluffs.

Scuba diving and rock climbing are other popular pursuits. Visitors will see diving flags, a requirement, on the surface of the lake. And while the most spectacular views of Devil's Lake are from the top of the broken-up summit cliffs, rock climbers should be experienced before making the ascent.

Hikers of all abilities can admire the area from above by following 15 different trails. Markers are color-coded and give hikers an approximate time needed to complete the loop, plus the degree of difficulty. For instance, the East Bluff trail (orange) is a medium trail which winds among bluffs and woods and has scenic views and dropoffs. This 75-minute hike goes to Elephant Cave and Elephant Rock.

For summer entertainment, consider Saturday night dances at the Chateau. Since the long wall of windows overlooks the lake, there is no better spot to view the bewitching waters by moonlight. Who knows, you might see something else on its moonlit surface. An appearance by the "spirits of the lake" may make the visit a hauntingly different journey.

BARABOO

After visiting historic Devil's Lake, it's time to head to historic Baraboo, a few miles to the south. It's a quaint place filled with Victorian houses. It is also an anachronism of sorts, since it has an old-fashioned city square bustling with activity.

Baraboo has a significant tourist attraction of its own: Circus World Museum, 550 Water Street, (608) 356-0800. The museum is a National Historic Landmark and a treasure trove of circus memorabilia. The 50-acre museum collects, preserves, and interprets circus history at the original winter quarters of the Ringling Brothers Circus. From 1886 to 1918, Ringling Brothers set up headquarters for "The Greatest Show on Earth" on the shores of the Baraboo River.

There are eight historic Ringling buildings and barns that once held the showy circus operations, including animals and train cars. Visitors are dazzled by such things as the world's largest collection (170 wagons) of gilt-edged circus wagons. The museum puts on the Great Circus Parade in Milwaukee each summer. Besides viewing circus memorabilia here, visitors enjoy a Big Top circus performance under a canvas tent. The variety show is aimed at "children of all ages." There is an admission fee. Circus World Museum, a not-for-profit operation, is owned by the State Historical Society of Wisconsin.

OTHER SITES AND ATTRACTIONS

Mid-Continent Railway, North Freedom (15 minutes southwest of Baraboo), (608) 522-4261. Historic steam train takes you for a ride into the scenic countryside.

Museum of Norman Rockwell Art, 227 South Park Street, Reedsburg, (608) 524-2123. Fifteen miles southwest of Wisconsin Dells. World's largest collection of its kind (about 4,000 selections) of Norman Rockwell work is on display. Framed and unframed prints for sale. Open daily May through October. Winter hours vary.

STEVENS POINT

An easy drive of about 75 miles separates Wisconsin Dells from the city that marks the very center of the state, Stevens Point. Drivers can opt for the I-39/Highway 51 route, or they can meander up County Z from a point about 20 miles north of the Dells to Wisconsin Rapids, then on to Stevens Point on Highway 54. The nice thing about the more rural route is that it shadows the Wisconsin River, a waterway steeped in history and closely tied to the economic development of the state.

The river is fascinating, whether for the Portage-based scheme to connect the Mississippi with Lake Michigan using the lower Wisconsin, or for the

The opulent Al Ringling Theater in downtown Baraboo was built in 1915 and was a popular venue for vaudeville acts; today, it hosts live performances and movies.

widths that the river attains before plunging through the narrows that form the Dells. Dotted with county parks and seasonal and permanent residences, the Wisconsin is said to be among the hardest working rivers in America. Fed by smaller rivers such as the Baraboo, the Lemonweir, the Yellow, the Big Eau Pleine, the Rib, and the Eau Claire, this large, natural stream is by far the most important water between the big lake and the big river.

A present-day bicyclist takes a breather on the Elroy-Sparta Bike Trail.

Stevens Point is almost exactly between the top of the state and the bottom, as well as being central between east and west. It is a city with a population of around 37,000 (including nearby Plover and Whiting). "Point" is in Portage County, one of the state's four original counties, founded in 1836.

In the 1830s, John B. DuBay started a trading post on the Wisconsin River, in the area now known as Stevens Point. By 1836, when the United States signed a formal treaty with Native Americans, the primitive settlement along the riverbanks had become a permanent community.

Around the same time, George Stevens, a lumber entrepreneur, began using the Wisconsin River for moving supplies between lumber operations. Stevens' headquarters on the river soon was named after the aggressive river trader who plied its waters.

The sawmills that brought the first settlers here eventually brought more people in as paper mills began thriving. But it wasn't until the Old Wisconsin Railroad (the Soo Line) made Stevens Point a scheduled stop that the area became easily linked to the rest of the state, as well as to the rest of the country.

Today, at the end of Main Street, you will see a marker noting the spot where George Stevens set up shop back in the first half of the 19th century. The lumber mills and trading posts are long gone along the Wisconsin River. But other industries, such as insurance and construction, have replaced the riverfront activities.

The area around Stevens Point is known as a vigorous agribusiness community. This rich farming area, called "Wisconsin's Central Sands," is home to several large canning facilities owned by such giants as Ore-Ida and Del Monte. Plover, a few minutes south of Stevens Point, is one of the most important potato-producing regions in the country.

For more information, contact the Stevens Point Area Convention & Visitor Bureau, 340 Division Street N., (715) 344-2556 or (800) 236-INFO.

Iola's main street: dusty, dirty, and bustling.

OTHER SITES AND ATTRACTIONS

Portage County Historical Museum, 1475 Water Street, (715) 344-4423. Built in 1905, this interesting structure was used as a synagogue until 1980. Since then it has been the home of the Portage County Historical Society and museum of Jewish heritage. Usually open 1 p.m. to 5 p.m., Saturday and Sunday only, June through August.

Portage County Historical Village, in Heritage Park, Madison Avenue and Willow Drive, nearby Plover, (715) 344-4423. A potpourri of authentic 19th-century buildings representing Portage County's earliest days. Open 1 p.m. to 5 p.m., weekedns only, June through September. Call about group tours.

Schmeeckle Reserve, North Point Drive, (715) 346-4992. This 275-acre reserve, supported by the University of Wisconsin–Stevens Point, is a research and teaching resource—within the confines of the city, open to the public. Visitors can view wildlife, boat, fish, jog, or hike the trails. Visit the Wisconsin Conservation Hall of Fame on the property. The UW–Stevens Point was the first university in the country to offer a degree in natural resources.

Stevens Point Brewery, 2617 Water Street, (715) 344-9310. Don't leave Stevens Point until you've visited this venerable small-town brewery. Founded in 1857, it is one of the oldest breweries in the state. Those in the know often point to Point beer as among the best beers in America. Tours are usually given several times a day. Call for times (small fee). Finish up with beer tasting, popcorn, and a visit to the gift shop. As the locals say, "When you're out of Point, you're out of town."

Flat tires and rutted roads were two of the many perils facing motorists in the early days of auto travel.

LODGING

The Amherst Inn, 303 S. Main Street, (715) 824-2326. Thirteen miles east of Stevens Point, in the small town of Amherst, is this wonderful Victorian home. Even if you don't stay here, it puts you in the mood of the past. The slow-paced, small-town atmosphere makes it easy to stop and smell the roses.

Dreams of Yesteryear B & B, 1100 Brawley Street, (715) 341-4525. The past is easy to envision when staying in this dreamy Victorian, not far from downtown. It is listed on the National Historic Register and featured in Victorian Homes magazine. Three floors of antiques and charm.

A Victorian Swan on Water, 1716 Water Street, (715) 345-0595. In downtown Stevens Point near the Wisconsin River, this 1899 home offers three comfy rooms, one with whirlpool and fireplace. It has nice architectural touches and a picturesque garden.

DINING

Pandy's, 1414 W. McMillan Street, (715) 387-3842. In an antique cheese factory in nearby Marshfield, this popular spot offers up atmosphere and good eats. Seafood, steaks, sandwiches. Open for lunch and dinner.

The Restaurant, 1800 North Point Drive, (715) 346-6010. Considered one of the best restaurants in the state. Upscale dining overlooking immaculate grounds at the Sentry Insurance Headquarters. Linen tablecloths, imaginative dinners like the savory chicken livers dish and spaghetti Caruso, one of the house specialties. Other choices include seafood, pasta, and veal. Dinners only.

The Silver Coach, 38 Park Ridge Drive, (715) 341-6588, serves great Cajun-influenced food in a restored train car with an original mahogany front.

SHOPPING

The Stevens Point area is known as the home of several big mail-order companies and a plethora of interesting shops.

Downtown antique shops, 1100 block of Main Street. Antique lovers can while away time roaming through a big building filled with about a dozen antique shops.

Figi's, 1302 N. Central Avenue, Marshfield, (715) 384-1128. One of the country's best known mail-order houses for Wisconsin products, namely sausage and cheese.

Herrschners Quality Needlecraft, 2800 Hoover Road, (715) 341-8686. This is the home of the largest mail-order craft catalog in the world. If that weren't enough, it is also the largest source of yarn in the country.

WAUSAU

Wausau, 34 miles north of Stevens Point, has long been associated with Wausau Insurance. The city also is considered the gateway to the North Woods. Wausau is dominated by the towering presence of Granite Peak, an imposing 1,940-foot mound that was known as Rib Mountain for many years. It is often referred to as the highest point in the state (the honor actually goes to Timm's Hill in Price County, near Ogema, at 1,951.5 feet). Rib Mountain State Park (its name didn't change) is a year-round playground featuring downhill skiing and

Motoring into the countryside and stopping for a picnic lunch was popular recreation in 1917.

other sports, and the Wisconsin River's ever-present path. The river, once used to power sawmills, doubles as a world-class whitewater kayaking course.

Wausau's history and development is directly associated with lumbering. In 1836, the U.S. government claimed a portion of land along the river from the hands of the Menominee Tribe. In 1838, St. Louis lumber barons sent George Stevens to the area to scout for a potential sawmill site. Stevens believed it to be the best mill site in the country.

After lumbering took hold, settlements sprang up all along the riverfront. For a while the area was called Big Bull Falls. Later it was changed to Wausau, which means "faraway place" in Chippewa. By 1850, fourteen mills were running in high gear, processing large shipments of logs floating into the area from the North Woods.

Many of Wausau's magnificent mansions, created in the sawmill heyday of the late 19th century, have been destroyed. Several still exist though, such as the extraordinary Cyrus C. Yawkey house, now used as the site of the Marathon County Historical Society. Including Wausau on a tour of historical places will enable visitors to browse downtown streets with beautifully preserved homes. Get a map from the Chamber of Commerce and take a walking tour of more than 60 area houses. Another reason to walk around Wausau: Red-bricked Washington Square offers shopping among the preserved buildings.

Incidentally, the vineyard-like agriculture in the area is ginseng. Approximately 95 percent of the U.S. crop is grown in Marathon County. Ginseng is a big deal for the state as a whole. It's the number one cash export crop of Wisconsin, with more than $90 million in annual production.

Why doesn't everyone grow ginseng? For starters, it is a quirky crop. Once planted, farmers feel lucky when it takes root, since it is highly sensitive to weather conditions. Once rooted, they feel even luckier if it reaches maturity, usually several seasons later. More bad news: When an acre of ginseng, about 2,000 pounds worth of the crop, reaches maturity, the acre dies off for a long time—about a hundred years. Visitors should respect the perseverance of ginseng farmers.

To learn more about ginseng, contact the Ginseng Board of Wisconsin, 16H Menard Plaza, (715) 845-7300. For other information, contact the Wausau Chamber of Commerce, 300 Third Street, (715) 845-6231.

OTHER SITES AND ATTRACTIONS

Cyrus C. Yawkey House/Marathon County Historical Museum, 403 Mc-Indoe Street, (715) 848-6143. This 1901 classical-revival mansion and former home of a lumber magnate is now the home of the Marathon County Historical Society. Architectural details, such as Ionic columns and beautiful woodwork, make stopping here worth the time. Lovely formal gardens. Usually open daily except Mondays.

Grand Theater, 415 Fourth Street, (715) 842-0988. There is nothing like seeing a musical or theater arts performance in the $2 million, beautifully restored 1927 Greek Revival opera house.

Leigh Yawkey Woodson Art Museum, 700 N. 12th Street, (715) 845-7010. A highly respected exhibit showcases Birds In Art—a fine tribute to birds in all forms of art, ranging from paintings to rare Royal Worcester porcelain. The museum, housed in a lovely old mansion, offers a rare look at birds as artistic creatures.

LODGING

Everest Inn, 601 McIndoe Street, (715) 848-5651. A mix of classic and contemporary in this charming Queen Anne. Billiards with fireplace suite.

Rosenberry Inn Bed & Breakfast, 511 Franklin Street, (715) 842-5733. This eight-bedroom, 1908 Prairie School home features large rooms and gorgeous leaded-glass windows, fireplaces, whirlpools.

DINING

Wagon Wheel Supper Club, 3901 N. 6th Street, (715) 675-2263. A Wausau landmark since the 1940s. Great selections include wild rice soup, steaks, bison, and seafood.

SHOPPING

Rib Mountain Antique Mall, 3300 Eagle Avenue, (715) 848-5564. One of the biggest antique emporiums in the state, there is something for everyone here.

CENTRAL WISCONSIN AT A GLANCE

MUSEUMS

Cyrus C. Yawkey House/Marathon County Historical Museum: 1901 classical-revival mansion, former home of a lumber magnate, is now one of the homes of the Marathon County Historical Society. Wausau.

Cranberry Expo Limited: Learn about the state's cranberry history and specialized cranberry harvesting machines. East of Warrens.

H. H. Bennett Studio and History Center: Museum opened in 2000, showcasing fabled 19th-century photographer H. H. Bennett and his hypnotic photographs of the Wisconsin Dells. The museum is located in Bennett's renovated studio.

Museum of Norman Rockwell Art: World's largest collection of Norman Rockwell's prints. Reedsburg.

Tomah Area Historical Society Museum: Displays of local cartoonist Frank King's syndicated comic strip "Gasoline Alley," plus history of area lumbering, railroads and cranberry business.

HISTORICAL SITES AND ATTRACTIONS

Al Ringling Theater: Listed on the National Register of Historic Places. Opened in 1915 and debuted first-run movies like "Birth of a Nation." Often called "America's prettiest playhouse," its lavish interior was inspired by the Grand Opera House of the Palace of Versailles. Courthouse Square, Baraboo.

Circus World Museum: A National Historic Landmark, this is a treasure trove of circus memorabilia, including the world's largest collection of circus wagons. Baraboo.

Devil's Lake State Park: Around 1,000 years ago, Effigy Mound Builders, the area's earliest settlers, built effigy mounds in the shapes of different animals in the area now occupied by the park.

Little Red Schoolhouse: Nineteenth century one-room schoolhouse. Gillett Park on Superior Avenue. Tomah.

Mid-Continent Railway: Historic 19th-century steam train takes passengers for rides in the country. North Freedom.

Natural Bridge State Park: The Paleo-Indians once inhabited this site said to be the oldest inhabited site in the Midwest. Southwest of Devils Lake State Park, near North Freedom.

Old Indian Agency House: Built in 1832 by the U.S. government for John Kinzie, an agent to the Winnebago (now Ho-Chunk Nation) Indians. Portage.

Portage County Historical Village: A composite of 19th-century buildings representing Portage County's earliest days. Portage County is one of the original four counties of the state. Plover.

Sauk County Historical Museum: Housed in a 1906 mansion, displays include pioneer and Indian artifacts, Civil War equipment, toys, and textiles. Baraboo.

Surgeon's Quarters: Early 19th-century home, built between 1819 and 1828 for Francois LeRoi. Restored home has a good collection of period furnishings. Portage.

OTHER HISTORICAL STOPS

Antique Mall of Tomah: Over 60 dealers offer diversified treasures. Tomah.

Burnstad's European Village & Cafe: Begun as the 1944 South Side Grocery, the family business now comprises a shopping village, grocery, and restaurant. Tomah.

Fort McCoy: Tour an Army base that spans 60,000 acres and more than 1,200 buildings. The base, originally called Camp McCoy, was founded in 1909. One-hour narrated auto tours for groups or visit the Historical Center on base. (608) 388-2407.

Grand Theater: Restored 1927 Greek Revival opera house now features musicals and theater arts. Wausau.

Locomotive No. 2713: An original locomotive of the old Soo Line. Southside Memorial Park, Stevens Point.

Mainstreet Historic District: Over 60 buildings in downtown Stevens Point comprise the Mathias Mitchell Public Square—the Mainstreet Historic District.

Point Brewery: Founded in 1857, it's one of the oldest breweries in the state. Stevens Point.

Rib Mountain Antique Mall: One of the biggest antique emporiums in the state. Wausau.

Walking tour of Wausau: Get a map from the Chamber of Commerce and take a walking tour of more than 60 area houses built in the heyday of the lumber barons.

Wisconsin Dells' Ducks: World War II amphibious landing craft now take passengers over wilderness trails and shallow samplings of the Wisconsin River. Wisconsin Dells.

HISTORICAL EVENTS AND FESTIVALS

APRIL

Yukon Trails Spring Rendezvous, Lyndon Station (Monroe County).

JULY

Monroe County Fair, Tomah.

AUGUST

Gasoline Alley Day, Tomah.
Badger Steam and Gas Engine Show, Baraboo.

SEPTEMBER

Baraboo River Rendezvous, Baraboo.
Central Wisconsin Antique Show and Sale, Wausau.

CHAPTER 6

SOUTHWESTERN WISCONSIN
THE UNGLACIATED UPLANDS

Wagons loaded with barrels of beer from the Potosi Brewery.

THE AREA BOUNDED by the Wisconsin River, the Mississippi River, the Illinois-Wisconsin line, and Interstate 90 is different from the rest of the state. Distinctly unglaciated, the land rolls, appearing to support more cows than people. It's also a pleasantly historic place to visit, making up for its lack of lakes and pine forests with ethnic villages and views that stretch for miles from one of many vantage points.

How travelers navigate their historic weekend trip in this area is up to them. With a distance of only about 75 miles from north to south, the region and its many attractions can be can be conveniently visited in two or three days. Probably the best place to begin or the excursion is at Spring Green, home to Frank Lloyd Wright, one the most famous and most controversial natives of Wisconsin. For those who crave city life, Madison is less than an hour away from most parts of the area.

SPRING GREEN

The spiritual home of Frank Lloyd Wright, Wisconsin's iconoclastic architect for the ages, is as good a place as any to begin a historic weekend. Spring Green lies between Highway 14 and the Wisconsin River, some 38 miles west of Madison. The village is 113 miles west of Milwaukee, 200 miles northwest of Chicago, and 255 miles southeast of Minneapolis-St. Paul. Approximately 1,300 people call Spring Green home.

The object of a historical visit is Taliesin, of course. The magnificent home designed by Wright for Wright is just outside of town and is open to visitors. But first some background, not all of it honorable, about the transcendentally talented fellow who is considered America's greatest architect.

Frank Lloyd Wright was born in Richland Center, Wisconsin, in 1867. The year is somewhat in doubt because Wright lied all of his adult life about his age, probably for reasons of vanity. But his birth was recorded by his large family, many of whom were Welsh Unitarians who migrated to this area west of Madison and took up farming.

Wright spent a year at the University of Wisconsin before heading to Chicago and tremendous success. There, his early genius flourished and his designs became much in demand. His penchant for controversy, especially in regard to fulfilling his financial obligations, also grew. The architect believed that great men like himself should not be bothered by monetary matters. No matter how much money he made, he was pursued all his life by creditors. Once, while walking down a street in Madison, Wright was struck by a workman he had stiffed, suffering a broken nose!

After spending a number of productive years in Chicago, Wright moved to Spring Green in 1911 and built Taliesin, which would serve as his home, studio, and classroom for years to come. He lived there with another man's wife, which caused quite a scandal at the time. Taliesin, which means "shining brow" in the Welsh language, is a low, prairie-style home with narrow halls, an expansive roof, even Wright-designed furniture. It was a home, a farm, a studio, and a school. Happily, visitors can tour the place today.

Taliesin can be visited any day, May through October, (608), 588-7900, or look up www.TaliesinPreservation.org. There are half a dozen Wright creations at the site. An admission fee is charged for one of four tours: Hillside, walking, house, or estate. The home is three miles south of Spring Green and just west of the junction of Highway 23 and County C. The Frank Lloyd Wright Visitor Center, which offers driving-tour maps and other helpful information, is at the same intersection and has the same telephone number. Other Wright creations can be seen on the driving tour.

By the way, Wright remained productive for an amazing number of years before dying at the age of 91 in 1959. There are 41 Wright structures presently standing in Wisconsin. Most are private homes and all are in the southern half of the state.

LODGING

Hill Street Bed and Breakfast, 353 W. Hill Street, (608) 588-7751. This Queen Anne Victorian dates from 1904 and offers a choice of seven rooms plus a full breakfast.

DINING

The Post House and Dutch Kitchen Restaurant, Jefferson Street, (608) 588-2595, features a bar designed by a Frank Lloyd Wright disciple. Open for lunch and dinner.

Riverview Terrace Cafe, Highway 23 and County C, (608) 588-7937. The Cafe, a part of Taliesin, offers lunches from May through October.

Spring Green Cafe and General Store, 137 S. Albany Street, (608) 588-7070, is the kind of place Wright might have visited. It offers homestyle food in a converted cheese warehouse.

MINERAL POINT

After Spring Green, head to Mineral Point, a town that is even older and steeped in more history. The drive to this village of 2,500 is a brief one—26 miles. Head south on Highway 23, then south again on Highway 151 and you're there. You can, of course, take less direct routes, perhaps combining them with the Frank Lloyd Wright driving tour (see above).

Settlers began arriving in the Mineral Point area with divining rods in the early 1800s because the word was out—lead, or "mineral," as it was called then, had been discovered in the surrounding hillsides. Mineral Point, so named because of the specific point where mineral was discovered, brought in many optimists looking for a strike. In 1827, Henry Dodge was one of them. When he mined a ton of ore, the news got around. More hopefuls showed up in this southwestern corner of the state. In 1836, the Territory of Wisconsin was established in Mineral Point, and Dodge was its first governor.

Mineral Point in the 1830s was bursting at the seams. Skilled hardrock miners from Cornwall, England, heard of Wisconsin's mining bonanza and arrived in droves. Several hundred settling near the Merry Christmas mine brought more than mining skills to their adopted home. From area limestone they built functional, small stone cottages in tidy rows. Local residents coined the phrase "Shake Rag Under the Hill (now Shake Rag Street)" to describe the miners' quaint neighborhood. The name aptly described how miners' wives called their husbands to dinner. They shook a rag out the window or door to summon their spouses.

While lead mining was the prime reason for the town's growth, it was eventually replaced by zinc mining, which kept Mineral Point in business until the Great Depression of the 1930s called a halt to mining. For many years, the stone cottages were neglected and in various stages of deterioration.

Then in 1970, the state purchased and renovated the buildings. The main attraction is Pendarvis, a cottage on Shake Rag Street, which was turned into a

Interior of one of the cottages at Pendarvis.

museum by the State Historical Society at the time. Here visitors can gain insight into the daily lives of mining families in the 1830s and 1840s when they tour this Cornish miners' colony. The tour of the painstakingly preserved stone and log houses is led by knowledgeable, costumed guides. There is also the opportunity to take a walking tour of the nearby Merry Christmas Mine Hill; admission is free. Pendarvis is operated by the State Historical Society and is open from early May through late October, (608) 987-2122.

Pendarvis and Trelawny, two of the houses that comprise the Pendarvis State Historical Site.

Enterprising artists and entrepreneurs discovered the town in the 1940s and 1950s and began renovating many of its tired buildings. In 1971, Mineral Point's downtown was deemed a historic district—the state's first—and was listed on the National Register of Historic Places. Walking through the historical district, look for Walker House, the oldest hotel in town (constructed between 1836 and 1860); the Mineral Point Depot (1857); and many interesting buildings along High Street and Jail Alley (named for the jail at the back of the courthouse on this street). A visit to Pendarvis, plus a chance to enjoy Welsh cooking at area restaurants, are reasons why Mineral Point is a favorite place with visitors.

For more information, contact the Mineral Point Chamber of Commerce, Water Tower Park or 237 High Street, (608) 987-3201.

LODGING

Brewery Creek Inn, 23 Commerce Street, (608) 987-3298. Ever fantasize about sleeping over a brewery? Brewery Creek makes such dreams come true.

This 1854 stone warehouse houses a brewery and pub. Guests stay "above the store" in the second and third floor guest rooms.

The House of the Brau-Meister, 254 Shake Rag Street, (608) 987-2913. This cozy 1900 Queen Anne is on one of the town's most historic streets.

Walker House, 1 Walker Street, (608) 987-3794. At least one trip to Mineral Point should include a stay at Walker House, purported to be not only the oldest hotel (1836) and restaurant in town, but also the oldest hotel-restaurant operation in the state. Lots of ambiance, plus Cornish dishes.

DINING

Brewery Pub, in the Brewery Creek Inn, 23 Commerce Street, (608) 987-3298. This is more than a brew pub that produces some great beer. It also features a varied and ever-changing menu, including some unusual and tasty sandwiches, plus daily soup specials.

Mineral Spirits Saloon, 20 Commerce Street, (608) 987-3682. This restaurant and lounge used to be the Chesterfield Inn, a Mineral Point landmark since 1834.

The town has more than 25 galleries and studios, and several antiques shops, most of them located in the 1840s buildings along Jail Alley house shops and the Mineral Point Civic Center and Theater.

MOUNT HOREB

Many Wisconsin towns have strong ethnic ties to their early German, Polish, Welsh, Swiss, Swedish, Finnish, and Italian settlers. More than a few places also herald their Norwegian heritage. Mount Horeb, about 30 minutes west of Madison, showcases its Norwegian roots, a connection that has been celebrated since the first settlers arrived in the 1840s.

From Mineral Point, drive east on limited-access Highway 151 for 28 miles. The drive is through a part of southwestern Wisconsin known as the Blue Mounds, so called because early settlers looked out across vast distances from certain hilly vantage points and pronounced the distances blue in color. It is no accident that Norwegians ended up settling here. Wisconsin's unglaciated uplands consist of splendid hills and valleys, winding gulches and glens, and a rugged landscape so wrought with raw beauty, it reminded the early Norwegian settlers of the places they left behind.

Mount Horeb looks, smells, and feels like a small Norwegian village. The emphatic sign at the edge of town leaves no doubt that this is a village proud of its roots: "Velkommen to Mount Horeb." Before visitors can get out of their cars they are assaulted by the sight of legions of carved wooden trolls. These gnomes come in a variety of shapes and frames of mind, and they engage in

A wooden troll guards the front of Opera House Imports in Mount Horeb.

everyday activities like accordion playing, chicken snatching, and gardening. Indeed locals call the commercial district "the troll stroll." Wide, gawking, good-natured grins accompany these longhaired, odd-looking creatures lurking behind trees, standing close to sidewalks, and crouching close to the heart of the village.

Although trolls are not historical figures, they are part of Scandinavian legend and make a visit to Mount Horeb an even more pleasant experience. Long ago, so the story goes, their prime purpose was to guard underground jewels such as precious metals and minerals. Because trolls were busy keeping track of out-of-sight treasures, they seldom showed themselves to the outside world.

Many of these local guardians are the work of Master Troll Carver Mike Feeney, who creates these magnets of curiosity and goodwill. When visitors encounter a troll in an unexpected location, it is akin to finding a lost keepsake in a drawer. Troll spotting brings out a sense of euphoria and good luck.

Mount Horeb wants travelers to spot trolls, so they have put together a list of some of the area's most elusive creatures in a visitor's guidebook. Of course the "Key To Troll Locations" map won't guarantee spotting all the trolls in the area. The downtown trolls, for instance, do not mind preening for visitors, but those in the deep forests surrounding the town cannot be lured out of hiding quite so easily.

Many visitors stop first at Open House Imports, a large Victorian home doubling as a gift shop and decorated with Mount Horeb's favorite art form: rosemaling. This is an ancient Norwegian decorative art that incorporates rose painting on wood. Other items of interest include Scandinavian clogs and Solje jewelry. Frequent visitors know that the six-foot troll on the lawn in front of the shop has long been a part of this location at 308 E. Main, but most do not know the story of the Peddler. Call (608) 437-5468.

Legend says the Peddler, Mount Horeb's first troll, stumbled upon the village a long time ago while he was journeying from town to town, selling his pack of odds and ends. He liked the area so much he decided to put down his sack of goods and stay a while. That was a hundred years or so ago, and so far, the Peddler seems in no hurry to leave.

Had enough troll spotting? Head to the heart of town. Those who know where to find country cooking and Scandinavian recipes stop at Schubert's Cafe & Bakery on Main Street. Not many restaurants have been around for more than a century, so stop in just to take a look around.

Once inside, however, you'll be hooked on its warmth, good food, and reasonable prices. Schubert's built its reputation on creating Scandinavian favorites like lefse and lutefisk, plus baked goods such as Swedish rye bread and rosettes. The place has been a staple of the downtown area for so long there is no street address on the menu. It's just Main Street, Mount Horeb, Wisconsin.

Those unfamiliar with or unwilling to try any of the Scandinavian fare (such as lutefisk, a pungent herring concoction) can choose among many simple country dishes, including burgers, fried chicken, and pot pies. But be careful. To get served, travelers must wedge themselves tightly into those old-fashioned wooden drugstore-type booths. Overeaters will find it a challenge to remove themselves from a booth's viselike grip.

Trolls are everywhere on Mount Horeb's Main Street.

Across the street is a well-known whimsical attraction. It is the Mount Horeb Mustard Museum, and the story behind it is as fascinating as the town itself. According to Barry Levenson, a former Wisconsin assistant attorney general and owner of this unusual museum, mustard collecting happened by accident.

When Levenson's beloved baseball team, the Boston Red Sox, lost the 1986 World Series, Levenson sought comfort by combing his local grocery store in search of food that would satisfy his saddened spirit. Only then, in the condiment aisle, coming from the mustard section, did he hear a voice say, "If you collect us, they will come."

Levenson wasted no time in collecting mustards. His museum and store on Main Street now displays more than 3,500 mustards from all 50 states and more than 50 foreign countries. While tasting, viewing, and purchasing mustard from the world's largest mustard collection may not seem like exciting sightseeing, the novelty of the shop, plus the chance to absorb Levenson's wacky humor, is worth a trip to a place that supports the owner's contention that "The world is a better place with one less lawyer and a lot more mustard." The museum is located at 109 E. Main Street, (608) 437-3986 or (800) 438-6878.

OTHER SITES AND ATTRACTIONS

Blue Mound State Park & Military Ridge State Trail, Mounds Park Road off of County K, (608) 437-7511 or (608) 437-7393. This is the highest point in southern Wisconsin. The park features two 40-foot lookout towers, camping, picnic grounds, and large heated outdoor pool. The 39-mile Military Ridge State Trail is a scenic stretch, perfect for biking, hiking, snowmobiling, and cross-country skiing. Call for trail fees and conditions.

Cave of the Mounds, (608) 437-3038. Discovered in 1939, now registered as a National Natural Landmark, the cave features underground caverns with a year-round temperature of 50 degrees Farenheit. Open mid-March to mid-November and every winter weekend. Three miles west of Mount Horeb, there's no missing the signs.

Little Norway, County JG, (608) 437-8211. Guided tours of a Norwegian pioneer village, homesteaded in 1856. The Norwegian Stave Church is more than one hundred years old. This Norwegian complex includes the impressive Norwegian Pavilion, which was showcased at Chicago's 1893 World Columbian Exposition. Beautiful setting and educational. Open May through October. Three miles west of Mount Horeb.

DINING

Schubert's Cafe & Bakery, 128 E. Main Street, (608) 437-3393. Old-fashioned soda fountain, Norwegian pastries, and bread. Hearty breakfast, lunch, and dinner menus.

NEW GLARUS

After absorbing Mount Horeb's Norwegian influences, it's time to head south and get a taste of another European culture that took roots in a southwestern Wisconsin town. This, of course, would be New Glarus, a community of 1,900 residents that looks and feels more like a transplanted slice of Switzerland than a small Wisconsin village.

The drive from Mount Horeb to New Glarus is an easy one of about 20 miles Head east on Highway 151 for a few miles to Highway 92, then turn right and go to Highway 69, a thoroughly pleasant drive amid gently rolling hills and picturesque woodlands.

As with most Midwestern towns, visitors will discover New Glarus history and roots through its architecture. Here are Queen Anne, Victorian, Gothic, Carpenter Gothic, log, and limestone configurations. Notice, too, a predominance of Swiss architecture in New Glarus homes and buildings—particularly the distinctive Bernese Mountain Chalet with its brown-stained wood walls, decorative flower boxes (red geraniums are the flower of choice), and detailed woodwork. Not long ago Wisconsin Trails readers named New Glarus "the most picturesque small town in Wisconsin" and "the town most resembling a Norman Rockwell painting."

That charm and the town's link to yesteryear are due to a pervasive sense of Swiss culture. It can be seen everywhere. Downtown, commercial buildings display their ties to Switzerland through fine examples of Swiss architecture. Buildings such as the Bank of New Glarus, the Village Hall, Anderson's Ben Franklin, and the First National Bank and Trust all appear to have been moved here from Swiss villages.

Visitors who wander into one of the town's restaurants, such as the Chalet Landhaus, will have a chance to try Swiss specialties including Kalberwurst and landjaegers, Schnitzel, geschnitzeltes, Swiss meatballs, roesti potatoes, and, of course, fondue featuring New Glarus cheese.

Travelers are apt first of all to gravitate to the Swiss bakeries. And they are not just selling long johns and doughnuts. Here there are varieties of traditional Old World desserts. A smorgasbord of temptations not often found at the visitors' hometown bakery includes stollen, meringues, pralines, nougats, Swiss pastries, European breads, and an abundance of Swiss chocolates.

Ambling along New Glarus's main streets (the main shopping area covers a few blocks and is easy to get around without driving), travelers continue to be reminded of the town's Swiss roots. Colorful flags and shields representing the 26 cantons, or counties, of Switzerland fly over lamp posts and street signs. Villagers feel that, while they may be a short distance from the interstate, they are not far from the heart of Switzerland.

That is the way the original settlers planned it. Swiss adventurers, 193 of them from the canton of Glarus, set out for a better life in America on April 16, 1845. Glarus was home to the great textile industries in Europe. At their peak, 22 factories made fabric in the Glarnese Valley in Glarus. But by the 1840s, social and technological change caused a crisis in the textile industry. Increased competition and modern technology forced most of the factories to close.

The Swiss from the canton of Glarus faced two choices: Stay put and face misery in their homeland or start over someplace else. Unlike some groups of immigrants, who often settled in certain areas of the United States by default, the Swiss knew exactly what they wanted.

Backed by the government of Glarus, a team of scouts was sent across the ocean. Their search carried them through more than 5,000 miles of roads in

One of the many quaint buildings that reflect New Glarus's Swiss heritage.

several Eastern and Midwestern states, in the mining regions of nearby Galena, Illinois, and Mineral Point. But when they found the Little Sugar River Valley, in the heart of Green County, they knew this was what they were looking for. The abundance of streams, forests, fertile soil, and rolling hills reminded them of home.

So the story of New Glarus began with the purposeful journey of 108 scouts who purchased 1,200 acres of land in Wisconsin. There was one major problem: New Glarus's original inhabitants were artisans, trained to work with Swiss textiles. None of the early settlers had a background in farming. Yet their survivalist spirit carried them through the early years as they adapted their skills to the "New" Glarus. They began to make cheese, and when this new industry proved successful in its first decade, community survival in the New World was assured.

Roberts Imports, housed in another of New Glarus's Swiss-style buildings.

Among Old World traditions still going strong is the creation of Sapsago, a green herb cheese, originally made in the Alps of Old Glarus. Another tradition is the beautifully loomed lace from the area. Those who have neither the time nor the budget to go to Switzerland should visit New Glarus, "America's Little Switzerland." For more information, contact the New Glarus Visitor Information at (800) 527-6838 or (608) 527-2095.

OTHER SITES AND ATTRACTIONS

Chalet of the Golden Fleece, 618 Second Street, (608) 527-2614, was built as a private chalet in 1937. Visitors can roam three floors of unusual collections, including painted furniture, Swiss dolls, Swiss scissors pictures, quilts, pewter and antique silver, Swiss woodcarvings, Swiss porcelain, and much more. Admission fee.

Sugar River State Trail. New Glarus is at the northern entry point to the trail. Part of Wisconsin's Ice Age Trail, the Sugar River Trail meanders for 23 miles, from New Glarus to Brodhead, through rolling valleys, wildlife refuges, and farmland. The trail features 32 campsites and 11 miles of hiking paths. Bikes are available for rent.

New Glarus's Chalet of the Golden Fleece contains several collections of Swiss artifacts and home furnishings.

Swiss Historical Village Museum, 612 7th Avenue, (608) 527-2317. A pioneer village showcasing Swiss customs and history. The 12-building museum features a log church, a general store, a blacksmith shop, a cheese factory, and a Swiss-style bee house.

LODGING

New Glarus offers several fine accommodations; the following have a strong historical flavor.

Chalet Landhaus, 801 Highway 69, (608) 527-5234 or (800) 944-1716. Some suites have whirlpools.

Jeanne-Marie's Bed and Breakfast, 318 10th Avenue, (608) 527-5059. Convenient location in the midst of the city, this red brick, early 1900s home has three guest bedrooms.

New Glarus Hotel, 100 6th Avenue, (608) 527-5244. In the heart of town, this charming Old World Inn (it also features excellent cuisine) has been a New Glarus institution since 1853. Beautifully preserved, visitors feel as if they are in Switzerland the moment they open the door. This also is the place for polka music and dancing.

Spring Valley Creek Bed & Breakfast, N 9098 Old Madison Road, (608) 527-2314. Fresh country air is among the benefits when staying at this 1880s Swiss farmstead. Three guest bedrooms.

DINING

Do not leave New Glarus without trying some of the town's Swiss cuisine.

Deininger's (King's Mountain), 119 5th Avenue, (608) 527-2012. Plenty of atmosphere here as the restaurant is in an old mansion. German and Swiss specialties include Konigsberger Klopse, a beef and veal meatball dish, served at the table with white wine. Lunch and dinner, Sunday brunch.

Glarner Stube, 518 First Street, (608) 527-2216. Lots of traditional fare, like the veal dish, geschnitzeltes. The restaurant has been a favorite with those who love Swiss food since 1901.

New Glarus Bakery, 534 First Street, (608) 527-2916. Features breakfast pastries and lunch items, including outstanding soups and sandwiches. In the summer, this is a good place to linger a while over coffee and dessert. It's hard to resist the bakery with its imaginative goodies, which include bread (their Alpenbread is as good as it gets), rolls, and desserts.

New Glarus Hotel, 100 6th Avenue, (608) 527-5244. Hearty, authentic Swiss cuisine—expect to find cheese and beef fondue, roesti potatoes, and many other traditional items, as well as some continental choices. Desserts, including traditional Black Forest cake, are lavish and beautifully decorated and presented. The glass-enclosed porch offers views of village activities. Lunch and dinner, Friday night buffets.

SHOPPING

Roberts European Imports, 102 5th Avenue, (608) 527-2517 or (800) 968-2517. The largest importer of Swiss and other European merchandise in New Glarus. How does Roberts sell its merchandise at the same or lower prices as in Switzerland? The reason is simple: Jack Roberts goes to the sources. Typical of Roberts's dedication to finding distinctive items are the intricately carved, one-of-a-kind milk buckets. These are a 1,000-year-old tradition, and Jack has found the only person left in the country who knows how to make them. Other imports include an array of raclette ovens (small tabletop ovens to make traditional melted cheese dishes), fondue pots, linens, Langethal china, and cowbells in every size. Roberts has been a New Glarus landmark for more than 50 years. Next to the Swiss Church.

The Swiss Church in New Glarus was built in 1900; it was preceded by two other churches built by Swiss immigrants and their descendants.

EVENTS

William Tell Festival, (608) 527-2095. This famous Friedrich Schiller play, rich with Swiss heritage, tells the story of Switzerland's independence in the 13th century. Presented during a colorful weekend. Other events going on over Labor Day include an art fair and Alpine Festival with traditional dancing and music. The play is presented in English and German. Call for times. (608) 527-2095.

MONROE

For quick diversion and a trip that will make you appreciate Wisconsin cheese making and all that it's meant to the state's economy, head 16 miles south of New Glarus to Monroe, which lies just 11 miles north of the Illinois border.

Head first for the square, with its Romanesque courthouse and other historic buildings, in the center of town. Like New Glarus, many Swiss settled here, giving Monroe the onetime nickname of Swiss Cheese Capital of the U.S. To learn more about the cheese tradition, visit the Green County Welcome Center and Historic Cheesemaking Center, Highway 69 and 21st Street, (608) 325-4636 or (888) 222-9111. The center has a nice display of cheese making history and is the best source in the county for visitor information. For more about sites and attractions in Green County, see the Web site at www.greeen-county.org.

LODGING

Chenoweth House Bed and Breakfast, 2004 10th Street, (608) 325-5064. This 1887 Queen Anne property is on the National Register of Historic Places. Each of the four guest rooms includes a parlor and a private bath.

Ludlow Mansion Bed and Breakfast, 1421 Mansion Drive, (608) 325-1219. Five suites are available in this stately old home on four acres.

DINING

Baumgartner's Cheese Store and Tavern, Courthouse Square, (608) 325-6157. A basic but atmospheric place, Baumgartner's has been dispensing beer from the local brewery and cheese sandwiches as long as anyone can remember.

SOUTHWESTERN WISCONSIN AT A GLANCE

MUSEUMS

Chalet of the Golden Fleece: Built in the style of a Swiss mountain home, the museum has three floors of unusual collections of Swiss dolls, Swiss scissors pictures, Swiss porcelain, and much more. New Glarus.

Green County Welcome Center and Historic Cheesemaking Center: Special emphasis on cheese making history. Monroe.

Mount Horeb Mustard Museum: World's largest seller of mustard varieties. Mount Horeb.

Swiss Historical Village Museum: The 12-building pioneer village includes a log church and general store. New Glarus.

HISTORICAL SITES AND ATTRACTIONS

Cave of the Mounds: Registered as a National Landmark, the cave, discovered in 1939, is open year-round. Blue Mounds.

Downtown Mineral Point: The small town's downtown buildings were the first in the state (1971) to be deemed a historic district. Several buildings of note include Walker House, the oldest hotel in town (built between 1836 and 1860) and the Mineral Point Depot (1857).

Gundry House: A distinctive 1868 sandstone house displaying Victorian furnishings and memorabilia of old Mineral Point. Mineral Point.

Little Norway: A Norwegian pioneer village originally homesteaded in 1856. The dramatic Norwegian Stave Church is more than a century old. Three miles west of Mount Horeb.

Pendarvis and the Merry Christmas Mine: Six carefully restored stone and log houses built by Cornish lead miners in the early 19th century. A slice of life during the town's lead mining days. Abandoned mine shafts on 43 acres behind the village. Operated by the State Historical Society and open to the public. Costumed guides. Mineral Point.

Shake Rag Alley: Reconstructed homes and businesses of the Cornish community dating from around 1830. Mineral Point.

Taliesin: Magnificent home, school and studio designed by Frank Lloyd Wright, considered America's greatest architect. Frank Lloyd Wright Visitor Center. Spring Green.

OTHER HISTORICAL STOPS

Chalet Landhaus: Old World Swiss cuisine and lodging. New Glarus.

Deininger's: Old mansion dining features authentic German and Swiss specialties. New Glarus.

Jail Alley Shops: A row of 1840s buildings now house gift and artisan shops. Situated where the town's jail and courthouse used to be. Mineral Point.

New Glarus Hotel: A New Glarus dining and lodging institution since 1853. Hearty Swiss specialties served up with plenty of atmosphere. New Glarus.

Open House Imports: Large Victorian house (note the rosemaling, or Norwegian rose painting, on the entrance) doubling as a Scandinavian gift shop. Mount Horeb.

Roberts European Imports: A New Glarus landmark since the 1940s, the store is brimming with imports, mostly from Switzerland. One such find: intricately carved milk buckets made in a 1,000 year-old tradition. New Glarus.

Sugar River State Trail: A 23-mile trail carves its way between New Glarus and Brodhead. The low-grade terrain is part of the Ice Age National Scenic Trail. Near Brodhead, on an offshoot of the main trail, you'll find the landmark "Halfway Tree." This was used as a halfway marker by the Winnebago Indians who knew this spot was midway between Lake Michigan and the Mississippi River.

HISTORICAL EVENTS AND FESTIVALS

JUNE

Real Antiques Show, Mineral Point.

SEPTEMBER

William Tell Festival, New Glarus.
Buckskinners' Rendezvous, Spring Green.

OCTOBER

Cornish Festival, Mineral Point.

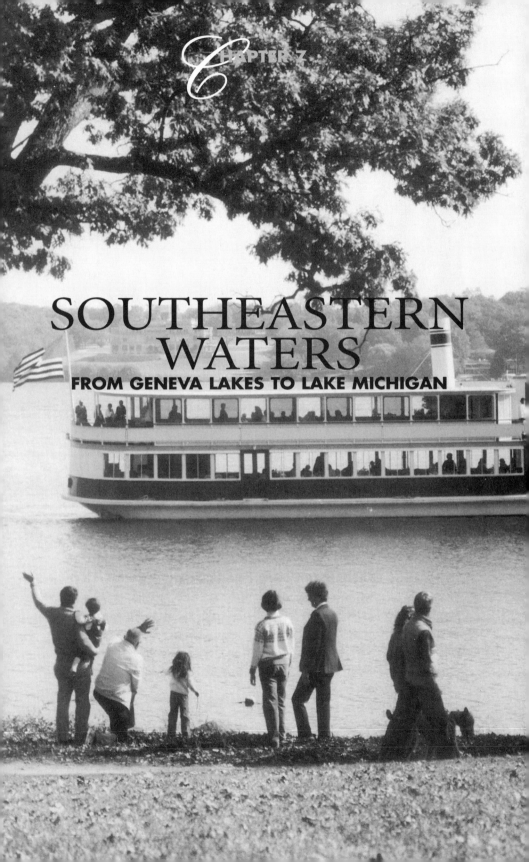

CHAPTER 7

SOUTHEASTERN
WATERS
FROM GENEVA LAKES TO LAKE MICHIGAN

The French Country Inn is an inviting retreat with a colorful past.

WHEN I WAS GROWING UP, my family had a summer home in what is now called the Geneva Lakes area. This was a place where, I like to tell my kids who look at the lake crowded with watercraft and wonder when jet skiers and water-skiers will run out of room, you could drop one water-ski (to practice slalom skiing) and leisurely pick up the floating, dropped ski a half hour later. No one would consider doing that today—there are too many boats. That once-unhurried existence on the lake and in the midst of town during peak summer months is, unfortunately, no more. But the Lake Geneva area still has its history, and it's a special kind.

Since the 1870s, Lake Geneva has been a playground for the rich and famous, particularly Chicago industrialists and their families such as the Wrigleys, Swifts, and Armours. They built palatial homes here, bringing household staff (you can see artifacts from their luxurious homes, like butlers' bells, at the Lake Geneva Museum downtown) to their summer palaces. The east end of the lake has so many magnificent estates, the area was called "Newport of the West," a nickname still heard today.

Today, Lake Geneva is packed with strolling tourists on a summer day. Visitors driving the mile or so from one end of town to the other might spend half an hour in traffic. On the plus side, the town offers fine restaurants, shops, tremendous lake views from many locations, and a pleasant ambiance. One of my favorite spots to sit back and take in the panorama is, surprisingly, at the local library, slightly west of the middle of town on the main drag.

One reason Lake Geneva is so popular is that it's within easy striking distance from Chicago (77 miles), Milwaukee (45 miles), and Madison (66 miles —almost as far as Chicago!); Minneapolis-St. Paul is a less convenient but still manageable 320-mile drive. Since not many Badgers travel south to vacation in the summer, out-of-state residents may have the area to themselves.

For those dying to get an exterior peek at the Wrigley mansion and other historically interesting homes ringing the lake, the best bet is one of the lake tours offered by Geneva Lake Cruises. Purchase tickets at the Riviera Dock in downtown Lake Geneva. My favorite cruiser, Lady of the Lake, is a beautifully detailed old wooden boat that has been carrying passengers for decades.

Lake Geneva was not only a favorite getaway for wealthy Chicagoans, it was a popular retreat for Chicago gangsters. Back in the 1920s, gangsters, including Al Capone, George "Bugs" Moran, "Machine Gun" Jack McGurn, and John Dillinger, drove north for rest and relaxation, away from the scrutiny of law enforcement and the threats from rival gangs. They headed to Lake Como, a few miles north of Lake Geneva, because the woods offered seclusion and good lakeside views.

One of the hideaway retreats was the Lake Como Hotel, now The French Country Inn. Locals tell stories about the place when it was a favorite gangster hideaway, especially about the underground speakeasy called the Sewer and the secret tunnels connected to the building for fast getaways. The hideaway feeling is still evident. Practically invisible from the street, the only way in is via a narrow, wooded road.

In 1986 the resort was purchased by the Navilio family, who revamped it and gave it a European flavor. The main guest house was shipped from Denmark at the turn of the century and is a masterpiece of craftsmanship. It originally was showcased at the Chicago World's Fair in 1893. The 24-room inn has superb accommodations. Kirsch's, the smartly appointed restaurant, offers award-winning dinner entrees, including Chateaubriand and Chilean sea bass. The restaurant also puts on a wonderful brunch.

There are many intriguing places like this surrounding the Lake Geneva area. After all, a playground that has historically been catering to the rich and famous for nearly a century and a half has stories to tell.

For more information, contact the Lake Geneva Chamber of Commerce, (262) 248-4416 or (800) 345-1020. Whether a fancy mansion or a tiny eatery is on a visitor's itinerary, Lake Geneva is best explored on foot. The 26-mile path around the lake will provides a close-up view of elegant old homes, lavish boats and piers, and charming shops and restaurants.

Incidentally, tycoons, gangsters, and tourists aren't the only ones who like this area. The first choice for the location in the 1950s of the U.S. Air Force Academy was the south shore of Geneva Lake. The idea was less popular among local residents, whose protests played a part in establishing the military school in Colorado Springs!

OTHER SITES AND ATTRACTIONS

Belfry Theater, Highway 67, Williams Bay, (262) 245-0123. It was a great treat to come to summer productions here when I was a kid. Since the 1940s, the Belfry has been dishing up musicals and dramas in a delightful old building. Oldest summer stock theater in the country.

Geneva Lake Cruise Line, Riviera Docks, (262) 248-6206 or (800) 558-5911. Travelers visiting Lake Geneva should get on the lake. Those without a boat can ride on these cruisers, which provide snippets of information as well as a pleasant trip. For a decidedly different journey, ride the mail boat as it makes its way around the lake (the mail person delivers the mail on the docks while jumping from the boat to the pier—the boat never stops). This is the oldest mail boat extravaganza in the U.S. Check out the Web site at www.cruise-lakegeneva.com.

Yerkes Observatory, Highway 67, Williams Bay, (262) 245-5555. The world's largest lens-type telescope, operated by the University of Chicago for testing the latest equipment, is in an old, stunning, and architecturally interesting building west of downtown. Call for times of tours.

LODGING

French Country Inn, W 4190 West End Road, Lake Geneva, (262) 245-5220. Bursting with colorful history, the 34-room inn, now a country retreat on Lake Como, housed a speakeasy and gambling casino when Chicago mobsters frequented the area. It is filled with touches like the beautiful hand-carved staircase and parquet floors, built in Denmark in the 1880s. These extraordinary examples of craftsmanship were shipped to Chicago for the 1893 Columbian Exposition, then incorporated in the inn's present location. Whirlpools, fireplaces, and balconies offering panoramic lakeside views. Bountiful breakfasts, afternoon teas, sherry, and homemade pastries. West off Highway 50 (follow the winding road until you reach the lake).

Pederson Victorian Bed & Breakfast, 1782 Highway 120 North, (262) 248-9110. A magnificent 1880 home features the splendor of yesteryear mixed with the artistry of today. Setting offers line-dried linens, natural soaps, vegetarian dishes, and plenty of porch places to spread out and read. Three miles north of Lake Geneva in Springfield.

Roses Bed & Breakfast, 429 S. Lake Shore Drive, (262) 248-4344 or (888) 767-3262. This four-bedroom, English country inn is one block from

The French Country Inn's intricately carved staircase was built in Denmark in the 1880s.

Lake Geneva. A marvelous wraparound porch.

T.C. Smith Inn B & B, 865 W. Main Street, (262) 248-1097. An 1845 estate, complete with fireplaces and fashionable antiques from the 19th century. Great location not far from the town's central activities.

The Watersedge, W 4232 West End Road, (262) 245-9845; Web site is watersedgebb.com. Once the favorite spot of the gangster, Bugs Moran. This B & B has six guest rooms with balconies and many antiques.

DINING

The Abbey, Fontana Boulevard and Highway 67, Fontana, (262) 275-6811. Our family used to motor over from Williams Bay on a Sunday morning for brunch. A terrific Sunday brunch is presented in the Monaco Dining Room (also lunch and dinner), a tall-windowed room with waterside views of the marina. La Tour de Bois Dining Room features continental and American cuisine, often with tableside preparation.

The magnificent parquet floor in the original wing of the French Country Inn.

Fitzgerald's Genoa Junction Restaurant, 727 Main Street (County B), Genoa City, (262) 279-5200. In an 1885 octagon house loaded with antiques and fireplaces, the restaurant does not disappoint. Specialties include honey barbecued chicken, barbecued pork ribs, and a Friday night, only-thing-on-the-menu, fish boil. Call for hours. Sunday brunch.

Kirsch's Lakeside Restaurant in the historic French Country Inn (for more information, see above), West End Road, (262) 245-5756. Traditional European-style menu, including excellent appetizers, soups, entrees, and desserts. In summer, enjoy the lovely outdoor terrace for views at the water's edge.

Popeye's, Broad Street and Wrigley Drive, (262) 248-4381. A busy spot, especially in summer, for enjoying a Bionic Burger on rye or other fare. Hearty cafe-style food and Greek specialties, since 1959. On the waterfront, across from the Riviera docks.

The Red Geranium, 393 N. Edwards Boulevard, (262) 248-3637. Not a historical spot (it opened in 1985), but one that must be included in a guidebook to the best dining in the area. The restaurant has several dining rooms covered in red geranium wallpaper—necessary expansion as the word about this establishment spread. It is well known for specialties such as duck with Door County cherry sauce and foods cooked on an open-hearth grill, including charcoal-grilled steaks. Accompaniments include excellent homemade buttermilk biscuits. Unusually large selection of wine by the glass. Open seven days a week for lunch and dinner.

St. Moritz, 327 Wrigley Drive, (262) 248-6680. Fine dining in a turreted 1885 mansion. Tantalizing, creative cuisine presented in extraordinary ambiance, overlooking Lake Geneva. The ever-changing menu features such house specialties as Wasabi Dusted Tuna, and Roulade of Salmon. Among other entrees to consider: Peanut-Crusted Rack of Lamb, Vegetable Strudel, and Grilled Beef Tenderloin. Open for dinner Tuesday through Sunday.

SHOPPING

Lake Geneva is full of places to shop. One of the newer ones is Geneva Village Shops, 727 Geneva Street, albeit in a historical town landmark. Cafe, gifts shops, art gallery in a restored building.

DELAVAN

For a quick change of pace from Lake Geneva's bustle and high-living past, consider heading to Delavan, a mere 10 miles northwest on Highway 50. The town has long been linked to the circus—for more than 50 years in the 19th century, the town was home to various circuses.

The first inhabitants in the area, though, were middle to late Woodland Indians from approximately 1800–2000 B.C. Mound builders lived in the area between 500 and 1000 A.D., constructing 105 effigy mounds around Delavan Lake.

In 1840, Edmund and Jeremiah Mabie, along with partner Seth Howes, founded their circus in Brewster, New York. Seven years later they moved the show to Delavan, beginning a 12-year reign, from 1847 to 1859, of having the largest circus in America. They launched the circus on 400 acres of land that they bought for $3,200; it is now the property of Lake Lawn Lodge (see below).

In 1882, the Mabie Circus was sold to Barnum and Bailey and it left Delavan, but not before it had created legendary stories that draw attention to this day. One story goes that when one of the circus elephants died in the winter of 1862, the circus used the frozen lake to get rid of the remains. Workers took the animal out on the ice, sawed a circle around it, and let it sink. Some 70 years later, when the resort was dredging a swimming area, the crew discovered a giant leg bone. That bone and others found homes with the Chicago Natural History Museum.

Who would have thought that pink lemonade was invented here—with the aid of red circus tights? One summer, when an enterprising circus performer with a lemonade stand ran out of water and came upon a bucket, he used it. A bareback rider had washed her red tights in it, giving the water a pink tinge. The pink lemonade has the same recipe today: Water, tartaric acid, and a little red dye. It was an instant hit.

Today, Delavan still sports a circus veneer. Tower Park has large fiberglass circus animals, and along the main street of town the old, red-brick, paved street seems to echo the rattle of long-ago circus wagons.

LODGING

Allyn Mansion Inn, 511 E. Walworth Avenue, (262) 728-9090. If there is one Wisconsin home that personifies 19th-century magnificence, this might win the grand prize. In fact, it did win the grand prize in the National Trust's Great American Homes Awards. It is one of the finest restorations anywhere. Ten marble fireplaces, two grand pianos, lavish yet comfortable living. Listed on the National Register of Historic Places. Eight guest rooms.

Lake Lawn Resort, Highway 50, (262) 728-7950. This year-round resort, on 275 wooded acres, has been a Delavan institution for more than one hundred years. It has 284 guest rooms, many with fireplaces, a golf course, indoor and outdoor swimming pools, its own airport and plenty of other amenities. Nonguests can enjoy the resort's restaurants and gift and clothing shops. The lunch buffets are bountiful in the Frontier Restaurant, facing the lake.

DINING

Millie's Restaurants and Shopping Village, County O, (262) 728-2434. Since 1964, when Millie's started offering Pennsylvania Dutch–style dinners in former farm buildings, hungry diners could not get enough of the place. They now serve 17 different types of pancakes, as well as other fare. Lots of kitsch and coziness in different themed rooms (brimming with antiques), including the Victorian Room, the New England Room, and the Williamsburg Room. Extensive gift shop. Not the easiest place to find.

The Allyn Mansion Inn in Delevan is a beautifully restored nineteenth-century B&B.

KENOSHA

*I*n marked contrast to the elegant and sedate past of Lake Geneva, the gritty, industrial cities of Racine and Kenosha, a few miles to the east on Lake Michigan, have histories chock full of social and political import. These are union towns, where factory workers pushed for improved working conditions, while their wealthy employers often resisted their efforts. These two dissimilar areas are linked by Highway 50, which runs east from Delavan to Kenosha, a distance of about 40 miles.

The Wind Point lighthouse pictured against a backdrop of a lake steamer.

Unlike other Lake Michigan cities, Kenosha began attracting settlers in 1835 not for the water, but for the farming opportunities. As the years rolled by, it became apparent that the city harbor would not accommodate ships as large as those that routinely docked in Milwaukee, Racine, and Chicago. Nevertheless, the city thrived because of its abundance of hardworking and creative Italian, Polish, Bohemian, Czechoslovakian, and Lithuanian immigrants, who swarmed into the area between the Civil War and the early 1900s.

Immigrants and first-generation Americans were hired by the Nash Company, a carmaker that began business in 1925. The folks at Nash, together with the Kohler family of plumbing fame, formed the Stalwarts. This group conspired to kill off Robert La Follette's Progressive movement in the Republican Party. They paid for that by having to battle left-leaning unions, not always successfully, for a number of years. Nash, which became American

Motors, eventually sold its old plant to Chrysler, which made engines here until around 1990.

Today, Kenosha is known for its recreational offerings, particularly the excellent lakefront parks. The large, lakeside Kemper Center should not be missed. Fishing enthusiasts can try landing Great Lakes treasures with the help of more than two dozen charter fishing companies. Another recreational endeavor (yes, shopping is entertainment in our culture) is the factory outlet shopping scene. Lakeside Mall and the Factory Outlet Center are minutes from each other off Interstate 94.

Many 19th-century homes can be seen in the Library Park area, between 61st and 66th Streets, along Seventh Avenue. Note the 1880 home at 6116 Seventh Avenue. It is the birthplace of Orson Welles, famous stage and film actor, director, and producer.

For more information, contact the Kenosha Area Visitor & Convention Bureau, (262) 654-7307 or (800) 654-7309, or the 24-hour hotline, (262) 658-4FUN.

OTHER SITES AND ATTRACTIONS

Kemper Center, 6501 Third Avenue. Large, lakeside county park offers lots to do. Listed on the National Register of Historic Places, the park's amenities include a tennis court, arboretum, cultural center, and arts center.

Kenosha County Historical Center & Museum, 6300 Third Avenue, (262) 654-5770. Nicely displayed exhibits, including folk art and toys, in a 19th-century mansion.

LODGING

In 2000 there were 14 inns, motels, and hotels in the area. Most are national chains and are along the Interstate 94 corridor, west of the downtown area. Contact the Kenosha Area Visitor & Convention Bureau for further information, (800) 654-7309.

DINING

Kenosha's Italian roots run deep, so the city has a number of better-than-average Italian restaurants. There are also a variety of superb restaurants representing other cultures and cuisine. If the weekend stay includes lodging somewhere else, do not overlook Kenosha for dining opportunities.

Bombay Louie's, 2227 60th Street, (262) 657-9314. A Kenosha institution for one hundred years, this popular restaurant features cuisine from around the world served with gusto. Lunch and dinner.

The Hobnob, 277 S. Sheridan Road, (262) 552-8008. When The Hobnob opened in 1954, its fancy decor and excellent rotation of Italian specialties attracted well-heeled customers to its location, midway between Milwaukee and Chicago. The veal scallopini is in a league of its own. No extra charge for those waterfront views of Lake Michigan. Open for dinner.

Mangia Trattoria, 5717 Sheridan Road, (262) 652-4285. It has not been around that long, but this restaurant, which opened in the late 1980s, has garnered a reputation for flavorful Italian dishes. Diners who enjoy informal (trattoria implies casual) Italian restaurants love this place. Nicely done pizza, lamb, fish, and chicken. Open for lunch and dinner.

Ray Radigan's, 11712 Sheridan Road, (262) 694-0455. Traditional food you can count on. Supper club lovers have been flocking to this family-owned spot, complete with start-up relish tray, since 1933. Succulent steaks, baked duck, New Zealand veal, and fine seafood are the main draws, but it is a fun place to people-watch, too. Close to the Illinois state line, it often attracts Chicago politicos and celebrities. Open for lunch and dinner.

Taste of Wisconsin, 7515 125th Avenue, (262) 857-9110. You really can get a taste of Wisconsin here. Everything on the menu is produced by a Badger farm or manufacturer. Charming decor includes renovated architecture and accoutrements found on Wisconsin farms. Open for breakfast, lunch, and dinner.

HISTORIC EVENTS AND FESTIVALS

This city likes its festivals, ranging from a coho fishing derby, usually held in June, to the annual Polkafest, usually in full swing in August. Here are two events that are among the more unique in a city rich with a host of ethnic traditions.

Danish Brotherhood Lodge Breakfast, 2206 63rd Street, (262) 657-9781. When the air is nippy and gray skies are the rule, usually in late April and mid-November, Kenosha's Danish Brotherhood Lodge (purported to have the most members in the country) holds a breakfast laden with Danish pastries and other traditional Danish fare. Worth the wait at the door.

Ye Olde Englishe Christmasse Feaste, St. Mark's Alstadt Auditorium, (262) 942-2230. A robust Scottish celebration which emulates dining in the Middle Ages. Bagpipers entertain the diners who partake in a multiple course banquet which includes traditional wassail, Cornish game hen, and flaming plum pudding.

RACINE

When it was announced in 2000 that J. I. Case Company of Racine would phase out tractor production here, many compared it to Chrysler departing Kenosha. After all, Case had been a part of Racine since 1844, when it was a booming wheat port. Regardless, this onetime industrial mecca is becoming a postindustrial city, thanks in part to the happy fact that Lake Michigan will always be here. This is a city with plentiful historical buildings and a super waterfront that travelers should not ignore while on the I-94 between Chicago and Milwaukee.

This pier lighthouse once stood where the Root River flows into Lake Michigan.

Racine has plenty of structures that history lovers will appreciate. Along the main streets in the downtown area is some of the best 19th-century architecture anywhere in the state. One of the structures that did not survive belonged to Joshua Glover, a runaway slave. He and friends were playing cards one night when federal marshals burst in, bludgeoned Glover, and hauled him away in a wagon. A mob of white "freemen" broke into the local jail, set Glover free, and moved him to Canada. This incident brought the federal Fugitive Slave Act home to many lily-white Wisconsin residents for the first time.

For what remains an industrialized city (more than 300 industries are in Racine County), Racine has a lakefront that is truly breathtaking. Located closer to Milwaukee than Chicago, the city is the opposite of what visitors would expect. Beautiful parks have sprung up along the lakefront, and even those who show up without a boat will appreciate the magnificent marina—purported to be the largest on Lake Michigan, with more than one hundred acres devoted to launching and storing boats.

For a city of about 80,000 residents, Racine has a much bigger feel to it. Maybe that is because it has long been the home of many national companies, such as Johnson's Wax, Hamilton Beach, Jacobsen lawn mowers, and Horlick's malted milk.

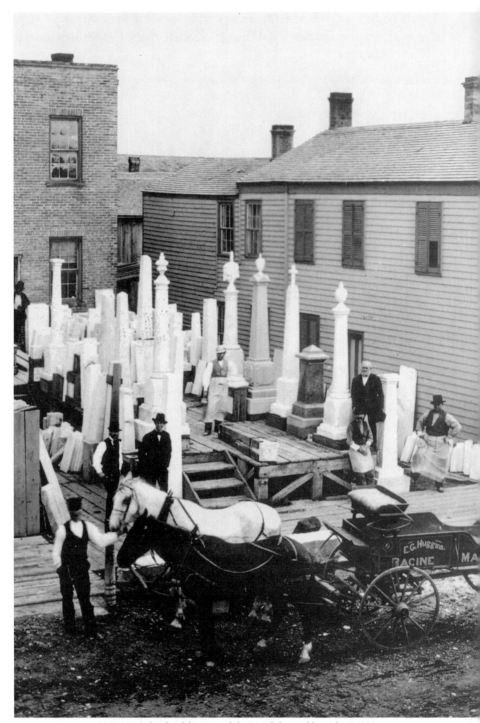

Racine was a bustling lake port and the site of this marble works in 1880.

There is a lot to see and do for history seekers over a weekend. Many of the homes of early entrepreneurs have been beautifully restored. Some of the more intriguing historical structures are found along Main Street. For instance, check out the turreted Joseph Miller house at 11th and Main Streets and the Henry Miller house at 1110 Main Street. For more information, contact the Racine County Convention & Visitor Bureau, (262) 634-3293 or (800) C-RACINE.

OTHER SITES AND ATTRACTIONS

Dillinger Exhibit, 730 Center Street. If an interest in history includes cops and robbers, then this exhibit is for you. Dillinger and three cronies robbed the local American Trades Bank (now the M & I Bank) of $27,000 on November 20, 1933. During their getaway, they grabbed a Model 1928 Thompson submachine gun from one of the police officers at the scene. Later, the gun, with Dillinger's signature on it, was captured and is now part of this popular display. Racine Police Department lobby.

Old Engine House No. 3 Museum, 700 Sixth Street, (262) 633-4305. Fire engine buffs should show up here. Visitors get a chance to see antique fire-fighting equipment in a former fire station. The museum usually is open Sundays. Free admission.

Racine County Heritage Museum, 701 Main Street, (262) 636-3926. This 1902 Renaissance Revival building, originally Racine's public library, was constructed with a grant from Andrew Carnegie and is now on the Register of Historic Places. Renovated, the museum moved into the building in 1963. Exhibits and information abound about the people and the products manufactured in the area.

S. C. Johnson Golden Rondelle Theater, 1525 Howe Street, (262) 260-2154. Definitely worth the short ride to the city's south side. The spaceship-like theater, designed by Frank Lloyd Wright's legacy, the Taliesin Associate Architects, was an instant hit when it was presented at the New York World's Fair in 1964. The movie shown at the fair, *To Be Alive*, won an Academy Award in the short documentary department. The theater was eventually moved to the grounds of S. C. Johnson Wax, designed by Wright. Visitors can tour the administration building as well as the theater and enjoy the award-winning documentary. Call for reservations.

The Southside Historic District, listed on the National Register of Historic Places, brims with elaborate homes and beautiful churches. Architecture represented includes Queen Anne, Victorian, Federal, Gothic, and Italianate styles. Note College Avenue, with its 1897 red brick paved street. The historic area, defined by Lake Michigan on the east, lies between 8th Street on the north,

DeKoven Avenue on the south, and College and Park Avenues on the west.

Windpoint Lighthouse, between Three and Four Mile Roads, is a picturesque lighthouse. Built in 1880, it is said to be the oldest lighthouse of any on the Great Lakes. Visitors aren't allowed inside (it is still being used), but it makes for a nice photo op. North of town.

LODGING

Linen & Lace Bed & Breakfast, west of I-94 on Highway 20, (262) 534-4966. Cozy, comfortable, romantic country charm on more than four acres. This hundred-year-old farmhouse, with three guest bedrooms, offers quaint touches and a good place to unwind.

Lochnaiar Inn, 1121 Lake Avenue, (262) 633-3300. This posh lakeside inn, built by a Scotsman in 1915, features many updated amenities, such as whirlpools and fireplaces in some of the rooms.

Mansards on-the-Lake, 827 Lake Avenue, (262) 632-1135. If staying on the lake is a requisite, here is another opportunity. This stately Second Empire home, now a bed and breakfast, has a complete mansard roof and is a graceful choice. Four residential suites with private baths and kitchenettes. On a picturesque hillside overlooking Lake Michigan and Pershing Park.

DINING

The Corner House, 1521 Washington Avenue, (262) 637-1295. Since 1945, this fine restaurant has been serving popular items like duck, prime rib, and veal in a formal, but not stuffy, atmosphere. The food is expertly presented. Open for dinner.

O & H Danish Bakery, 1841 Douglas Avenue, (262) 637-8895. Known for superb Danish kringles, like the fruit-filled varieties. Do not attempt to leave Racine without sampling these fine European pastries.

THE SOUTHEASTEN LAKES AT A GLANCE

MUSEUMS

Dillinger Exhibit: All about the escapades of Dillinger and his cronies. Racine Police Department lobby.

Heritage Hall Museum of Barbershop Harmony: Visitors get a look at barbershop harmony's rich history in this museum located in a stylish mansion. 6315 3rd Avenue, (262) 653-8440. Kenosha.

Kemper Center Lakeside country park is included on the National Register of Historic Places. The park has a tennis court, arboretum, cultural center, and arts center. Kenosha.

Kenosha Country Historical Center and Museum: Nicely displayed exhibits in a 19th-century mansion. Kenosha.

Old Engine House No. 3 Museum: Antique firefighting equipment in a former fire station. Racine.

Racine County Heritage Museum: The 1902 Renaissance Revival building, originally Racine's public library, was constructed with a grant from Andrew Carnegie, and is now on the Register of Historic Places. Racine.

HISTORICAL SITES AND ATTRACTIONS

Belfry Theater: Oldest summer stock theater in the country. They've been dishing up musicals and dramas since the 1940s. Williams Bay.

Library Park: Many 19th-century homes between 61st and 66th Streets, including the birthplace of Orson Welles, along Seventh Avenue. Kenosha.

S. C. Johnson Golden Rondelle Theater: The Frank Lloyd Wright-designed Administration Building was the former home of the Johnson family. Visit the spaceship-like theater on the property, an instant hit when it was presented at the New York World's Fair in 1964. Racine.

Southside Historic District: Listed on the Register of Historic Places, this area is filled with elaborate homes and beautiful churches. Racine.

Windpoint Lighthouse: Built in 1880, it's said to be the oldest lighthouse on the Great Lakes. North of Racine.

Yerkes Observatory: The world's largest lens-type telescope is located in an interesting old landmark building. Williams Bay.

OTHER HISTORICAL STOPS

Allyn Mansion Inn: Magnificent 19-century home now serves as a bed-and-breakfast inn. It took grand prize in the National Trust's Great American Homes Awards. Delavan.

Footpath around Geneva Lake: This 26-mile trail connects with ancient Native American arteries around the perimeter of the lake. Retrace history and see stately old lakeside mansions close up. Lake Geneva.

French Country Inn: Country retreat on Lake Como once housed a speakeasy and gambling casino. Known as a frequent hangout for Chicago gangsters during Prohibition. The main building has an extraordinary hand-carved staircase and parquet floors built in Denmark in the 1880's. West of Lake Geneva.

Lady of the Lake: Old wooden cruise boat glides passengers around Geneva Lake. Narrated tours and champagne Sunday brunch on white linen tablecloths.

Lake Lawn Resort: The first inhabitants of this area were Woodland Indians and Mound builders. Artifacts are on display throughout the lodge. The first inn was built in 1878; now the low-slung resort encompasses over 275 acres. Delavan.

Mail boat ride: Ride along on the mail boat as a mail "jumper" delivers the mail to mailboxes on piers on Geneva Lake. The boat never stops during the jumped deliveries. A way of life on Geneva Lake for nearly a century. Only passenger-carrying mail boat with a jumper in the country.

Millie's Restaurants and Shopping Village: A nice spot to unwind at the edge of the country. Millie's has been serving Pennsylvania Dutch–style food in former farm buildings, since 1964. Seventeen different types of pancakes. Delavan.

Racine Harbor: Renovated harbor includes an observation deck, boardwalk, lighthouse, and restaurants. The area hosts the largest on-the-water boat show on the Great Lakes.

Ray Radigan's: Since 1933 this popular family-owned supper club has been serving fine food to crowds of fans, including Chicago politicians and celebs. Kenosha.

St. Moritz: Fine dining in a turreted 1885 mansion. Lake Geneva.

HISTORICAL EVENTS AND FESTIVALS
APRIL

Antique Flea Market, fairgrounds, Elkhorn (Walworth County).

JULY

Cruise Nights, Classic Cars, Kenosha.

AUGUST

Top Collectors Convention, Burlington.
Pike River Rendezvous, Kenosha.

DECEMBER

Ye Old Englishe Christmasse Feaste,
St. Mark's Alstadt Auditorium, Kenosha.

CHAPTER 8

MADISON
THE CAPITAL, THE CAMPUS, AND MORE

A view of the second capitol building around 1870; it was destroyed by fire in 1904.

WISCONSIN RESIDENTS TAKE their history seriously. How else to account for the fact that the State Historical Society in Madison was founded in 1846, two years before Wisconsin became a state? The society, which is housed in a handsome stone building on the University of Wisconsin campus, became a state agency in 1949. It is a repository of all things Wisconsin. In fact, it's safe to say that if an event of any significance occurred in the state, there is a thorough record of it in the State Historical Society.

While Wisconsin's recorded history is relatively brief when compared to that of some other states, it is more interesting than most. All of the political and much of the social goings-on have taken place in Madison, which was named the capital shortly after Wisconsin became a territory in 1836. Native Americans called the area Taychopera, or Four Lakes, in recognition of the four local lakes: Mendota, Monona, Waubesa, and Yahara. The abundance of fresh water, lush valleys, and open prairie lured settlers into the area.

Interestingly, Madison did not have any inhabitants when Judge James Doty wooed legislators to move the capital from Belmont, southwest of Madison, to a site he deemed much better for development. He encouraged followers to give the area a try by offering free land. The idea took hold, even though many settlers who ventured to the wilderness inhabited by large encampments of Winnebago thought Madison too wild to survive. History briefly proved them right. In 1842, six years after the capitol was built, there were only about

125 people living in the new settlement. Once Wisconsin became a state and the University of Wisconsin was founded, both in 1848, approximately 7,000 residents became citizens.

Less than fifteen years later, Camp Randall emerged as a 53.5-acre martialing area for the 70,000 Wisconsin residents who marched off to the Civil War. The camp, which included a hospital and a stockade for Confederate prisoners, now is part of the university. An arch commemorating the camp was erected in 1912. These days, the site is mostly devoted to athletic activities, including the 78,000-seat football stadium named after the camp.

Wisconsin's most famous political leader, Robert M. "Fightin' Bob" La Follette Sr. (1855–1925), was born just outside of Madison. As governor, he led the Progressives, a third-party alternative to the Democrats and Republicans, to enact legislation that included workers' compensation, primary election laws, tax reform, and conservation. La Follette ran unsuccessfully for president in 1924 as an independent.

Meanwhile, the university, which now has more than 40,000 students, was growing. It became known for its research and education in medicine, genetics, chemistry, and agriculture. A popular university fact: The UW has the oldest radio station still in operation in the world—WHA radio was founded in 1917 and now is Madison's public-broadcasting affiliate. Over the past 150 years, the university has grown immensely, from the two students that comprised the first graduating class in 1854, to the thousands of graduates that are churned out each year. Those in search of the oldest campus building, which dates from 1851, should check out North Hall, near the State Historical Society.

The school has developed a well-earned reputation for political and social activism. This was no more evident than when it became a leading campus center in the 1960s for radical anti-Vietnam War activity. Riots filled the streets and tear gas filled the air from 1967 into the 1970s, though an incident in 1970 sobered both sides of the issue. Radicals attempted to blow up a campus ROTC building, killing a student in the process. Both the antiwar protesters and the war eventually ran out of energy.

Yet for years Madison has been a place to enjoy a high standard of living. In 1947, Life magazine showcased Madison with a full-length article and a cover showing a mother playing with her baby in the land of "the good life." There have been many honors bestowed upon Madison over the years, but a recent one stands out: In 1996, Money magazine designated the city the best place to live in America because of its high quality of life, its cold weather notwithstanding.

The magazine was right. The city's rich cultural, intellectual, and artistic diversity is evident everywhere. Dane County, home to Madison, has more than 25 parks and thousands of acres of parkland, ranging from rugged and wild beauty to fully developed entertainment facilities, like Vilas Park with its concession stand, zoo, and swimming beach on Lake Wingra.

At almost any destination around the lakes, there are places to picnic, hike, bike, walk in the woods, boat, or watch boating activities. A good place to rent boats is at the Memorial Union boat ramp. The Hoofers, a sports club associated with the UW, operates and maintains about one hundred sailboats and dozens of canoes, offering instruction as well as rental. Best advice for a summer afternoon: Rent a canoe or sailboat, then navigate over to Picnic Point on Lake Mendota. The half-mile-long peninsula, which can also be reached via a walking trail, offers spectacular lake views.

Travelers bent on exploring the Madison area for historic sites and related activities will not be disappointed. Because the city of 210,000 has so many places of historical interest, consider spending several weekends here. Here are just are a couple of sites and attractions that should not be missed. For more information, contact the Greater Madison Convention and Visitors Bureau, 615 E. Washington Avenue, call (608) 255-2537 or (800) 373-6376.

Wisconsin's State Capitol is the focal point of the entire town. Its prominence in the downtown area, built high on an isthmus of land between Lakes Mendota and Monona, makes it visible from almost any spot in the surrounding city. A replica of the U.S. Capitol building in Washington, the State Capitol was completed in 1917. The structure is the third on this site; the first was replaced by a second that burned down. The latest structure cost $7.25 million and took 11 years to complete. It has been called the country's most magnificent state capitol building. It is also used as a location for Hollywood movies. Entering the main floor rotunda, it's easy to see why the capitol commands attention. There are 43 types of stone used in the building, glass mosaics, and gorgeous murals.

The dome inside the rotunda showcases Edwin Blashfield's mural, "Resources of Wisconsin." Albert Herter, who painted the imposing Supreme Court mural, wanted his family to have a place in history. He painted his son and his dog in the picture. Below the largest granite dome in the country, 6.5 acres of lawn surround the building with beautiful gardens that bloom throughout spring, summer, and fall. In April and May, more than 50,000 tulips light up the lawn. Free tours are available. Check with the information desk on the ground floor.

Afterwards, head over to the Mansion Hill Historic District just north and east of the capitol. Also known as Yankee Hill and Aristocrat Hill, this is where

The interior of the 34-foot-wide capitol dome celebrates Wisconsin's many natural resources.

the privileged upper class built homes in the mid-1800s. Queen Anne, German Romanesque Revival, and Italianate architectural styles are represented in the many homes still standing. This historic district includes interesting homes between Butler and Henry Streets and the parallel streets of Gorham and Gilman. Close to Lake Mendota and the UW campus.

You'll then want to visit the University of Wisconsin–Madison campus, beginning with the Memorial Union and Memorial Union Terrace, 800 Langdon Street, (608) 265-3000. This is the heart of the campus, where a visitor can easily absorb the flavor of the university and its impact on Madison. The union was built in 1928 with money from a successful post–World War I fundraising drive. Since then, it has been the cultural, political, and artistic heart of the university. The Rathskeller, with its muraled walls reflecting an old German beer stube, draws students, faculty, and others to eat, drink beer, study, and people watch. Some of the best views in Madison are gleaned from the Terrace, a multilevel stone outdoor gathering place with some 600 metal chairs with their sunburst design. On a nice day, this is the place to watch sailboats and sunsets on Lake Mendota. Visitor information on the second floor.

OTHER SITES AND ATTRACTIONS

Madison has a huge number of attractions that make it a perennial favorite among writers, editors, and readers of national magazines. Take a tour of the places to see and things to do and you will know why pollsters consistently rank Madison among the nation's favorite cities to visit and live.

Art Fair on the Square. The capitol grounds adjacent to the four perpendicular streets of the Square—Mifflin, Carroll, Main, and Pinckney—make a splendid backdrop for the July weekend event that brings to town more than 500 artists from around the country. Expect terrific art but also enormous crowds, particularly on Saturday, opening day.

Dane County Farmers Market. From April through October, the Square on a Saturday morning (approximately 6 a.m. to 2 p.m.) is awash with every Midwest farm product imaginable. The market has been going strong since the 1960s, and is one of the first and biggest such markets in the country. More than 200 area farmers bring their wares, which range from fresh vegetables, plants, and flowers to just-picked morel mushrooms in spring and trucks full of pumpkins and squash in the fall. Downtown Capitol Square.

Elvehjem Museum of Art, 800 University Avenue, (608) 263-2246. Travelers cannot miss this museum and its large outdoor sculpture at University Avenue and Park Street. The museum was named for Conrad A. Elvehjem, from 1958 to 1962 the 13th president of UW–Madison. Founded in 1970, the arts and cultural center encompasses three floors and has an enormous permanent col-

A biology lab at the University of Wisconsin–Madison around 1900.

The capitol building under construction around 1914; it took 11 years to build.

lection, including Egyptian and Greek porcelain and Japanese prints, amid 26,000 feet of exhibition space. Call for current revolving shows. Free admission.

Executive Residence (also known as the Governor's Mansion), 99 Cambridge Road, (608) 266-3554. The governor's home in the tiny hamlet of Maple Bluff is on the Lake Mendota waterfront. Built in 1927, the 34-room home has many interesting features, including seven fireplaces and a stately, wrought-iron fence which originally encompassed the capitol grounds in Madison. Free tours are given from April through August of a portion of the residence.

This mill once stood where the Yahara River meets Lake Mendota on Madison's east side.

Gates of Heaven Synagogue, 302 E. Gorham Street, (608) 266-4711. Built in 1863, the German Romanesque Revival sandstone building was the first synagogue in Madison. It is considered one of the oldest synagogues in the country still in existence. When it was doomed to the wrecking ball at its original location at 214 W. Washington Avenue, locals helped save the building and move it to its current location. Owned by the City of Madison, it is now used for special events, such as weddings.

Grace Episcopal Church, 116 W. Washington Avenue, (608) 255-5147. The bright red door of the Gothic Revival–style church immediately draws attention. Built in 1858, it is the oldest surviving building on the Capitol Square. Stained glass fans take note: One of the church's beautiful windows is an original 1899 Tiffany glass, made and designed by the famous New York design firm.

Madison Art Center, 211 State Street, (608) 257-0158. Major shows, featuring mostly contemporary artists, run about a dozen times a year. Free admission. The Gallery Shop, connected to the Art Center, has a nice selection of jewelry, gifts, and accessories. In the Madison Civic Center.

Monona Terrace Community & Convention Center, 1 John Nolen Drive, (608) 261-4000. Completed in July, 1997, the project, designed by the distinctive Frank Lloyd Wright, was on the drawing board for nearly 60 years. Not all visitors or locals like it, but to drive north on John Nolen Drive and see it coming up on Lake Monona is an impressive sight. It is even more dramatic in early evening, when the building's curlicue forms reflect on the water. A rooftop garden offers great lakeside views. Call for tour hours.

A row of commercial buildings on Madison's east side around 1875.

The "Red Gym," Langdon Street. An extensive renovation reestablished this 1892 building as one of the university's most interesting structures. Now a student resource center, the fortress doors conceal another place in time. The renovation beautifully preserved brick walls, wooden floors, and architectural treasures, adding touches such as the photos on glass panels suspended from the ceiling above the main staircase. If only these walls could speak. William McKinley, Eugene Debs, Upton Sinclair, and William Jennings Bryan are among the historical personages who have orated here. Next to the Memorial Union.

State Historical Museum, 30 N. Carroll Street, (608) 264-6555. Related to the State Historical Society of Wisconsin, the museum is filled with resources about the state's history. Four floors examine Wisconsin's past. Exhibits pertaining to the lifestyle of Native Americans and their role in state history are particularly poignant. Free admission.

State Street. For many, this is the heart of Madison, where locals take out-of-town guests for a glimpse of what differentiates Madison from rural Wisconsin. The street also draws huge crowds when anything is worth noting—when the Badgers win a football game, or when students want to protest another nation's human-rights record, for example. In the 1970s, the city put an end to automobile traffic from the end of State Street, at the University of Wisconsin Library Mall, to the start of the street, near the capitol building. Besides having a fine collection of 19th- and 20th-century architecture, the street has an intriguing urban mall flavor, a magnet for some of the city's most interesting art galleries, bookstores, specialty shops, and restaurants.

Workers for the Conklin Ice House cut and collect ice on Lake Mendota in 1912.

Unitarian Meeting House, 900 University Bay Drive, (608) 233-9774. Next to Monona Terrace, some say this is Frank Lloyd Wright's most stunning building. Of the 32 Wright buildings in greater Madison, eleven were constructed and eight remain standing. Most are private residences. The Meeting House, built in 1946, invites visitors to a building constructed with interlocking triangles. The innovative design again demonstrates Wright's ability to integrate the outdoors with the interior. Guided tours are usually offered May through September. A small donation is requested.

LODGING

The following accommodations were selected mainly because of their historical interest, longevity on the Madison scene, or some other unique quality. Most of Madison's more than 6,000 rooms are in hotels, motels, and inns concentrated in and around the downtown area, along East Washington Avenue, and along the Beltline, especially on the rapidly expanding far west side.

Annie's Garden Bed & Breakfast, 2117 Sheridan Drive, (608) 244-2224. Not historical (the home is about 30 years old), this is a lovely place to round out a weekend. The two-bedroom suite has nice views of meadows and marshlands, and it offers close-by walking paths along the lakeshore. Secluded, serene, restful.

Arbor House, An Environmental Inn, 3402 Monroe Street, (608) 238-2981; Web site is www.arbor-house.com. An award-winning inn for its role in creating space that beautifully fits with urban ecology. Built in 1853, the home has a second house, the arbor house, adjacent to it. Across from the UW Arboretum, guests enjoy canoeing nearby Lake Wingra. Fireplaces, whirlpools, not far from biking and ski trails, and 10 minutes from the UW and downtown.

Best Western Inn on the Park, 22 S. Carroll Street, (608) 257-8811 or (800) 279-8891. A favorite place with visitors and politicians since 1871. Indoor pool and fitness center. Comfortable first-floor restaurant plus elegant dining and spectacular views of Lake Mendota and Lake Monona from the Top of the Park Restaurant. There are 213 guest rooms, including suites. Airport and campus shuttle service. On the Square downtown.

Canterbury Inn, 315 W. Gorham Street, (608) 258-8899. This is the place for book lovers. The building was erected in 1924. The inn is above Canterbury Booksellers Cafe, a fine establishment for buying books and enjoying pastries and good coffee. Each of the inn's six guest rooms features a character from Chaucer's Canterbury Tales. Near the university and half a block from State Street.

Collins House, 704 E. Gorham Street, (608) 255-4230. Listed on the National Register of Historic Places, this beautiful Frank Lloyd Wright–style prairie home on Lake Mendota was built in 1911. Whirlpools, fireplaces, lakeside views. Comfortable setting with Arts & Crafts furnishings and handmade quilts. Yummy pastries baked on the premises.

The Edgewater, 666 Wisconsin Avenue, (608) 256-9071 or (800) 922-5512. The Edgewater was built in 1948. The list of celebrities who have stayed here is mind-boggling: Elvis Presley, President John Kennedy, Prime Minister Nehru and his daughter, Indira Gandhi, Elton John, Bob Hope, Tony Bennett, Betty Ford ... the list goes on and on. The Edgewater has 110 comfortable rooms and is the only hotel on Lake Mendota. Free underground parking. Free limousine service. Dining room and lounge. The Edgewater pier, where guests sit over the water and enjoy snacks and meals, opens as soon as weather permits. The earliest pier opening on record was April 16. At the top of Langdon Street, a few blocks from downtown and the university.

The Livingston Inn, 752 E. Gorham Street, (608) 257-1200, is a Gothic

Crowds gather on the capitol square to celebrate the nation's centennial on July 4, 1876.

Revival–style mansion within walking distance of Lake Mendota and the downtown area. The luxurious 1857 home looks like an imposing historical structure seen in the movies. Room sizes vary, ranging upward in size and price to a mammoth suite that includes a library (with fireplace), conservatory, bedroom (with another fireplace), and Victorian soaking tub.

Mansion Hill Inn, 424 N. Pinckney Street, (608) 255-3999 or (800) 798-9070. On the Register of Historic Places, this magnificently restored 1858 Romanesque Revival mansion has 11 guest rooms, each with its own distinctive flavor. Wonderful architectural details, including hand-carved marble fireplaces and a circular stairway. This is where to go for a special weekend. Amenities include 24-hour valet service, whirlpools, fireplaces, and stunning private baths. A couple of blocks off the downtown Square.

University Heights Bed & Breakfast, 1812 Van Hise Avenue, (608) 233-3340. In a historical, residential area a few blocks from the campus, this charming inn was built in 1923 in the craftsman style. The great room features original oak trim. Four guest rooms with private baths, one with double whirlpool bath.

A carriage maker and his workers outside their Madison factory.

LODGING

For years, Madison has been heralded for having more restaurants per capita than any other city in the country. While that fact has not been substantiated (San Francisco, for instance, also claims the top spot on this somewhat arbitrary list), Madison does have hundreds of restaurants. Many are in restored buildings, serving fare ranging from stylish haute cuisine to fabulous burgers.

The following eateries are those that are either housed in noteworthy history buildings or, because of their longevity on the Madison scene, have become historic landmarks. Unless noted, they are within city limits.

Blue Marlin, 101 N. Hamilton Street, (608) 255-2255. A young server here heard me talk to my dining partner about the jazz concert we were to attend after our meal. When we arrived at the concert, a few blocks from the restaurant, I realized I had left the "doggie bag" at my table. As if by magic, our kind-hearted server appeared to deliver the carry-home bag. Just off the Capitol Square, this charming place, at the triangle of Mifflin, Pinckney, and Hamilton Streets, is reminiscent of seaside restaurants in Greece and Italy. The menu is almost all seafood; choices change as availability changes. Offerings include shrimp, scallops, Alaskan halibut, Chilean sea bass (my favorite), seafood pasta, and, of course, blue marlin. Dine outdoors in warm weather. Lunch and dinner.

The water tower on Madison's East Washington Avenue was the focal point of commercial activities in the 1890s.

Fyfe's Corner Bistro, 1344 E. Washington Avenue, (608) 251-8700. Early in the 20th century, the large brick building was home to a farm implement store. Today, the restaurant features imaginative cuisine in a bistro style (pick and choose individual selections) of dining. This is one of those places where the old brick walls lend character to superb cuisine, ranging from pasta and chicken dishes to oven-roasted pork tenderloin. The desserts are ravishing. Lunch and dinner.

The Great Dane Pub & Brewing Company, 123 E. Doty Street, (608) 284-0000. Madison's first grand hotel was built in 1858 and this place is the current

The Fauerbach Brewery was a Madison institution from 1868 to 1966.

tenant. The site brims with historical ambiance, including stories of gunfights and family feuds. A block from the capitol, the hotel was a hub for visiting dignitaries. Carriages regularly toted visitors to and from the train depot on West Washington Avenue. The Fess family owned the hotel through three generations, until 1976. In 1994, the property changed hands and was transitioned into a European brewpub, complete with pub food, including fish and chips and great sandwiches. The walled outdoor courtyard is a delightful place to dine. Lunch and dinner.

Kennedy Manor, 1 Langdon Street, (608) 256-5556. The swank restaurant, housed in a 1930s apartment building, is a throwback to a pre–World War II bistro. A gilded elevator takes diners to the lower level restaurant and bar. Black and white photos add style, jazz and blues provide background pleasure, and white linen tablecloths extend the mood. Jean Harlow or Bette Davis should appear any minute. Beef tenderloin, pasta, and salmon are favorites. Open for dinner.

Monty's Blue Plate Diner, 2089 Atwood Avenue, (608) 244-8505. Lots of neon and chrome, with an interesting history to boot. Transformed from Severson's Gas Station by Linville Architects of Madison, known for their snazzy restaurant interiors, the Blue Plate exudes a chic ambiance. An arty, trendy, people-watching place with hearty food like meat loaf, roast turkey and mashed potatoes, and milk shakes and malts. My favorite breakfasts are the potato zucchini pancakes with homemade cranberry apple sauce and fresh cinnamon swirl French toast. Breakfast, lunch, and dinner.

Paisan's, 80 University Square, (608) 257-3832. In 1950, when the restaurant opened its doors, its pizza pies drew the crowds, not only from campus but from town. People could not get enough of the distinctive blend of Italian cuisine, with big, fancy salads. Cozy booths, stained glass, fun. Open for lunch and dinner.

Porta Bella, 425 N. Frances Street, (608) 256-3186. A visit here is akin to visiting an atmospheric villa. Diners have been taking in the abundance of ornate chandeliers, stained glass, and private dining coves since 1970. Nicely prepared and presented Italian and continental dishes. This is casual dining in elegant surroundings. Expect long waits on the weekend. A block off University Avenue. Open for lunch Fridays only and dinner.

Quivey's Grove, 6261 Nesbitt Road, (608) 273-4900. History lovers adore Quivey's. Listed on the National Register of Historic Places, the original 1855 house is an Italianate fieldstone mansion with 18-inch-thick walls, 13-foot ceilings, and unstained hemlock floors. The Stable Tap, once the site of 19th-century livery, has antique furnishings, including old sheet music (notice the replica of the 1855 flag) and lithographs from 1846. The Stable is open for lunch (casual dining includes great salads, burgers, and chicken entrees) and has a limited menu for dinner. An underground stone tunnel (added in 1980), built with 50 tons of stone, connects the Stable to Quivey's Grove Stone House. The 1885 house is filled with antiques in each of the six intimate dining rooms. Open for dinner only. Located off Highway 151, two miles south of the Beltline on the way to Verona and Mount Horeb. Right on County PD, left on Nesbitt Road.

Smoky's Club, 3005 University Avenue, (608) 233-2120. According to at least one published list, Smoky's is considered one of the top 10 steak houses in the country. There is little doubt that the ranking and its reputation among many travel writers is well deserved. Smoky's has great charcoal-broiled entrees. It has been a Madison hot spot since 1936, but since the Schmocks, the current owners, bought it in 1969, they have quadrupled the size of the original restaurant. Diners congregate in this cavernous spot with memorabilia hanging about because it is festive, fun (loud, too), and features some of the best steak anywhere. Open for dinner.

Stamm House at Pheasant Branch, 6625 Century Avenue, Middleton, (608) 831-5835. Dane County's oldest tavern, the old stagecoach stop was constructed in 1847 in the town of Pheasant Branch, now part of Middleton. Diners swarm here on Friday nights for the all-you-can-eat fish fry. Good burgers, chicken and dumplings, and other casual dining. Grab a table upstairs and look for an anachronism near one of the exterior walls. That is the original "dumbwaiter secret compartment" used to bring food and utensils up from the kitchen. Look for the bright red building with its white silhouetted horse and stagecoach. Open for dinner.

MADISON AT A GLANCE

MUSEUMS

Elvehjem Museum of Art: The museum, named for UW–Madison's 13th president, Conrad A. Elvehjem, encompasses three floors of exhibits.

State Historical Museum: Related to the State Historical Society of Wisconsin, the museum is filled with resources about the state's history. Four floors examine Wisconsin's past.

Wisconsin Veterans Museum: Artifacts, clothing, memorabilia commemorating veterans who served in wars. Three galleries are on one floor. One gallery is devoted to 19th-century exhibits, another to the 20th century, the third has rotating exhibits. Open year-round, (608) 267-1799. 30 West Mifflin.

HISTORICAL SITES AND ATTRACTIONS

Camp Randall: A 53.5-acre martialing area for the 70,000 Wisconsin res-

A view of the corner of State & Mifflin Streets through an archway decorated to honor Wisconsin's 50 years as a state in 1898.

idents who marched off to the Civil War. It once included a hospital and stockade for Confederate soldiers. The site of the encampment, at Monroe Street and Randall Avenue, is now part of the university and is mostly devoted to athletic events. Listed on the National Register of Historic Places.

Edgewood University Campus: This was once Governor Washburn's estate. The site, recognized with a marker by the Dane County Historical Society, was deeded to the Sinsinawa Dominican Sisters in 1881.

First Capitol: A few buildings remain in what was once the seat of the Wisconsin Territory in 1836. The legislature and capitol were moved permanently to Madison in 1838. The museum is funded by the Wisconsin Legislature to help people better understand the creation of government and law when the state of Wisconsin was still in its infancy. It is open Memorial Day through Labor Day. Three miles northwest of Belmont. (608) 987-2122.

Mendota County Park: The Dane County Historical Society has recognized this site. It was where the St. Cyr trading post was located, and where Governor Dodge negotiated with the Winnebago during the Black Hawk War of 1832. On County M, one-quarter mile east of County Q.

North Hall: Built in 1851 of native sandstone, it is the oldest building on campus. The world-famous naturalist John Muir lived here while he was a student. Several of his inventions are on display. In the Bascom Hill Historic District.

State Historical Society of Wisconsin: This handsome stone building on the University of Wisconsin campus is a repository of all things Wisconsin.

WHA Radio at Radio Hall: Oldest radio station still in operation in the world. Founded in 1917, it's Madison's public broadcast affiliate.

OTHER HISTORICAL STOPS

Collins House: Built in 1911, and listed on the National Register of Historic Places, this beautiful Frank Lloyd Wright–style prairie home, now doubling as an inn, overlooks Lake Mendota.

The Edgewater: Built in 1948, the list of celebrities who have stayed here is mind-boggling. The hotel has 110 rooms and is the only hotel on Lake Mendota.

Gates of Heaven Synagogue: Built in 1863, the German Romanesque Revival sandstone building was the first synagogue in Madison. It is considered one of the oldest synagogues in the country still in existence.

Governor's Mansion: This is the executive residence of the governor of Wisconsin. Built in 1927, the 34-room home has many interesting features, including seven fireplaces and a stately, wrought-iron fence which originally encompassed the capitol grounds in Madison. Free tours from April through

August. Maple Bluff.

The Livingston Inn: A 1857 Gothic Revival-style mansion is within walking distance of Lake Mendota and the downtown area. The luxurious home looks like an imposing historical structure seen in the movies.

Mansion Hill Historic District: Also known as Yankee Hill and Aristocrat Hill, this is where the privileged upper class built homes in the mid-1800s. Queen Anne, German Romanesque Revival, and Italianate architectural styles are represented. Close to Lake Mendota and the UW campus.

Mansion Hill Inn: On the Register of Historic Places, this magnificently restored 1858 Romanesque Revival mansion has 11 guest rooms, each with its own distinctive flavor.

Memorial Union and Memorial Union Terrace: This is the heart of the UW–Madison, where a visitor can easily absorb the flavor of the university and its impact on Madison. The union was built in 1928 with money from a successful post-World War I fund-raising drive. Since then, it has been the cultural, political, and artistic heart of the university.

Monona Terrace Community & Convention Center: This impressive Lake Monona lakefront building was built in 1997, sixty years after it was designed by Frank Lloyd Wright. A rooftop garden offers great lakeside views.

Otis Redding Memorial: The memorial honors the rock and roll legend whose plane went down in Madison's Lake Monona in December 1967, only three days after he recorded the hit "Dock of the Bay." In the rooftop garden of the Monona Terrace Community and Convention Center.

Quivey's Grove: Listed on the National Register of Historic Places, the original 1855 house, now a restaurant, is an Italianate fieldstone mansion with 18-inch-thick walls, 13-foot ceilings, and unstained hemlock floors. The Stable Tap, once the site of a 19th-century livery, has antique furnishings, including old sheet music and lithographs from 1846.

The "Red Gym": This "castle" on the lake, built in 1892, is a UW student resource center. Many famous people, like Upton Sinclair and William Jennings Bryan, have orated here. Next to the Memorial Union.

Stamm House: Built in 1847 as a stagecoach stop and tavern. Today, the old stone restaurant specializes in traditional American food. Middleton, just west of Madison.

State Capitol: Replicating the nation's Capitol building in Washington D.C., Wisconsin's State Capitol was built in 1917. This building is the third on this site; the first was replaced by a second that burned down. It has been called the country's most magnificent state capitol building and is often used for Hollywood movies.

Tenney Locks: Old stone locks maintain the water depth of Lake Mendota, allowing boat navigation between Lake Mendota and Lake Monona. Recognized as a historical point of interest by the Dane County Historical Society. Located at Tenney Park at Sherman Avenue and the Yahara River.

Unitarian Meeting House: Of the 32 Frank Lloyd Wright designed buildings in Madison, eight remain standing, including this 1946 structure. The innovative design incorporates interlocking triangles, demonstrating Wright's ability to integrate the outdoors with the indoors. Guided tours.

HISTORICAL EVENTS AND FESTIVALS
APRIL THROUGH OCTOBER

Dane County Farmers Market: One of the oldest and biggest farm markets in the country, it's been going strong since the 1960s. More than 200 area farmers bring their wares to the downtown Capitol Square Saturday mornings.

CHAPTER 9

GREEN BAY AND BEYOND
MANY LINKS TO THE PAST

In 1912, Green Bay was a thriving port for shipping lumber, paper, and agricultural products.

HISTORY BUFFS HEADED for the Green Bay area have a decision to make. They can stay mobile, visiting not only this port city but also nearby attractions spread out in several directions; they can stick with the city itself; or they can choose several sites from throughout this chapter and pay them a reasonably quick visit. Regardless, travelers will find that northeastern Wisconsin has more than just professional football.

GREEN BAY

No matter how a visitor feels about pro football, the Packers are an obsession in Green Bay (and throughout the state, for that matter), and they do have a long and colorful past as one of the teams that formed the basis of the National Football League, having been founded in 1919. The team is also a well-known anachronism. The Pack is the oldest team in professional football, but more interesting is the fact that it is the only team in all of professional sports owned by a community. That, of course, is Green Bay, which also happens to be the oldest community in Wisconsin.

Green Bay originally was named La Baye by French trappers and explorers. It later evolved to La Baye Verte, which means green bay. After the French and Indian Wars, the British named their prize Fort Howard. Visitors will see all of these names throughout Green Bay history and when visiting local historical sites.

On arrival, travelers can see why Green Bay was a magnet for voyageurs and adventurers. Those early settlers were drawn to the area because the mouth of the bay was a natural gateway to western land and waters beyond. It was a lively yet rugged outpost, a favorite stopping point for trappers, traders, and Jesuit missionaries.

In 1669, the loosely established community (near the city of De Pere and adjacent to today's Green Bay) became a permanent settlement named New France. That settlement, guided by legendary Jesuit priest Claude Allouez, would have the distinction of being the first community on the northwestern frontier, which later would be known as the territory, then the state, of Wisconsin.

Through the early 1800s, the fur trade was the dominant business. But in 1825, when the Erie Canal opened, it gave the territory access to more travelers. News that Green Bay offered cheap land and easy living traveled fast. While some early settlers may have found land at bargain prices, they soon learned that living on the raw frontier bay, with the winds and squalls whipping the landscape at a moment's notice, was not as easy as they had imagined. Logging, farming, and iron smelting were where the work was, and it was hard work.

Nevertheless, immigrants from Europe swelled the area in the 19th century, allowing manufacturing, shipping, and the paper industry to grow and prosper. Most came from all parts of Germany, plus Holland, Poland, and Belgium. Native Americans, in the form of Oneida tribespeople, settled just west of the city, where there is a large reservation to this day.

Proof positive that Green Bay offers something besides football exists at Heritage Hill, 2640 S. Webster Avenue, (920) 435-2244, a living history museum with roots dating from 1938, when Beaupre Place, an 1842 Greek Revival home, was moved to this site. Several years later, between 1975 and 1977, other area historical buildings were brought here.

The museum showcases the history of northeastern Wisconsin from 1672 to 1905 through 25 exceptionally reconstructed buildings. On site, too, are 11,000 artifacts that help tell the stories of the pioneers who carved out this area of the state. At the gate of this beautiful property, which slopes to the Fox River, travelers enter a world of yesteryear. This theme world includes French fur trappers, blacksmiths, a 1901 Belgian farmstead, and, during the Christmas season, re-creation of a holiday dinner at the 1871 Beaupre House.

Heritage Hill is divided into four time lines. They include:

➤ Pioneer Heritage Area: Highlights are a maple sugaring house, a replica of the area's first courthouse (1824), and a 1671 bark chapel, reflecting the type of construction and style built for Jesuit missionaries.

➤ Military Heritage Area: This 1836 area includes the original Fort

Howard Hospital and kitchen, as well as the Fort Howard School and officers' quarters.

➤ Small Town Heritage Area: Here are the 1871 Tank Cottage, the oldest wooden frame home in the state, the De Pere News office, a Moravian church, the law office of Henry Beard, the Franklin Hose Company firehouse, a blacksmith shop, and other authentic buildings.

➤ Agricultural/Ethnic Heritage Area: This 1905 Belgian farmstead has many interesting buildings to explore, including a summer kitchen and a horse and dairy barn. Also at the site are several outbuildings, a chapel, and a cheese factory.

Expect crowds during the school year. More than 35,000 visitors roam the grounds annually, including about 1,900 school groups.

GREEN AND GOLD HISTORY

Yet Green Bay remains a football town, with evidence of the Packers nearly everywhere in the area. But kids who normally regard history with the same sentiments they reserve for brussels sprouts will enjoy their time at the Packer Hall of Fame, with its team memorabilia. Located at 855 Lombardi Avenue, (920) 499-4281, the well-laid out facility contains over 70 years' worth of film clips, wall-sized posters, and lots of memorabilia pertaining to Green Bay's favorite team. Visitors gain insight into early coach Curly Lambeau's vision of creating a world-class football team, and memories of 1960s greats, including Vince Lombardi (who is practically a saint in this town), Bart Starr, and Paul Hornung. Interactive opportunities including jumping in the hands-on area and making a winning field goal. The facility is open daily; there is an admission fee.

Then walk over to nearby Lambeau Field, (920) 499-4281, to see where it all happened. Who could leave Green Bay without touring the famous Lambeau Field? Tours show off nearly every nook and corner of the stadium. There is an admission fee. Tours given daily June through Labor Day.

For more information, contact the Green Bay Area Convention and Visitor Bureau by dialing (920) 494-9507 or (800) 236-3976.

OTHER SITES AND ATTRACTIONS

Bay Beach Amusement Park, 1313 Bay Beach Road, (920) 448-3365. It has always seemed strange to see this carnival atmosphere right next to the bay. Nevertheless, it is a great gathering place for families and folks who want to take in the picnic and amusement park atmosphere, including 12 rides. Usually open daily from Memorial Day through late August. Free park admission.

Bay Beach Wildlife Sanctuary, 1660 E. Shore Drive, (920) 391-3671. A 700-acre spread, up the road from the amusement park, with a wide selection of animals indigenous to Wisconsin. There is a timber wolf house, a nature

The basics of camping haven't changed much in the last 50 years.

center, and many trails to explore. Open mid-April to mid-September.

Charles A. Grignon Mansion, 1313 Augustine Street, Kaukauna, (920) 766-3122. This magnificent, white-columned mansion was built in 1837 as a wedding gift from Charles A. Grignon to his bride, Mary. The home sits on the site of a fur-trading post dating from about 1760. The Grignon family had been involved in fur trading for more than one hundred years. Costumed guides help re-create the period when Charles Grignon lived here, from 1837 to 1862. A museum shop and an apple orchard also are on the premises. Off Highway 41, 20 minutes south of Green Bay.

This Green Bay gas station, built in Norwegian–style architecture, is a far cry from today's minimarts.

Hazelwood Historic House Museum, 1008 S. Monroe Avenue, (920) 437-1840. In the historic Astor District, this restored 1837 Greek Revival mansion (and museum) sits on a bluff above the Fox River. Hazelwood is surrounded by other stately homes. For more than a hundred years the Morgan L. Martin family, community leaders, lived here. Morgan's wife, Elizabeth, chronicled life by writing intriguing Civil War diaries and memoirs. Hazelwood is definitely worth a tour. Many notable furnishings are represented, including authentic Empire, Sheraton, and Duncan Phyfe pieces; several played roles in Wisconsin history. On the National Register of Historical Places, Hazelwood is open May through August. Donation. Call for hours.

National Railroad Museum, 2285 S. Broadway, (920) 437-7623. Travelers who like old-time railroad artifacts will love this place. With nearly 80 assorted railroad cars and engines, the museum is a railroad palace. Some of the historical bits include the Dwight D. Eisenhower World War II Train, the Union Pacific Big Boy, and the Rock Island Aerotrain. Train rides, theater with railroad videos. Admission fee. Open year round but daily from early May through December.

Neville Public Museum, 210 Museum Place, (920) 448-4460. Fascinating, changing exhibits of art, history, and science. Two floors to roam.

LODGING

The area has many fine lodges, inns, hotels, and motels, including several national chains. The following represent interesting places with historical ties.

Astor House, 637 S. Monroe Avenue, (920) 432-3585. The first bed and breakfast in Green Bay, this 1888 home, in the Astor Neighborhood, features plenty of amenities, including whirlpools, fireplaces, and refrigerators. Each of the five guest rooms offers decor reflecting these themes: Victorian, Country French, Southwestern, Asian, and Gothic. Evening bed turn-downs are typical of attention to detail.

DINING

Eve's Supper Club, 2020 Riverside Drive, (920) 435-1571, has been a Green Bay institution for nearly four decades. Eve's has one of the best views in town from the fourth floor atop the Riverside office building. The Fox River Valley below is breathtaking, and Eve's food is good to boot. Steak (the most popular item offered), seafood, and chicken dishes are featured. Open for lunch and dinner.

Bistro John Paul, 1244 Main Street, (920) 432-2897. Termed one of the state's finest French restaurants, visitors will see why once they sample the cuisine. Beautifully prepared entrees include duck, lamb, veal, chicken, and beef. Save room for creme brulee, one of my favorite desserts. Open for dinner, Tuesday through Saturday.

Fuzzy's Number 63, 2511 W. Mason Avenue, (920) 494-6633. To grab the flavor of what it is like to live in Packer Land, visit Fuzzy's. This place, named for a former Packer legend, is what football frenzy is all about. Lively atmosphere.

Kroll's East, 1658 E. Main Street, (920) 468-4422. (The two Kroll's restaurants are run by two cousins.) This is the original Kroll's, featuring great food like charcoal-grilled burgers and seafood plates.

Kroll's West, 1990 S. Ridge Road, (920) 497-1111. The place to be for those hoping to rub elbows with football greats or, at the very least, football fans. Close to Lambeau Field, Kroll's has a football atmosphere and plenty of hearty food. Patrons love the goofy yet effective buzzers on the walls so they can get waitstaff attention. Try cheese steak sandwiches or fried perch.

Rock Garden Supper Club, 1951 Bond Street, (920) 497-4701. A big, bountiful menu that will have travelers wondering where the time went. Choose from
succulent steaks, chicken, or ribs. A wide selection of popular choices.

The Wellington, 1060 Hansen Road, (920) 499-2000. The restaurant features a rich ambiance, not unlike dining in a lavish Old English residence.
Specialties include chicken Marsala and fresh salmon. Since Door County is
nearby, this imaginative restaurant often weaves ingredients associated with
Door products, such as cherries, into its blend of tastes and textures. Case in
point: Salmon dressed in cherries and port wine. Open for lunch and dinner.

DE PERE

This village, which bumps up against the city of Green Bay on the southeast, has some of the richest history in the state. In 1634, Jean Nicolet became
the first white man to come to the area when his 1,000-mile canoe trip ended
amid rapids in an area later named De Pere. Following Nicolet was Father
Claude Allouez. He established St. Francis Xavier, a mission that was a religious
settlement between 1670 and 1687. Visitors to this historic spot included
Marquette and Joliet, who spent a few days here on their journey to become the
first Europeans on the upper Mississippi River.

Modern De Pere started in 1829 when William Dickinson realized that
water could be used to power manufacturing. A dam was built in 1849, and the
De Pere Manufacturing Company was constructed. Today the city is a gateway
to Green Bay and the North Woods.

While in De Pere, stop in at the White Pillars Museum, 403 N. Broadway,
(920) 336-3877. This unique place has a long and colorful history. Originally
built as the mainstay of the Fox River Hydraulic Company, it also was the first
bank building in Wisconsin. Subsequently, it became a private residence in
1912, and now it serves as the home of the De Pere Historic Society, with collections of historic area artifacts. There is no admission fee.

DINING

The Union Hotel, 200 N. Broadway, (920) 336-6131. The Maternowski family has been running this landmark establishment since 1918. History fans will
find the architectural details in this kitschy place intriguing. Lots of wood and
wallpaper. Two dining rooms, each featuring steak, panfried walleye, and pork,
plus salads, soups, and heavenly homemade pies. Open for lunch and dinner.

History buffs who run out of activity in Green Bay have a number of
attractive choices. They can head northeast on Highway 57 to Door County
(see Chapter 1); they can drive southeast on Interstate 43 to the tidy lakeside
towns of Manitowoc and Two Rivers; they can head west-southwest on

Ho-Chunks playing the mocassin game, which involved guessing the mocassin that held a small object.

Highway 54 to history-conscious New London; or they can head north on Highway 41 to the towns of Peshtigo and, on the Wisconsin-Michigan border, Marinette. The latter drive is most attractive, providing glimpses of Green Bay and hints of the great forests that once were.

PESHTIGO

Most people who visit here are attracted by the history of the great Peshtigo fire. It began on October 8, 1871, the same day fire ravaged Chicago. Ironically, the Peshtigo fire was more devastating, but because Chicago was more prominent and more populous, it got more attention. But the Peshtigo inferno was by far the more disastrous in terms of lives lost.

Six years after the Civil War, Peshtigo was a boomtown with a population of 2,000. A river and a narrow-gauge railroad helped move lumber to Green Bay for shipment to Chicago. Besides sawmills, there were retail stores, a Catholic church, and a newspaper. Chicago & North Western railway crews were laying track north of Peshtigo in an area that had recently been logged and, therefore, had lots of rubble and brush.

Workers loading kilns with hardwood logs to produce charcoal on the Fox River near De Pere.

The summer and fall had been dry and several forest fires were noted as early as September. The train crew may have set the fire intentionally, to clear brush or otherwise. A relentless wind blew the fire south, and the inferno became so powerful it created its own hurricane-like weather. Some 800 residents died, while others saved themselves by jumping into the river. The terrifying fire also burned northward, leaping the Menominee River and burning 14 miles deep into the state of Michigan. The town of around 3,500 residents today has survived, but there seems to be a pall still, due to the worst forest fire in U.S. history.

The Peshtigo Fire Museum, 400 Oconto Avenue, (715) 582-3244, pays homage to the people who died as well as to the survivors. Aptly placed, the museum is in the first church constructed after the 1871 fire. The museum does a fine job showcasing remnants from that tragic day, plus photos and news articles relating to the terrible tale. Nearby is a graveyard for the fire victims. Free admission. Open daily, Memorial Day through early October.

DINING

Schussler's Supper Club, west of town on County B, (715) 582-4962. Good German fare.

MARINETTE

Marinette, 53 miles north of Green Bay, is situated in a beautiful area, with the Lake Michigan lakeshore and the Menominee and Peshtigo Rivers (this is big rafting country) winding through the forests. Like Peshtigo, it was big timber country for more than half of the 19th century. Marinette was spared in the big 1871 fire due to the presence of a couple of sandy ridges between the town and the inferno. Lumbering continues in the area, but the main draw is summer tourism.

Those who want to explore the nearby Nicolet National Forest or take in the gorgeous back-country have come to the right place. Outdoor activities are the main game in town. Marinette, named for a daughter of a Menominee chief, has more waterfalls than any other area in the state.

One of the most historically significant sites in the area is the Marinette County Logging Museum, Stephenson Island, (715) 732-0831. The facility provides a chance to see replicas of two complete logging camps, which offer a look at what life was like in these parts more than one hundred years ago. The museum is open Memorial Day through Labor Day, and there is a small admission fee. Stephenson Island is just off Highway 41.

For more information about other area attractions, contact the Marinette Chamber of Commerce and Visitor Center. Dial (715) 735-6681 or (800) 236-6681.

LODGING

M & M Victorian Inn, 1393 Main Street, (715) 732-9531. This is one of the state's most splendid inns. The 115-year-old site is European to the core (expect to be greeted with "Bonjour!"), being a tall-towered Queen Anne with five guest rooms, lavish baths, and wine cellar.

NEW LONDON

Head due west of Green Bay about 40 miles on Highway 54 to the town of New London, where you'll find, among other sites, the Heritage Historical Village, 900 Montgomery Street. Five historical buildings, including an Octagon house, Triangle School, railroad depot, village chapel, and log cabin, have been moved to this site to commemorate the city's heritage. It is adjacent to Memorial Park and about three blocks from the library. Open the first and third Sundays in June, July, and August, the site also can be visited by appointment. Call Bob Polaske for arrangements, (920) 982-5186 or (920) 982-8557.

The New London Museum and Library, 406 S. Pearl Street, (920) 982-8520, was built in 1914 and renovated in 1986. The museum was founded in 1932 by one of the city's first librarians. Free admission. Call for hours.

Lake Michigan has gained a well-deserved reputation for being unkind to small boaters, as well as to larger craft.

MANITOWOC

For another interesting glimpse into Wisconsin's past, take the 45-minute drive southwest of Green Bay on Interstate 43 to Manitowoc. This community of 35,000 residents was long known as the "Clipper City" because of the number of clipper ships it produced in the 19th century. The town continued to be a shipbuilding center through World War II, when it became one of the country's prime naval shipyards. There are numerous vestiges of that rich heritage evident throughout the city, but it now has an industrial base that goes beyond strictly maritime interests. Commercial fishing, once a major industry, still exists, but charter fishing has become a big operation, primarily in April and May.

The Wisconsin Maritime Museum, 75 Maritime Drive, (920) 684-0218, honors the town's past with a fascinating look at one hundred years of maritime history along the Great Lakes. World War II submarine, photographs, model ships, plenty of exhibits. This is as good a place as any to determine the approximate location of any given Lake Michigan shipwreck. Open daily.

A classroom of serious students at the Van Dyne School in Fond du Lac County 1905.

OTHER SITES AND ATTRACTIONS

Pinecrest Historical Village, Pinecrest Lane, (920) 684-5110 or (920) 684-4445. Nearly two dozen historical buildings, some pre–Civil War, were moved to this location and lovingly preserved. Admission fee. Open early May through Labor Day. Off County JJ.

LODGING

Westport Bed & Breakfast, 635 N. 8th Street, (920) 686-0465 or (888) 686-0465. A charming 1879 Italianate home with four guest rooms and porches for loafing. Shops and restaurants are a short walk away.

TWO RIVERS

A visitor won't be able to escape the fact that Two Rivers, population 13,030, bills itself as the place the ice cream sundae was invented in 1891. Take Highway 42 north for about seven miles from Manitowoc and take time to see what the fuss is about. This is also a waterfront town named for the East and West Twin Rivers. The "twins" end up mixing with Lake Michigan, making for a water-lover's sort of place.

It is also a great place to stop and take in harbor views and to enjoy the friendly, small-town atmosphere. Even the McDonald's, smack in the middle of town, is pretty nifty. Lots of info on the three-dimensional map inside about Lake Michigan, its reefs, fish, and shoreline.

LODGING

Lighthouse Inn on the Lake, 1515 Memorial Drive, (920) 793-4524 or (800) 228-6416. Tremendous views of Lake Michigan, since the inn is practically on top of the waves. Indoor pool, sauna, and Water's Edge restaurant.

Red Forest Bed & Breakfast, 1421 25th Street, (920) 793-1794 or (888) 250-2272. Charming hospitality in this four-bedroom home with beautiful stained glass windows and loads of antiques.

DINING

Berner's Ice Cream Parlor in the Washington House, 1622 Jefferson Street, (920) 793-2490. This is where it all started: the world's first ice cream sundae saw the light of day here. Funky atmosphere, very good ice cream.

Kurtz's, 1410 Washington Street, (920) 793-1222. How many restaurants have been going strong since 1904? This well-known spot falls into that category. Hearty fare, especially known for really good sandwiches.

A GLANCE AT THE GREEN BAY AREA

MUSEUMS

Green Bay Packer Hall of Fame: Film clips, posters, memorabilia pertaining to Green Bay's favorite team. Over 70 years' worth of interesting football material. Interactive opportunities for becoming a football hero. Green Bay.

Heritage Hill State Park: A living history museum featuring an 1842 Greek Revival home and 25 reconstructed buildings. Visitors enter a world of French fur trappers, blacksmiths, a 1901 Belgian farmstead and, during the Christmas season, a re-creation of holiday dinner at the 1871 Beaupre House. Green Bay.

History Museum of Two Rivers: This former convent houses religious artifacts pertaining to German, French, Polish, Lithuanian heritage. 1810 Jefferson Street. (920) 793-1103. Two Rivers.

Marinette County Logging Museum: Two complete logging camps give visitors a look at what life was like during the area's logging boom heyday. Marinette.

National Railroad Museum: This railroad palace includes nearly 80 assorted railroad cars and engines and lots of old-time railroad artifacts. Green Bay.

Neville Public Museum: Changing exhibits of art, history, and science on two floors. Green Bay.

New London Heritage Historical Village: Five historical buildings, including an Octagon house, Triangle school, railroad depot, village chapel, and log cabin have been moved to this site to commemorate the city's heritage. Adjacent to Memorial Park. New London.

New London Museum & Library: Built in 1914 and renovated in 1986, the museum was founded in 1932 by one of the city's first librarians. New London.

Peshtigo Fire Museum: Appropriate placement of this museum—it's in the first church constructed after the 1871 fire that ravaged the town. Photos, news articles relating to that terrible event. A graveyard for the fire victims is nearby. Peshtigo.

Rahr-West Museum: Housed in a grand 1891 Victorian mansion, the museum contains an exceptional collection of art, period furnishing, Indian artifacts, dolls, and porcelain. 610 N. 8th St. (920) 683-4501. Manitowoc.

White Pillars Museum: This place has a long and colorful history. Built as the mainstay of the Fox River Hydraulic Company, it also was the first bank building in Wisconsin. Now, its serves as the home of the De Pere Historical Society. Extensive collections of area artifacts. De Pere.

Wisconsin Maritime Museum: A fascinating look at more than a century of maritime history along the Great Lakes. Photos, model ships, maps, plenty of exhibits. Manitowoc.

HISTORICAL SITES AND ATTRACTIONS

Charles A. Grignon Mansion: This 1837 home, built by Charles A. Grignon as a wedding gift to his bride, Mary, is on the site of a 1760 fur trading post. The Grignon family had been involved with fur trading for more than one hundred years. Kaukauna.

Hazelwood Historic House Museum: In Green Bay's historic Astor District, this restored 1837 Greek Revival mansion (and museum) sits on a bluff above the Fox River. Listed on the National Register of Historic Places.

Oneida Nation Museum: A collection of Oneida history and culture in the main hall on the Oneida Reservation. Outbuildings include a stockade. W892 EE Road, west of Green Bay. (920) 869-2768.

Pinecrest Historical Village: Nearly two dozen historical buildings, some pre–Civil War, were moved to this location and lovingly preserved. Manitowoc.

OTHER HISTORICAL STOPS

Astor House: The first bed and breakfast in Green Bay, this 1888 home in the Astor neighborhood features plenty of amenities. Green Bay.

Berner's Ice Cream Parlor: This is where the first ice cream sundae was invented in 1891. Two Rivers.

Lambeau Field: A visit to Green Bay isn't complete until you've toured the famous Lambeau Field. Tours show off nearly every nook and corner of the Packer stadium. Green Bay.

M & M Victorian Inn: One of the state's most splendid inns, this 1885 site is European to its core. Marinette.

The Union Hotel: Family owned and run since 1918, this kitschy restaurant serves popular items like steak and panfried walleye in an atmosphere with lots of intriguing architectural details. De Pere.

HISTORICAL EVENTS AND FESTIVALS
JUNE

Bayfest: Large summer festival drawing some of the country's finest musicians. Billed as the biggest mix of food and music north of Milwaukee. Green Bay.

AUGUST

Heritage Days & Rail Fest, New London.

SEPTEMBER

French and Indian War Encampment: Green Bay.

CHAPTER 10

THE FAR NORTH
BAYFIELD AND BEYOND

A bountiful apple harvest on display near Bayfield.

IT'S ALMOST UNFAIR TO PITCH the far northwestern corner of Wisconsin as a weekend destination. For one thing the drive from Chicago to Bayfield, as an example, is a daunting 445 miles, while it is 356 miles from Milwaukee, 300 from Madison, and almost 200 from Minneapolis-St. Paul. For another, there are so many historically significant things to see and do that a full week is probably more realistic for a visit that does justice to the area. But wherever you're coming from and however long you're staying, the trip is well worth it.

BAYFIELD

To understand Bayfield, the northernmost thumb of Wisconsin, a visitor must understand Lake Superior's importance to the Bayfield peninsula. The largest freshwater lake in the world, Lake Superior has been a gateway to exploration, adventure, and to some of the most glorious sailing available anywhere.

During the time Columbus was searching for a new route to India, the Ojibwa Indians migrated to nearby Madeline Island. French and British explorers arrived at La Pointe, the trading post on the island, in the 1600s. They were followed by fur trappers and missionaries in the mid-1600s. In 1659, two Frenchmen, Radisson and Groselliers, from Three Rivers, Canada, first penetrated into northern waters. They were guided by Indians across Lake Superior to the mouth of Chequamegon Bay and the Chippewa settlement of Lac Courte Oreilles.

Over the next 300 years, the number of sailors plying Superior's waters grew as optimistic entrepreneurs realized Bayfield was a good place to seek their fortunes. Towns mushroomed along the mainland shore, supporting fishing, lumbering, and quarrying. A common denominator of the Bayfield scene is that the lake has always been a major source of the economy. Leisure travelers from several states in the Midwest regularly gravitated to the area during the 1880s. Lavish hotels and inns were built to accommodate their needs. Wealthy vacationers built opulent summer homes on Madeline Island, but Bayfield, too, had its share of grand homes. One of the finest was built by a Civil War general who loved Bayfield for the crisp lake breezes that helped ward off his asthma. Industries, as well as tourism, boomed in the late 1880s, then steadily declined around the turn of the century. In the 1950s, tourists began to rediscover the area.

In 1970, the Apostle Islands National Lakeshore was established to protect the beauty of 21 Apostle Islands, 12 miles of unspoiled coastal property, and a startling number of lighthouses, more than any other shoreline in the country. Although not part of the official national lakeshore (because of its preexisiting settlers), Madeline Island is a 20-minute ferry ride from Bayfield and home to about 180 year-round residents. The numbers swell to 2,500 in summer. Many islanders have maintained homes here for several generations.

Bayfield's economy still revolves around the area's natural beauty and water. Rugged, rocky shorelines, legendary shipwrecks, breathtaking sunrises and sunsets, billions of stars—they are all here. Visitors are drawn here because of the history, beauty, and utter peacefulness, reasons why the Chicago Tribune termed Bayfield "Best Little Town in the Midwest" in 1997, after a search of 139 towns and 8,000 miles of travel.

For a hands-on trip into Bayfield's nautical past, there are few things that can match sailing on a classic, two-masted wooden ketch among the islands. You can get the experience aboard the Sandpiper, a meticulously maintained sailboat owned by Craig and Sharon Locey of the Thimbleberry Inn Bed & Breakfast in Bayfield. Once they made the decision to buy the boat, they realized they were buying more than a sailboat—they were buying a legend. The wooden boat was well known in the world of sailing, particularly in New England. The Sandpiper began with Swift Custom Boats of Exeter, New Hampshire, who built her. She was originally designed by Winthrop L. Warner in 1930, and built and finished off in 1978 by Bill Page, a wooden-yacht broker in Camden, Maine.

An exceptional boat in many ways, the Sandpiper, which sleeps five, has been featured in the book Classic Yacht Interiors and in Wooden Boat magazine. Those who know boats like the craft's detail. Everything has its place. The linens and sheets are stored in efficient color-coded order. When visitors come onboard, Craig shows the sailboat's intriguing features, such as the built-in silverware drawer in the dining room table, the special holder for binoculars, and the depth finder, which swings out and can easily be read from the cockpit, then secured in place.

Up close, the boat shows exotic shades and textures—elegantly varnished woods, including cherry, butternut, and locust. It was easy to see why this lovely wooden craft lends a distinctive presence to the summer scene in Bayfield, a piece of paradise on Lake Superior's south shore.

For more information, contact the Bayfield Chamber of Commerce, open year-round at Manypenny and Broad Streets,(715) 779-3335.

OTHER SITES AND ATTRACTIONS

Apostle Island Cruise Service, Rittenhouse Avenue, (800) 323-7619; Web site is www.apostleisland.com. They do a Grand Tour of the islands from summer through early October. On one narrated tour, our guide was quick to point out a bear swimming to Stockton Island, the bears' retreat for berries and campers' discarded food. The Islander cruise takes visitors to Stockton or a historic fish camp on Manitou Island. The cruise service also offers an Inner Island shuttle to Sand or Raspberry Islands. Reservations are necessary, particularly for those who want to sit on the upper deck. The lower, enclosed deck has concession stand and comfortable seating. This is an excellent way to get to know the Apostle Islands and the sea caves (about two hours into the journey) close up.

Apostle Island National Lakeshore, (715) 779-3397. Many historical sites throughout the Apostle Islands, including guided tours of historic fishing camp on Manitou Island, one of numerous archaeological sites in the Apostles.

The Bayfield Winery and Hauser's Superior View Farm, County J, (715) 779-5404. A glorious family orchard that has been going strong since the Hauser family started the operation in 1908. Enjoy the orchard, pick apples, tour the historic Sears & Roebuck barn. Apples, jams, jellies, plants, and flowers for sale. Open May through October. Overlooks Lake Superior. Two and one-half miles northwest of Bayfield.

Big Top Chautauqua, Ski Hill Road, (715) 373-5552 or (888) 244-8368. Don't leave Bayfield without taking in at least one show under the tent, affectionately called Big Blue. There is no experience quite like it. Since 1985, Chautauqua founder and artistic director Warren Nelson has been presenting "culture under canvas." The nonprofit arts organization spotlights area history

Ed Lane was the lighthouse keeper on Michigan Island from 1901 to 1939.

Every October, as many as 50,000 visitors cram into tiny Bayfield for its Apple Festival.

through song and drama, sponsoring musicals, dramas, and big-name draws. Shows run as often as nightly and change daily during mid-July through August. Call for dates. Open late May through mid-September. At the base of Mt. Ashwabay, three miles south of Bayfield, just off Highway 13.

LODGING

Old Rittenhouse Inn, 301 Rittenhouse Avenue, (715) 779-5111 or (888) 578-4667. A cross between a museum and a mansion, this large inn—the inn is actually made up of three historic homes—includes 20 guest rooms. Each room has a fireplace, a private bath, and an assortment of marvelous antiques. Suites and whirlpools also are available. Travelers are astounded at such finery when they take a self-guided tour. Check with desk for availability. A few blocks from the harbor.

Pinehurst Inn at Pikes Creek, Highway 13, (715) 779-3676. Lovely six-bedroom, 1885 sandstone home. It would be hard not to notice the wondrous architectural details. Whirlpool suite on the third floor. Country setting.

The Silvernail Guest House, 249 Rittenhouse Avenue, (715) 779-5575. Built in 1887, the Silvernail is a charming place to catch up on quiet time. The two-bedroom suite with its mix of pretty antiques, courtyard, and scrumptious pastries waiting in the morning, is especially charming.

The Thimbleberry Inn Bed & Breakfast, 38300 Robin Run Road, (715) 779-5757 or (800) 881-5903. A contemporary three-bedroom inn (named for the thimbleberries that grow on the property), with breathtaking views of five of the Apostle Islands. Award-winning cook Sharon Locey's luscious breakfasts are often accompanied with bowls of freshly picked raspberries and strawberries. Try wild rice and mushroom quiche, accompanied by Craisins (dried cranberries) and poached pears, or stuffed cream cheese and peach French toast. Craig Locey takes guests (no need to stay at the inn) on inter-island, half-day and full-day sails aboard the Sandpiper (previously mentioned). Sailing fees are extra. A few minutes north of town.

DINING

Greunke's First Street Inn, 17 Rittenhouse Avenue, (715) 779-5480. Old 19th-century structure where locals go for fish. As a matter of fact, legend says this is where the fish livers fan club started (frugal fishermen's wives are also given credit for using that part of the fish, heretofore thrown away) at the turn of the century. This place runs the gamut from pancakes to sandwiches to steaks. Open for breakfast, lunch, and dinner.

Maggie's, 257 Manypenny Street, (715) 779-5641. Not a historic place, but a fun place that should not be overlooked. A friendly, trendy place that is smack out of a "beach blanket" movie. The popular restaurant is covered in pink flamingos. An array of casual offerings, including terrific burgers.

Old Rittenhouse Inn, 301 Rittenhouse Avenue, (715) 779-5111 or (888) 578-4667, is among the most photographed homes in Bayfield, or all of Wisconsin. This 1890 Queen Anne mansion, on a hill overlooking Lake Superior's shore, has been beautifully restored by Mary and Jerry Phillips, who opened the inn in the 1970s. It was one of the first bed-and-breakfast inns in Wisconsin. The dining rooms, filled with extraordinary art and decor, are marvelous places to pull up an antique chair and indulge in wonderful food. Dinner selections include regional specialties like chilled lake trout or spring lamb, while lunches have a variety of imaginative entrees, soups (the red raspberry soup is a knockout), and salads. Always, the desserts are to die for. The white chocolate torte with fresh raspberries was far better than a similar torte in Brussels. Lunches, dinners, and Sunday brunch are open to the public.

No other view of Bayfield shows off its splendor quite as well as the one from Lake Superior.

SHOPPING

Bert Vanderventer Gallery, across from the ferry, (800) 475-0660. Travelers should chat with Rita Vanderventer, proprietor of this shop; they are in for a treat. When I stopped, Rita, a Red Cliff native who lives on the area reservation, was making baskets strung with sinew on her porch. Her birch bark baskets, among other gifts and accessories, are sold here.

The Candy Shoppe, 217 Rittenhouse Avenue, (715) 779-3668. In one of Bayfield's historic buildings in the midst of town, don't miss this old-fashioned shop. Beverly Ellested's selection of English toffee and fudge is heavenly. Everything is made from scratch. The home-baked pies are so high, travelers will want to carry a carload home.

MADELINE ISLAND

For hundreds of years, Lake Superior carried adventurers to their destinations. Madeline Island, named for the daughter of a local chief who was christened Madeline by the Protestant missionaries when she married a British fur trader, was one of them. The original inhabitants of Madeline Island, settled in the late 1400s, were the Ojibwa people. Then came the French voyageurs and explorers, fur traders, fishermen, and lumberjacks.

Across the strait is Madeline Island, reachable by ferries that leave Bayfield every half-hour during the summer, (715) 747-2051. The largest of the 22 Apostle Islands at 14 miles long and three miles wide, Madeline has a state park, Big Bay State Park, and a town park. Both have very nice beaches. At Big Bay Town Park, seven miles from La Pointe, the tiny town at the heart of the island, a long strip of beach is connected by lagoons beneath a rustic wooden footbridge.

Also here, near the ferry docks, is the fascinating Madeline Island Historical Museum, one of 10 Wisconsin Historical Sites. Surrounded by thick stands of birch, balsam, aspen, and spruce, the compact museum displays items that guide a visitor from the first Ojibwa villagers through several centuries that saw voyageurs, explorers, fishermen, and lumberjacks. With its pioneer barn, Old Sailor's Home, the old La Pointe jail on the property, this is a great place for the entire family. Hours are 10 a.m. to 4 p.m., Memorial Day to October 1, (715) 747-2415. For more information, check www.shsw.wisc.edu/sites/madisle on the Web.

To learn more about Madeline Island, contact the Madeline Island Chamber of Commerce (open Memorial Day through Labor Day), (715) 747-2801.

LODGING

Brittany Estate and Cottages, Old Fort Road, La Pointe, (715) 747-5023. Built in 1905, this is the island's oldest lodging establishment. The country estate, in the style of the great Adirondack compounds, has been beautifully restored, maintaining the green and yellow exterior color scheme as well as original architectural details and fixtures. The snazzy grounds include the dock at water's edge, a croquet court, swimming at the inn's beach, a teahouse, and formal gardens. Visitors who wonder what a luxurious life must have been like in the 1920s should see the three antiques-laden cottages that are open to guests. A must-stay for anyone who loves historical properties. Stay in the

The Madeline Island Historical Museum houses a fascinating collection of artifacts, including items related to the fur trade.

Brittany, Normandy, or Burgundy Cottages, original to the property.

White Seagull Bed & Breakfast & Island Home Rental, (715) 747-5595 or (800) 977-2624. Captains Quarters and Balcony Over Water are great spots for taking in the splendid seaside views from this very special setting. The White Seagull also rents the Treasure House, an updated, 1900s home in La Pointe, as well as the Carriage House, a lovely home on the south side of the island.

DINING

There are a few places in La Pointe, such as the Bell Street Tavern and Grampa Tony's, that offer a good variety of food and drink; just about all of them are open only during the summer months.

WASHBURN

Heading south out of Bayfield on Highway 13, you'll soon arrive in Washburn. Referred to as "the little city on the big lake," it was a boomtown between 1880 and the 1920s when lumbering, iron ore, and the quarrying of brownstone brought thriving industries to the town. One of the interesting facts about Washburn is that its timber supply helped rebuild Chicago after the 1871 fire. Because of its location on Lake Superior, shipping also was a viable industry during the city's early years. Logging began to wane around 1905 because local supplies had been overharvested. City growth slowed. Today, the town is known as "the charter fishing capital of Lake Superior."

Washburn's rich past is highlighted in the exceptional Washburn Historical Museum and Cultural Center, 1 E. Bayfield Street, (715) 373-5591, housed in a massive, gabled structure in the heart of town. Built with local Lake Superior sandstone in 1890, the building is on the National Register of Historic Places. Once known as the "old bank building," it houses an array of local history and artifacts on three floors. There is a small admission fee. Call for hours.

For more information about the area, contact the Washburn Chamber of Commerce at (715) 373-5017 or (800) 253-4495.

LODGING

Bodin's Resort, (715) 373-2359. This mainstay of the North Woods (housekeeping cabins and small resort) has been greeting visitors since 1936. Nearby kayaking and sandy beach.

Pilgrim's Rest Bed & Breakfast, Maple Hill Road, (715) 373-2964. This 10-acre retreat has splendid views of the nearby Penokee Mountains, plus private baths, and even a hot tub.

DINING

It's A Small World Family Restaurant, 144 W. Bayfield Street, (715) 373-5177. Rotating weekly specials promoting countries around the world does make it seem like a small world. Interesting ethnic-themed food, served for breakfast, lunch, and dinner.

Steak Pit, 125 Harbor View Drive, (715) 373-5492. Since the mid-1970s, the Steak Pit has been one of the North Woods' most popular places to enjoy sizzling, certified Angus steaks. A nice selection of prime rib, chicken, Lake Superior trout, and whitefish round out the menu at a picturesque marina location. Open for dinner daily.

A logging crew takes a break to admire its work in this 1875 photo taken near Washburn.

ASHLAND

Farther south and east about 10 miles is Ashland, situated on Chequamegon Bay. With about 8,600 residents, is a hardscrabble town with a rich history. A woman who lived here a few years back said her husband was one of the few people in town whose job lasted all 12 months of every year. "We were celebrities," she reported.

More than any other town in the north, Ashland's "color" is immediately noticeable. Many of its historic buildings were constructed of the distinctive, reddish, Lake Superior sandstone. The town also has mansions, old banks, a railroad depot, and ore docks.

One must-see attraction for anyone interested in Lake Superior's impact on Ashland's history is Superior Water-Logged Lumber Company. This company is retrieving logs that sank more than a hundred years ago when they were being transported across Lake Superior on pulp rafts. After the logs are brought above water, artisans are transforming them into home furnishings, art, and accessories without having to cut down one more tree. The facility is located on Highway 2 East, (715) 685-9663.

Wild rice being harvested by hand in the Ashland area.

If you want to know more about Ashland's beginnings, be sure to visit the Ashland Historical Museum, 509 W. Main Street, (715) 682-4911. Maps, artifacts, exhibits, photographs all help fill in the history of the city during its first hundred years.

For more information about Ashland, contact the Ashland Chamber of Commerce, (800) 284-9484.

OTHER SITES AND ATTRACTIONS

Ashland Historic District. The city's downtown area includes City Hall, the courthouse, the Vaughn Library, ore docks, and several homes along Main Street, Vaughn Avenue, and Chapple Avenue.

Bad River Indian Reservation. Just east of Ashland, this big (124,234 acres), undeveloped area was established by treaty in 1854. The seat of tribal government is the hamlet of Odanah on Highway 2. Some 16,000 acres of the property is Lake Superior wetlands. Activities include the harvesting of wild rice and the operation of a fish hatchery that stocks lakes and streams with 15 million walleye each year. For more information, call (715) 682-7111.

Northern Great Lakes Visitor Center, 29270 County G (at the intersection with Highway 2 West), (715) 685-9983. General information services, but also a fine regional historical archive and research center. The Northern Wisconsin History Center, showcasing regional history, is also in the building.

Ore Dock. Construction of this mammoth dock began in 1916 and, at 1,800 feet long, 80 feet tall and 59 feet wide, is the largest concrete construction of its kind. Iron and ore were shipped from here until the mid-1960s.

Sigurd Olson Environmental Institute at Northland College, 1411 Ellis Avenue, (715) 682-1223. Sigurd Olson, a renowned author and conservationist, was an Ashland native. Born in 1899 (he died in 1982), he was vitally in tune with nature, communicating with birds and animals and urging others to preserve the wilderness.

LODGING

Hotel Chequamegon, 101 Highway 2 West (Lakeshore Drive), (715) 682-9095. This castle-like edifice, with its rounded twin towers on either end, has 65 rooms, complete with regal antiques. The gorgeous woodwork is worth a trip in itself. While the hotel appears historic (it was built in 1986), it is a redo of the original 1877 hotel that burned on New Year's Day in 1958. Indoor pool and sauna.

The Residenz, 723 Chapple Avenue, (715) 682-2425. This magnificent home (now a bed and breakfast), complete with belfry tower, was built in 1889 by a state senator. The three bedrooms with private baths are liberally decorated with period antiques. For those who admire old furnishings, this home has plenty to see.

DINING

L.C. Wilmarth's Deep Water Grill, 808 W. Main Street, (715) 682-4200. Nostalgic atmosphere features fine dining, steaks, and freshly caught Lake Superior fish. Open for lunch and dinner.

Golden Glow Cafe, 519 Main Street, (715) 682-2838. An old fashioned cafe/ice cream parlor that serves up hearty fare for breakfast, lunch, and dinner. A favorite local hangout.

Sirtoli's Italian Steak House at the Hotel Chequamegon, 101 Lake Shore Drive West, (715) 682-9095. Wonderful choices served in a very nice atmosphere. Open for lunch and dinner.

RED CLIFF CHIPPEWA RESERVATION

If you prefer to head west from Bayfield, you'll encounter a rich variety of historic attractions on the journey along Highway 13. The first is the Red Cliff Indian Reservation about 4 miles north. A fraction the size of the Bad River reservation east of Ashland, this site hugs the tip of the Bayfield Peninsula. It may be most well known for the photos of ice caves shot along the shore of Lake Superior each winter. Here, too, are campgrounds, a boat landing, pow-wow grounds, and facilities for everything from sea kayaking to snowmobiling. For more information, call (715) 779-3743.

To get a feel for what a commercial fishing operation looked like more than 50 years ago, visit the Hokenson Brothers Fishery. Go west on Highway 13 for 10 miles, turn north on County K, then go to Little Sand Bay Road; the fishery is next to the visitor center at Little Sand Bay. This commercial fishing operation was run by three brothers, Eskel, Leo, and Roy Hokenson, in the 1930s and 1940s. Sons of Swedish immigrants, the brothers created a commercial fishing complex that started from scratch and eventually became a significant operation.

The National Park Service took over the site in 1970. The two-story twine shed is where gill nets and pond nets are stored—nets that were strung out for miles, trapping whitefish, herring, and trout. There is an icehouse and an old, weathered dock that had been pieced together as the need for more space grew. Look, too, for the Twilite, a 38-foot, diesel-powered fishing boat built by the brothers. Still on the wall are marks showing the number of fish the men prepared to put on ice. The site is about 14 miles northwest of Bayfield. The visitor center is open from mid-May through Labor Day, and tours last approximately 45 minutes.

CORNUCOPIA

If you continue your journey for another 10 miles along the Lake Superior coastline, you'll come to the charming fishing village of Cornucopia, located at the west end of the Apostle Island National Lakeshore. The village was named for the abundance of fish from the sea, as well as the apples, berries, and vegetables grown in the area.

Don't let the "last outpost" feeling of the town fool you. The Village Inn, one of the best restaurants at the top of the state, is here, as is an enchanting harbor that has been important to the area's survival for hundreds of years.

Only about 85 people live here in winter; many of the kids are home-schooled. For a look into what life is and has been like here for nearly a hundred years, visit Ehler's, a general store operation in the heart of the village. The store opened on May 1, 1915. Though it has changed over the decades, Ehler's remains a good place to gain insight into this small fishing village.

For more information on Cornucopia, contact the Cornucopia Business Association by calling (715) 742-3282.

LODGING

The Fo'c'sle Bed & Breakfast, Highway 13 at Superior Avenue, (715) 742-3337. Wonderful views of Lake Superior. The two-bedroom inn lies on the South Shore of Siskiwit Bay.

The Village Inn, Highway 13 and County C, (715) 742-3941. The four-bedroom inn sitting room (above the restaurant) seems like an Old World country inn. Spick and span, country charming. Each room has a private bath and its own color scheme and decor. Continental breakfast.

DINING

The Village Inn has a restaurant that offers the opportunity to taste some of the most authentic of Lake Superior's old-time recipes, plus freshly caught fish and locally harvested ingredients. Visitors will find the only fish boil in town at this spunky restaurant (served in the adjacent screened pavilion.) Ruth and George Grubbe, who have owned the inn for more than 20 years, are committed to offering their guests a relaxing experience, good food, and spectacular sunsets.

SUPERIOR

Lake Superior, the largest of the Great Lakes and the largest body of fresh water in the world, boasts some impressive statistics. It is 350 miles long, 160 miles wide, and 1,333 feet at its deepest point. It covers an astonishing 31,700 square miles and exists beside three states and two countries. To many, the city that best reflects the rich maritime history of Lake Superior is the city of Superior situated on its far western shore.

The area was called the "Pittsburgh of the West" back in the 19th century, because of its importance as an ore-shipping port. Superior is still defined by its position on the lake, since it has one of the deepest harbors in the world. Today, the shipping industry thrives and the port continues to be one of the busiest in the country.

Visitors can enjoy a close look at harbor activity from Superior's focal point—Barker's Island, a combination 420-slip marina and family entertainment center just off Highways 53 and 2 on the city's shoreline, (715) 394-7716 or (800) 942-5313. From this vantage point, travelers can see the hills of Duluth and the twin-port harbor of Superior. You can experience some impressive maritime artifacts at the S.S. *Meteor* Maritime Museum, 300 Marine Drive, (715) 394-5712. The facility also is home to the only whaleback freighter in existence.

Also noteworthy for history buffs is the Fairlawn Mansion and Museum, 906 E. Second Street, (715) 394-5712 or (800) 942-5313. This is the lavish 42-room Victorian mansion of Martin Pattison, early lumber baron and Superior's second mayor. Besides exquisite furnishings and an elegant ambiance, the home showcases the link between maritime and local history, as well as Indian lore.

For more information contact the Superior/Douglas County Chamber of Commerce, 305 Belknap Street, at (715) 392-2773 or (800) 942-5313.

A crowd gathers to celebrate the launching of a whaleback freighter in Superior in 1891; the boat is the same type as the S.S. *Meteor* now on display on Barker's Island.

OTHER SITES AND ATTRACTIONS

Old Firehouse and Police Museum, 402 23rd Avenue E., (715) 398-7558. Restored early 1900s fire station houses a fine collection of antique firefighting equipment.

Vista Fleet Cruises, Barker's Island, (715) 394-6846. Cruise the harbor aboard the Vista King. This is a good way to see some of Superior and Duluth's interesting architecture, such as Duluth's Aerial Lift Bridge, as well as the area's busy grain elevators and lake freighters. Operates from mid-May through mid-October.

LODGING

The area has a number of chain motels and inns.

DINING

Sammy's Pizza and Elbo Room, 1309 Tower Avenue, (715) 392-3829. Homemade Italian entrees (the lasagna is always a good bet) served in a friendly atmosphere.

The Shack Smokehouse and Grille, 3301 Belknap Street, (715) 392-9836. Prime rib, tasty chicken, it's all here at one of the area's most popular supper clubs. Unlike some supper clubs, which tend to thrive in a dim atmosphere, this has a refreshingly lively and light garden theme. Excellent Caesar salad and homemade bread. Open for lunch and dinner.

A GLANCE AT BAYFIELD AND BEYOND

MUSEUMS

Ashland Historical Museum: Maps, artifacts, exhibits. Ashland.

Fairlawn Mansion and Museum: Lavish 42-room Victorian mansion once the home of Superior's second mayor, now showcases the link between maritime and local history. Superior.

Madeline Island Historical Museum: One of the Wisconsin Historical Society's sites, the museum guides visitors to the first Ojibwa visitor through the times of voyageurs, explorers, fishermen, and lumberjacks. Madeline Island.

Old Firehouse and Police Museum: Restored early 1900s fire station contains a fine collection of antique firefighting equipment. Superior.

S.S. *Meteor* Maritime Museum: On permanent display. Launched in Superior in 1896, it's the only whaleback freighter in existence. Superior.

HISTORICAL SITES AND ATTRACTIONS

Ashland Historical District: The city's historic downtown includes many public buildings like the Court House and City Hall, and many homes along Main Street, Vaughn Avenue, and Chapple Avenue.

Hokenson Brothers Fishery: A once-thriving commercial fishing operation in the 1930s and 1940s, the operation was created by two brothers who trapped whitefish, herring, and trout. Now operated by the National Park Service. Visitor Center Little Sand Bay.

La Pointe: The Ojibwa Indians migrated here in the 1400s. In the 1600s, the island settlement was a trading post and stopping point for British and French explorers. Madeline Island.

Northern Great Lakes Visitor Center: General information about the area, but also a fine regional historical archive and research center. Ashland.

Washburn Historical Museum and Cultural Center: The area's rich past is highlighted in this massive, Lake Superior sandstone building. Washburn.

OTHER HISTORICAL STOPS

Apostle Island National Lakeshore: To protect and preserve the islands and a strip of lakeshore, in 1970 Congress named 21 of the 22 Apostle Islands and 2,5000 acres of the peninsula a national lakeshore. The area is managed by the National Park Service. In 1986, Long Island was added.

Bayfield Winery and Hauser's: This family orchard business has been going strong since 1908. Apple picking, jams, and jellies. Tour the old Sears & Roebuck barn. Bayfield.

Big Top Chautauqua: This nonprofit arts organization spotlights area history through song and drama under a colossal tent. The seasonal nightly events are billed as "culture under canvas." At the base of Mt. Ashwabay, three miles south of Bayfield.

Brittany Bed & Breakfast: A beautifully restored country estate built in 1905. The Brittany is the island's oldest lodging establishment. Madeline Island.

Greunke's: Old 19th-century structure where locals go for fish. Legend says this is where the whitefish livers fad began at the turn of the 20th century. Bayfield.

Hotel Chequamegon: This is a redo of the original 1877 hotel that burned on New Year's Day in 1958. Ashland.

Old Rittenhouse Inn: One of the most photographed sights in Bayfield. The magnificent 1890 Queen Anne is a cross between a museum and a mansion. Stay a while or enjoy lunch or dinner. Bayfield.

Ore Dock: Built in 1916, the mammoth dock was at the center of the iron and ore shipping business until the mid-1960s. Ashland.

Red Cliff Indian Reservation: The Red Cliff Reservation of the Lake Superior Chippewa is located three miles north of Bayfield. The reservation has a campground and Isle Vista Casino.

Sea Caves: Centuries of waves combined with freezing and melting conditions, have created a series of arched, honeycombed, sea caves along Lake Superior. Visitors can see the carved-out colossal entrances to the caves on the north shore of Devils Island, Swallow Point on Sand Island, and north of Cornucopia on the peninsula. Visitors can explore the mainland caves during all seasons of the year. For winter weather conditions to the mainland sea caves call the Apostle Islands Ice Line at (715) 779-3398, ext. 499.

Superior Water-Logged Lumber Company: Absolute must for those interested in area history. The company is retrieving logs that sank in Lake Superior more than one hundred years ago. Ashland.

The Thimbleberry Inn. Not a historic inn, but the inn has a historic touch. Guests can take sailboat rides on The Sandpiper, a restored classic wooden ketch, the only one of its kind in the area. Bayfield.

HISTORICAL EVENTS AND FESTIVALS

JULY

Red Cliff Indian Powwow: Event is held over the Fourth of July weekend. Three miles north of Bayfield.

AUGUST

Wooden Boat Rendezvous, usually held the third weekend in August. Head to Bayfield's city dock to take in classic wooden boats, including canoes, kayaks, and runabouts. Festive atmosphere amid a nautical flea market.

SEPTEMBER

Apple Festival, Bayfield. The biggest event of the year, as well as the largest apple fest in Wisconsin, attracting some 50,000 visitors each year. Many unusual apple concoctions—pies, jams, turnovers, apple bratwurst, apple mustard. Events galore the last weekend of September or early October.

CHAPTER 11

THE MILWAUKEE AREA

A RICH ETHNIC HERITAGE

The Pabst Mansion, built in the early 1890s, epitomizes the wealth of Milwaukee's early industrialists.

THE HOME OF RICHIE and the Fonz in "Happy Days," America's traditional beer capital, the birthplace of a rich mix of people, ranging from William Rehnquist, chief justice of the U.S. Supreme Court, to Liberace, the late pianist and showman—Milwaukee is much more than a lakeside city somewhere north of Chicago. For travelers, it is so compact and well-laid-out that they can move expeditiously from one attraction to the next without experiencing bumper-to-bumper traffic. In fact, no two sites inside city limits are more than 20 minutes apart. The largest city in Wisconsin (population around 650,000, with the metro area more than 1.5 million), Milwaukee is 90 miles north of Chicago and 320 miles southeast of Minneapolis-St. Paul.

The city has a long and colorful history that its diverse population is proud to celebrate. The first settlers were various Indian tribes, particularly the Potawatomi, who called this area with plentiful water "Millocki," or gathering place by the waters. They were drawn here because of its excellent location at the confluence of three rivers and the big body of water later known as Lake Michigan. The area began to grow after Congress created the Territory of Wisconsin in 1836 and particularly after 1848, when Wisconsin became a state. At that time, land was available for $1.25 an acre. When European immigrants heard of the attractive location and the price of land, they began making their way here.

Milwaukee became a shipping center because of its prime location near water and railroads. Lead from Wisconsin's western mines was shipped through here, as were crops from the growing number of Wisconsin farms. Immigrant numbers swelled, and by the end of the 19th century, Milwaukee's population of Germans was one of the largest in the country.

In addition to the city's rich tapestry of cultural diversity, it has also been known as a beer lover's town. In the 1880s, the city was a magnet for breweries—there were more than 80. Now, just a handful survive, but Old World brewing techniques haven't been lost. To get a taste of Milwaukee's past and present, visit a brewery like the famous Miller Brewing Company or the smaller Sprecher Brewing Company.

Milwaukee is also identified by its profusion of colorful ethnic neighborhoods. Visitors have a chance to enjoy restaurants, bakeries, and shops in communities that are comprised of cultural traditions such as the Italian, Irish, Polish, Serbian, and German.

This ethnic pride is also reflected in its many large and boisterous festivals. Probably more than any other city, Milwaukee likes to celebrate its history and heritage with events the public can enjoy. No matter when a traveler might arrive, there is probably a festival going on somewhere in the area.

To get a quick immersion into Milwaukee's rich past, take a stroll through the Third Ward, just south of the downtown. In the 19th and 20th centuries, the Third Ward was the city's major wholesale and manufacturing hub. It sprang up in this location because of its proximity to the rivers, to Lake Michigan's harbor, and to nearby railroads.

A densely populated neighborhood that was home to several ethnic communities, the Third Ward suffered a severe blow when an evening fire broke out on the west side of Water Street in 1892. Horse-drawn fire trucks from as far away as Chicago and Oshkosh moved in to fight the terrific blaze, but the entire neighborhood was almost lost. More than 440 buildings were destroyed and more than 1,900 immigrants, mostly Irish, became homeless. Productivity in this area didn't slow for long, though. The community began immediately to rebuild, and today there are more than 75 buildings in the Third Ward.

Now that the area has been deemed historically significant, it has become a trendy haven. Lofts, galleries, restaurants, and artsy shops are here. You can't go wrong rummaging in this area, whether you buy or not. The atmosphere, which recalls Soho in London or the Left Bank of Paris, has managed to retain its quaintness and charm. It is also known as an off-Broadway neighborhood, since the Broadway Theater Center, with many local theater groups, has its home here. Everything for discretionary taste seems to come to life in these Old World shops. Specialty establishments range from jewelry and one-of-a-kind clothing to stylish restaurants. A walking tour of the Third Ward begin at 1 p.m. Saturdays at Chicago and Buffalo Streets. It is usually offered early June through mid-October.

To get a sense of the area's past in more compact and manageable settings, there are two museums you shouldn't miss. The Milwaukee County Historical Society, 910 N. Old World Third Street, (414) 273-8288, is housed in a 1913 neoclassical building that is listed on the National Register of Historic Places. Originally the Second Ward Savings Bank, museum includes wonderful collections of artifacts that furnish replicas of various 19th-century offices and shops. A doctor's office, typewriter shop, a bank, and many other vignettes offer a fascinating look at the daily life of this multiethnic city. The facility is open daily; call for hours. Admission is free; a donation is suggested.

The Milwaukee Public Museum, 800 W. Wells, (414) 278-2700; Web site is www.mpm.edu. This is a favorite among frequent visitors to the city and is considered a world-class museum. One of its show stoppers is "Streets of Old Milwaukee," where visitors feel like people in the 19th century as they walk the streets of long ago and peer into the merchants' windows. The walk-through concept was initiated at the museum in the 1890s. Another exhibit, albeit non-historical, features an up-close and personal look at a Costa Rican rain forest. There is also a two-story exhibit on butterflies. Open daily. Admission fee. There is a separate admission for the adjacent IMAX theater.

And no tour to the "City of Suds" would be complete without honoring its beer-making past. You can accomplish this mission at the Miller Brewery Company, 4251 W. State Street, (414) 931-BEER. Frederick Miller immediately began brewing beer in this country after arriving from Germany in 1855. His first effort was called Frederick Miller's Plank Road Brewery. That brewery produced about 300 barrels the first year, while Miller Brewing, the largest brewery in Wisconsin, now produces around nine million barrels annually. A visit offers insight into the history of brewing, as well as Miller's link to Milwaukee history. Historic brewing equipment can be seen at the Caves Museum, a segment of the original "cooler" where beer was stored. Tours are available; call for hours.

For more information about any of Milwaukee's attraction and activities, contact the Greater Milwaukee Convention & Visitors Bureau by calling (414) 273-3950 or (800) 231-0903.

HISTORIC ARCHITECTURE

Another way of appreciating Milwaukee's colorful past and rich ethnic history is to take in its fascinating architecture. The various styles evident in many of the city's buildings reflect the influence of architects from many ethnic backgrounds. Styles include Queen Anne, Victorian, Romanesque Revival, Flemish

The wagons are ready to head out of the Pabst brewery in the early 1800s.

Milwaukee's North Point lighthouse was erected about 1855.

Renaissance, Frank Lloyd Wright's Prairie style, Greek Revival, and Beaux Arts. The result is a city filled with intriguing architectural textures.

American National Bank Building, 526 E. Wisconsin Avenue. A downtown Milwaukee fixture since 1906, for a long time the French Renaissance building was known as the business it housed—the Northwestern National Life Insurance Company.

Astor Hotel, 924 E. Juneau Street, (414) 271-4220 or (800) 558-0200. Historic beauty built in 1920. Many of the fixtures are original to the hotel. Originally called Astor-At-The-Lake, it was constructed by Walter Schroeder, who also built Milwaukee's Hilton Hotel.

Basilica of St. Josaphat, 601 W. Lincoln Avenue. Designed by Erhard Brielmeier, the 1901 church, which seats 2,400, is the largest in the city. It was constructed from tons of stones recovered from the razed building that formerly housed the Chicago Post Office.

Frederick C. Bogk House, 2420 N. Terrace Avenue. This stark 1916 home, of massive proportions, was built by Frank Lloyd Wright and is characterized by his Prairie style. It is said to have been influenced by his simultaneous work on Japan's Imperial Hotel.

Button Block, 500 N. Water Street. This has nothing to do with buttons, but instead is a distinctive red monolith built by Charles Button as a tribute to his father, Dr. Henry Button. The red sandstone building shows a plaque at its peak officially declaring it the Button Block, 1892.

A. F. Gallun Mansion, 3000 E. Newberry Boulevard. A beautifully restored 1914 Tudor mansion, originally the home of the president of Gallun Tannery. The impressive ivy-covered residence once was severely decayed but has regained its original luster.

Henry Harnischfeger Home, 3424 W. Wisconsin Avenue. One of my favorite residences, this unusual German Renaissance Revival home is one of the few remaining structures depicting ornate baroque architecture. A complicated structure with a lot of style. Note the arched room over the driveway to allow cars to pass under it.

Charles L. McIntosh Mansion, 1584 N. Prospect Avenue. A great example of brick and brown stone used to accentuate the imposing 1904 home, built as a residence for the director of the Milwaukee Harvester Company. The property is now home to the Wisconsin Conservatory of Music.

Milwaukee City Hall, 200 E. Wells Street. This was a pricey project when it was built in 1895 for more than one million dollars. Interestingly, in 2000, the 11-ton bell was once again put back into service. It rings in its lofty 350-foot tower three times a day for the first time since 1925. It was originally silenced because it was feared that the vibrations might damage the building.

Milwaukee Public Library, between 8th and 9th Streets on Wisconsin Avenue. Built in 1895, the building has many interesting architectural details, including its landmark dome.

Iron Block, 205 E. Wisconsin Avenue. This is the only cast-iron building in the city. The iron was cast in New York, then sent to Milwaukee for reconstruction. The structure also is referred to as the Excelsior Block.

Pilings being driven for one of Milwaukee's many bridges in 1928.

Pabst Mansion, 2000 W. Wisconsin Avenue, (414) 931-0808. This should be at the top of the list for those interested in architectural treasures. Built between 1890 and 1892, this 37-room, 14-fireplace, Flemish Renaissance Revival mansion once was the home of the Captain Frederick Pabst family (his wife, Maria Best, was the daughter of the founder of Best Brewery). It was built by George Bowman Ferry. One of the home's features is its conservatory, so large it was originally used to display Pabst brewery items at the Columbian Exposition in Chicago in 1893. A stunning showplace, often referred to as Milwaukee's most palatial residence. Frederick's sons, Gustave and Fred Jr., must have enjoyed life in mansions, because they built mini-palaces of their own. Tours are available, and there is an admission fee. Call for hours.

Pabst Theater, 144 E. Wells Street. This 1895 red sandstone and orange brick theater has been restored to its original elegance.

Pfister Hotel, 424 E. Wisconsin Avenue, (414) 273-8222 or (800) 558-

8222. The cream city brick and terra cotta facade has been well known since the hotel was built in 1893. This is sumptuous elegance near the lake.

The Arthur L. Richards Houses, 2700 block of Burnham Street. Those interested in Frank Lloyd Wright will find this 1916 block of six prefab homes interesting. Wright designed these homes (developed by Arthur Richards) in conjunction with his American System Built homes project.

Schlitz Tavern, 2249 N. Humboldt Avenue. This 1890 edifice was cleverly built as a neighborhood tavern to promote Schlitz beer products. A good example of Romanesque Revival architecture.

The Pabst Theater, on Wells Street, built in 1895.

St. John's Roman Catholic Church, 802 N. Jackson Street. Built in 1847, this is one of Milwaukee's oldest churches. Even though much of it was ravaged by fire in 1935, it maintained the integrity of the earlier structure. (Formally, the church was the Cathedral of St. John the Evangelist.)

St. Stephen's Evangelical Lutheran, 1136 S. 5th Street. Of particular interest here is the fact that the keystone of this 1901 Gothic church also has a second date of 1854. The red brick spire covers the date of an older building.

OTHER SITES AND ATTRACTIONS

Allen Bradley Clock, National Avenue, between First and Second Streets. This is the city's premier clock—not just for telling time but as a landmark to boats on the waterways. Every big city has clocks on tall towers and skyscrapers, but not many cities can rival the scope and size of the Allen Bradley clock.

This beauty ranks second largest in the world, behind Big Ben.

Boerner Botanical Gardens, 5879 S. 92nd Street, (414) 425-1130. Here is your chance to see a formal garden, like those in merry old England. An indoor garden shows off bulbs and other hothouse favorites. Ongoing environmental educational events and historically interesting workshops. Open May through October.

Brady Street. Nineteenth-century buildings hold court in this old Italian neighborhood. The area's identity is directly connected with not only its Italian roots, but also the Milwaukee River and Lake Michigan. The artsy destination now is lined with Italian restaurants, coffee shops, bakeries, and markets on the city's near-north side.

Broadway Theatre Center, 158 N. Broadway, (414) 291-7800. Fans of local theater love this wonderful place, home to many theater groups. Call for current productions. In the historic Third Ward.

Milwaukee County Zoo, 10001 W. Bluemound Road, (414) 771-3040. The zoo originated as a small mammal and bird exhibit in downtown Washington Park in 1892. It has expanded several times over the years, moving to its present site in 1958. Often called one of the country's best zoos, it is consistently working to preserve and conserve endangered species. The zoo is also widely known for its breeding programs with animals such as Siberian tigers. The large penguin exhibit is a popular gathering spot.

Mitchell Park Domes, 524 S. Layton Boulevard, (take the 26th Street exit off Interstate 94, east of the new Miller Park), (414) 649-9830. There is a lot to see at the Domes at the Mitchell Park Conservatory, with 3 seven-story, curved glass spheres covering extraordinary botanical gardens.

While the futuristic-looking Domes are not historic works of architecture, their creation is directly connected to city history. In the late 1800s, Milwaukee was made up of many European immigrants, who loved flowers and conservatories. In 1898, in response to this love, Milwaukee built a botanical showplace known as the Old Conservatory and Sunken Gardens.

After 1955, when the Old Conservatory had to be razed, a new botanical park was already on the drawing boards. Land had been purchased from John Mitchell in the late 1800s, in anticipation of building a new park system down the road. Mitchell, who later became a senator and was the namesake for the new conservatory, also gave the city more than five acres of land for the proposed park project.

When the three connecting glass domes of Mitchell Park Horticultural Conservatory (part of the Milwaukee County Park System) opened in the 1960s the gardens were heralded as imaginative, innovative, and inventive. Each of the

A Milwaukee fisherman chips ice from his nets around 1900.

domes measured 140 feet wide by 85 feet high. They were considered an engineering marvel because they incorporated new methods of controlling heat, light, moisture, and ventilation. The Domes are still acclaimed for their design and function and continue to be the only botanical architectural structure of its kind. In addition to showcasing thousands of plants, the structure is home to more than 20 species of birds and a variety of lizards, frogs, and fish.

In the late nineteenth century, the unique community of Jones Island, on Milwaukee's waterfront, had few roads and was accessible only by water.

By stepping inside, visitors can cross the equator and visit the great deserts of the world. A good way to begin your exploration is by crossing the hall to the right of the entrance and opening the doors to the Tropical Dome, where you'll be met by perfumed air, cawing birds, rippling water, and more. This sultry rain forest setting is home to more than 750 species of tropical plants, dozens of species of birds, and a mixture of other creatures, including lizards and frogs. A 25-foot waterfall cascades over the exotic greenery. The magnificent plants in the Tropical Dome represent environments from the world over—the Amazon, the Congo, Southeast Asia, and Africa.

Across the world (or hall), the Arid Dome's dry atmosphere, nurturing more than 600 plants, is a sharp contrast to the humid tropics. If you like cacti, succulents, and showy bougainvillea, this is a good place to take it all in. Splendid examples of plant life representing the deserts of the American Southwest, Africa, Madagascar, South America, and Mexico are everywhere.

The third Dome, the Show Dome, is where themed shows, such as major flower shows, take place. Open daily; call for hours. Admission charge.

Pabst Brewery, 917 W. Juneau Avenue. The oldest brewery in the country, Pabst once was the sixth-largest brewery in the U.S. The brewery has closed its operation and tours, but visitors can still appreciate the Victorian buildings where this operation once made fine lagers.

St. Joan of Arc Chapel, Marquette University, (414) 224-7039. This is an actual medieval French chapel, which was carefully dismantled and sent to the U.S. in 1927. It has been reconstructed twice since arriving, first in New York and then another delicate rebuilding in 1965 at Marquette University.

Walker's Point. This small peninsula is named for George Walker, who first lived where the Milwaukee and Menominee Rivers come together. He dreamed that once the surrounding swamp was drained, the area would not only be habitable, it would be useful as an east-west traffic itinerary. Walker was right. The vicinity arose from the swamps; many of Milwaukee's prime industries and lavish residences came with the territory. Ethnically diverse neighborhoods also grew up on the Point. Almost every immigrant group that came to Milwaukee was at one time represented here.

MUSEUMS

Milwaukee has at least 30 fine museums, not counting those in the outlying areas. The following are excellent places to start a cultural and historical tour.

Charles Allis Art Museum, 1801 N. Prospect Avenue, (414) 278-8295. This impressive collection of 19th-century French and American artists, as well as Chinese, Korean, and Japanese ceramics, belonged to industrialist Charles Allis. He led Allis Chalmers, a major Milwaukee company, as its first president. His art collection of more than 1,000 pieces is housed in the stately 1909 Tudor mansion. Walnut and mahogany paneling were used in the mansion's decor. Small admission fee; call for hours.

Kilbourntown House, 4400 N. Estabrook Park Drive, (414) 273-8288. Art, furnishings, and accessories are nicely displayed in this mid-19th century Greek Revival house.

Milwaukee Art Museum, 750 N. Lincoln Memorial Drive, (414) 224-3200. This nationally acclaimed museum shows off more than 20,000 works of art representing the 15th century through the present. There are many recognizable pieces, such as Sun Prairie, Wisconsin, native Georgia O'Keefe's "Poppies."

Mitchell International Aviation Museum. An interesting retrospective of early aircraft, including several, such as the zeppelin, on site. Free admission. Open daily. Upper level, Mitchell International Airport.

Villa Terrace, 2220 N. Terrace Avenue, (414) 271-3656. A wonderful museum of decorative arts, showcased in an elegant 1923 home. Art, furniture, home accessories, and a large Italian garden. Rotating exhibits might include sumptuous displays of Wedgwood pieces and their history, a show I enjoyed in the past. Small admission fee. Call for hours.

FESTIVALS

Because Milwaukee is a city comprised of many ethnic neighborhoods, it celebrates its diversity with festivals throughout the year. For more information on events such as the Lakefront Festival of the Arts, Summerfest, Great Circus Parade, and the Grape Lakes Food & Wine Festival, call the Greater Milwaukee Convention and Visitors Bureau: (414) 273-7222 or (800) 231-0903. Here are a few of the city's many festivals.

German Fest. If you are here the last weekend of July, expect many folks to be heading to Gemutlichkeit, the largest German festival in North America. (How many cities can make that claim?) Expect to feel transplanted to the sights, tastes, and smells of Deutschland. German food, craftspeople, music, and merriment. The festival runs all weekend. Maier Festival Park, on the lakefront, just east of I-94.

Holiday Folk Fair International, Milwaukee Exposition Convention Center and Arena (MECCA), (414) 225-6220. No time, interest, or budget to visit a variety of countries? Then this festival is for you. Since 1943, the festival, celebrating cultural diversity, has highlighted the customs and traditions of dozens of ethnic groups. International food, crafts, exhibits, and music. Usually held the weekend before Thanksgiving. Call for hours.

Irish Fest, 1532 Wauwatosa Avenue, (414) 476-3378. The shenanigans, spread over the lakefront, often encompass a dozen or more stages of music and revelry. This is the next best thing to being in Ireland. Usually held the third weekend in August.

WALKING TOURS

Milwaukee has so many interesting neighborhoods, filled with architectural landmarks, it is hard to know where to start a walking or driving tour. Here are a few of the tours you can do on your own or with a guide.

Historic Yankee Hill. This is a personal favorite, perhaps because of the setting along Lake Michigan. Visitors are shown the churches and palatial estates of the area's early settlers. Meet in the foyer of the Astor Hotel at 1 p.m. on Sunday, early June through mid-October, 924 E. Juneau Avenue.

The Mansions of Lake Drive. Learn more about the people and architecture of some of the most sumptuous historical homes in Milwaukee. Set for 10 a.m. Saturdays, early June through mid-October. Meet at Lake and Memorial Drives.

Polish Heritage. See excellent examples of Polish influence in residential and commercial neighborhoods. Meet at 10 a.m. Saturdays at the picturesque

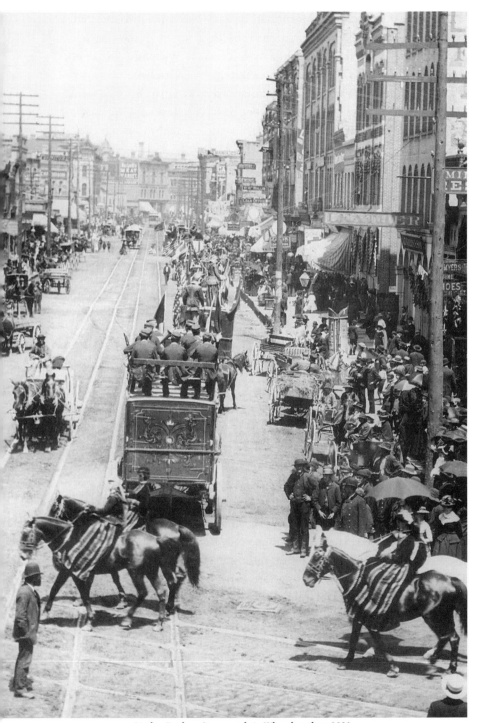

Ringling Brothers Circus parade in Milwaukee about 1890.

St. Stanislaus Church, 524 W. Mitchell Street. Early June through mid-October.

Riverwalk. Downtown tour covers the sites along the Milwaukee River and the new Riverwalk. Meet at 10 a.m. Saturdays at Wisconsin Avenue and Water Street, Bank One Plaza. Early June through mid-October.

Walkers Point. Participants tour the city's first National Historic District. Group meets at 1 p.m. Saturdays in front of M & I Bank, 414 W. National Avenue. Early June through mid-October.

Governor Robert La Follette (second from right) visits Milwaukee aboard his campaign train in 1900.

Water Tower Neighborhood. There are many different architectural styles in this unique neighborhood. Group meets at 1 p.m. on Sundays at the park fountain, Lake Drive and North Avenue. Special evening tours in the summer (call for dates and times). Early June through mid-October.

There is no need to register for tours in advance. Just show up at the meeting place and pay a small fee (student rates offered).

OTHER SPECIAL TOURS

The following tours are a sampling of special tours of historical sites around town:

In Search of Milwaukee's Beer Barons. Participants view homes and breweries of Milwaukee's great brewmasters—the Blatzes, Gettelmans, Millers, Pabsts, and Uihleins.

Milwaukee's Sacred Beginnings. The oldest churches in the city, including St. Joan of Arc Chapel, Old St. Mary's Catholic, and Grace Evangelical Lutheran are toured.

Milwaukee's Pre–Civil War Buildings. Many buildings were put up between 1830 and 1860. Join the tour and find out where these earliest buildings are located, as well as insight into how and why they were built.

Special group tours can be arranged via bus or at times conducive to your group's interests and time constraints. Historic Milwaukee, an organization dedicated to preserving the city's historical treasures, has many special tours throughout the year. For more information about the group and its tours, call (414) 277-7795.

LODGING

Many of Milwaukee's historic places are downtown hotels. They are some of the city's more interesting sites to spend a weekend. Several of the larger places specialize in weekend packages that also may include tickets to area attractions and events. Always ask about available packages before booking, and never take the "rack" rate without comparative shopping.

The Brumder Mansion Bed & Breakfast, 3046 W. Wisconsin Avenue, (414) 342-9767. This beautiful mansion was built in 1910. Guests (there are five guest bedrooms) enjoy elegance amid antiques and seven fireplaces. Lovely appointments include detailed woodwork.

Hotel Wisconsin, 720 N. Old World Third Street, (414) 271-4900. A half block from the Grand Avenue Mall downtown, this historic landmark hotel offers reasonable rates and has packages that often include tickets to area attractions and events. Restaurant on site.

Hyatt Regency Milwaukee, 333 W. Kilbourn Avenue, (414) 276-1234 or (800) 233-1234. This is a good place to stay for those who want to spend time downtown. With nearly 500 rooms, the hotel offers a number of amenities, including a rooftop revolving restaurant and an enclosed walkway to the Grand Avenue Mall. One thing I like about Hyatt hotels is that many of them, like this one, use indoor space to set off plants and light. The Hyatt Regency has an 18-story atrium that gives a feeling of airiness, even though this is a big but compact place.

Milwaukee Hilton, 509 W. Wisconsin Avenue, (414) 271-7250 or (800) 445-8667. A beautiful 1920s downtown hotel with plenty of marble and art deco touches. Many amenities, including indoor pool.

DINING

Milwaukee is a restaurant town—big time. Although not all of the following restaurants are landmarks, or have been around for one hundred years (not many restaurants fit that category), the following are on the list because they offer a special experience and are apt to make the weekend in Milwaukee even more memorable.

Coquette Cafe, 316 N. Milwaukee Street, (414) 291-2655. A flirty French bistro featuring soups, salads, pizza, and imaginative entrees like salmon roulade and oven-roasted pork loin with sauce piquant. Sassy desserts include the whipped-up chocolate mousse and pistachio cake.

County Clare, 1234 N. Astor Street, (414) 272-5273. Irish pub serving Irish food with an American spin. Sandwiches, soup (don't overlook their famous root soup), seafood, lamb chops.

Grenadier's, 747 N. Broadway, (414) 276-0747. A top name in restaurants for decades. A posh Victorian atmosphere. Highly imaginative European and ethnic entrees and continental favorites. Recent examples include char-grilled veal porterhouse with mushroom risotto. Many restaurants may have one type of creme brulee; here they offer two: chocolate and cherry vanilla bean. Open for lunch and dinner.

Historic Turner Restaurant, 1034 N. Fourth Street, (414) 276-4844. Built in 1882 as a meeting hall for the Turners (European gymnastics enthusiasts), this historic restaurant features American specialties, but it also offers an assortment of German dishes. Open for lunch and dinner.

John Ernst Cafe, 600 E. Ogden Avenue, (414) 273-1878. German and American entrees have been served to an appreciative crowd here since 1878. Highlights include Wiener schnitzel and brats, and the house specialty, a whole roast duck. Open for lunch, dinner, and Sunday brunch.

Mader's German Restaurant, 1041 Old World Third Street, (414) 271-3377. If you say "German restaurant" in Milwaukee, chances are you will hear Mader's mentioned. This has been a "no food like German food" attraction since 1902, when most people got here by horse and carriage. So what is the draw? The food, like the sauerbraten, is good, but the Bavarian kitsch atmosphere cannot be beat.

Mimma's Cafe, 1307 E. Brady Street, (414) 271-7337. Terrific pasta (the selection is enormous) and Italian dishes. This is where to go for a taste of Milwaukee's "in" crowd. A great people-watching place. On the lower East side.

Miss Katie's Diner, 1900 W. Clybourn Street, (414) 344-0044. Nostalgia, good eats, and a legacy of serving famous politicians, this spot has had international fame ever since President Bill Clinton and German Chancellor Helmut Kohl had lunch at the 1950s diner in 1996. (The restaurant was actually built in the 1980s.) Hearty diner fare served up in a fun atmosphere popular with the Marquette University crowd. Open for breakfast, lunch, and dinner.

Pieces of Eight, 550 N. Harbor Drive, (414) 271-0597. A mix of harbor mania with Victorian charm. Open daily for lunch and dinner. Sunday brunch. A big menu of choices includes seafood and sandwiches. The draw here is the

The Milwaukee waterfront in 1912 was the place to see and be seen.

chance to dine waterside, enjoying stellar views.

Karl Ratzsch's, 320 E. Mason Street (near Broadway and Milwaukee Street), (414) 276-2720. A robust, fun place. Another of Milwaukee's fine German restaurants. Diners delight in the liver dumpling soup, tender sauerbraten, prime rib, and goose shanks. Open for dinner.

Sanford Restaurant, 1547 N. Jackson Street, (414) 276-9608. This spot opened in 1989 and is adored by restaurant critics. Chef and owner Sanford "Sandy" D'Amato, who grew up here above his grandfather's Italian grocery store, was named one of the Top Ten chefs in the country by food guru James Beard. That's just one of the restaurant's national accolades. Superb Italian cuisine with an imaginative spin. Seafood, Italian dishes. Reservations recommended. Open for dinner.

Serb Memorial Hall, 5101 W. Oklahoma Avenue, (414) 545-6030. In town on a Friday night? Chances are, traffic on the southwest side of the city is heading toward this famous no-frills fish fry. At some places, atmosphere is part of the price of admission. Here, the draw is the reasonably priced, melt-in-your-mouth fish.

Third Ward Cafe, 225 E. St. Paul Avenue, (414) 224-0895. Historical spot serves fine northern Italian dishes. Chicken breast with artichoke hearts, chicken-filled ravioli. Open for lunch and dinner.

Three Brothers Restaurant, 2414 S. St. Clair Street, (414) 481-7530. This is a must for those who love landmarks. The 1897 building once was the pride and joy of the Schlitz brewery. This is where the famous brew was created, and the feeling of an Old World pub is still here. Serbian food choices include several decidedly good chicken dishes. A charming Bayview area and an ethnic neighborhood restaurant, but not easy to find. Look for St. Clair on exiting Russell Street.

SHOPPING

Milwaukee may not be as large as Chicago, but when it comes to shopping for old and unusual finds, the city is top-notch. Here are a few choice places to start your search.

Grand Avenue Mall, west of the river and south of Wisconsin Avenue. The original four-block shopping area opened its doors in 1915 to gasps that it was ahead of its time. When it reinvented itself and opened amid skylights, gardens, and glass in the 1970s (shops on the first level, restaurants on the second floor), it was a marvel of architecture, again heralded as an innovative palace of pleasures. Today, with all the grand malls dotting the country, it doesn't seem the superstructure it once did, but fine shops remain, connected by indoor walkways.

Milwaukee Antique Center, 341 N. Milwaukee Street, (414) 276-0605.

Milwaukee has some of the state's oldest establishments, and this is another one of those distinctive places. The oldest antique center in Wisconsin has three floors of odd, offbeat, and interesting antiques, collectibles, and art to peruse. Open daily.

Usinger's Famous Sausage, 1030 N. Old World Third Street, (414) 276-9105 or (800) 558-9998. If you want to take home sausages made from authentic, old German recipes, Fred Usinger's is the place. Usinger, a sausage maker in his native Germany, arrived in Milwaukee from Frankfurt in the late 1870s, with a little bit of savings and lots of sausage recipes. Since that time, "America's Finest Sausage" has been cooking up trademark sausages made from beef and pork. Visit the early 1900s store for a trip back in time. Just follow the scent of wood smoke in the air.

Gusty day in Milwaukee about 1912.

MILWAUKEE SUBURBS

If time allows during the Milwaukee weekend, get out in the suburbs to enjoy some of the attractions. You can either stay in the city and take the easy drives to some of these spots, or you can stay in one of the suburbs and come into the city for the day. Either way, here are just a few of many choice places that will round out a visit to the area.

HISTORIC STIES AND ATTRACTIONS

Clark House Museum, 206 E. Wisconsin Avenue, Pewaukee, (262) 691-0233. Home of the Pewaukee Historical Society, the museum, a former stagecoach inn built in 1844, has an assorted collection not often seen in other museums, including what was found in the home's walls during reconstruction a few years ago. The "how did they get there?" objects include well-worn shoes. A cutaway of the walls allows visitors to see the early construction. There are also interesting exhibits of arrowheads, toys, and clothing.

When visiting Pewaukee, travelers will be following the footsteps of visitors who have enjoyed this resort area west of Milwaukee since 1847. Pewaukee Lake attracts people to the area to fish, sail, swim, and enjoy the natural beauty of its shores. In the winter, the lake has the reputation of being the ice-boating capital of the world.

Genesee Woolen Mill, Highway 59, Waukesha, (262) 521-2121. An interesting countryside stop showing how freshly sheared wool is washed, dried, carded, and used for a variety of comforters, quilts, and other home accessories. Quilting material available for purchase. Call for tours.

Schlitz Audubon Center, 1111 E. Brown Deer Road, Bayside, (414) 352-2880. A 225-acre nature sanctuary, complete with hiking trails, ponds, and hands-on nature exhibits, this is a peaceful respite from the hustle and bustle of Milwaukee.

Sprecher Brewing Company, 701 W. Glendale Avenue, (414) 964-2739. Wisconsin's first and largest microbrewery. Micro simply refers to the size of the brewery: Micro means it is a smaller brewery as opposed to the brewery giants that made Milwaukee famous. One of the distinguishing features about Sprecher beer is that it is not pasteurized, in accordance with Bavarian Purity Law. To find out more about how this Old World beer is brewed, take a tour. Call for hours.

Trimborn Farm Park, 8881 W. Grange Avenue, Greendale, (414) 529-7744. This 1850 farm is the only historic park in Milwaukee County. Listed on the National Register of Historic Places, it features Victorian themes during special times of the year, such as a country Victorian Christmas.

SHOPPING

Inn at Pine Terrace, 351 Lisbon Road, Oconomowoc, (262) 567-7463. A large (13 bedrooms) beautifully restored Victorian inn. Architectural details are dazzling—hand-carved doors, double whirlpools, and marble floors. Breathtaking luxury amongst fine Eastlake furnishings.

DINING

Bartoletta's, 7616 W. State Street, Wauwatosa, (414) 771-7910. An excellent place to dine and take in one of the suburbs. Not a historical restaurant, but in a roundabout way, it has historical roots. Restaurant owner Joseph Bartoletta is the brother of Chicago's famous chef, Paul Bartoletta, of landmark

Revelers celebrate the end of Prohibition at the Schlitz brewery in 1933.

restaurant Spiaggia fame. A wide range of imaginative Italians dishes, plus pizza baked the "old country" way, in woodburning ovens. Open for dinner.

Cafe Vienna Fine Dining, 17700 W. Capitol Drive, Brookfield, (262) 783-6100. In the midst of the Early American Stonewood Village, this country cafe features classic Viennese dishes like schnitzel and many other European-influenced entrees and desserts. Call for hours.

Jack Pandl's Whitefish Bay Inn, 1319 E. Henry Clay Street (Highway 32), Whitefish Bay, (414) 964-3800. This superb spot has been here since 1915 and is designated an official Milwaukee County landmark. Probably best known for excellent German pancakes, but the long and legendary menu also features excellent whitefish and duck. Open for lunch and dinner. Sunday brunch is a champagne sit-down affair (not buffet).

Jerry's Old Town Inn, N116 W15841, Main Street, Germantown, (262) 251-4455. Historic landmark in an early 20th-century farm setting. Black Angus steaks, barbecue, Cajun cooking, baby back ribs. Open for dinner.

Red Circle Inn, N44 W33013 Watertown Plank Road, Nashotah, (262) 367-4883. If your goal is to eat in the oldest restaurant around, you've hit pay dirt here. The Red Circle, which opened its doors in 1848, is the oldest restaurant in Wisconsin. It opened as a stagecoach stop between Milwaukee and Watertown. Besides that, they serve gourmet selections, including veal, lamb, wild rice and duck, and seafood. Consider the lofty double-chocolate mousse for dessert. Open for dinner.

Sebastiano's Landing, W278 N2315 Prospect Avenue, Pewaukee, (262) 691-2622. Lakeside dining on the south shore of Pewaukee Lake. Soups, salads, pizza, burgers, fresh daily seafood, and steaks. Open for lunch and dinner. Take Exit 290 at I-94 to County SS and Pewaukee Lake.

SHOPPING

Just A Little Bit Country, N2 W22496 Bluemound Road, (262) 542-8050. This variety of country shops, featuring antiques and interesting new and old collectibles, is situated on an 1859 farmstead called the Solomon Conright Farm. It is a fun place to lose yourself for a while.

Pinewood Galleries, 9724 W. Forest Home Avenue, Hales Corners, (414) 529-3638 or (800) 472-4ART.

THE MILWAUKEE AREA AT A GLANCE
MUSEUMS

Charles Allis Art Museum: Art collection of Charles Allis, a founder of Allis Chalmers, a major Milwaukee company. His collection of more than 1,000 pieces spans 2,000 years, and is housed in a stately 1909 Tudor mansion.

Clark House Museum: Toys, clothing, arrowheads, and more. Pewaukee.

Milwaukee Art Museum: The museum has more than 20,000 works of art, representing the 15th century through the present.

Milwaukee County Historical Center: Listed on the National Register of Historic Places, this 1913 neoclassical building, originally the Second Ward Savings Bank, houses wonderful collections of artifacts set up as interior views of 19th-century offices and shops.

Milwaukee Public Museum: Among the highlights of this world class museum are a walk-through Costa Rican rain forest (the walk-through concept was initiated at this museum in the 1890s) and "Streets of Old Milwaukee."

Villa Terrace: A museum of decorative arts, including art, furniture, and home accessories, are in an elegant 1923 home.

HISTORICAL SITES AND ATTRACTIONS

Allen Bradley Clock: Landmark clock ranks as the second largest in the world, behind Big Ben in London. Not just for telling time, it's a landmark for boats on the waterways.

Boerner Botanical Gardens: Formal gardens like those in merry old England. Ongoing environmentally educational events and historically interesting workshops.

Historic Third Ward: A densely populated neighborhood that was home to several ethnic communities in the 1890s. It's now a trendy place with artsy shops, restaurants and a theater district.

Walkers Point: This is Milwaukee's first National Historic District.

OTHER HISTORICAL SPOTS

Historic Turner Restaurant: Built in 1882 as a meeting hall for the Turners (European gymnastics enthusiasts), this historic restaurant features American food and German specialties.

Mader's German Restaurant: A "no food like German food" attraction since 1902. Bavarian kitsch atmosphere.

Miller Brewery: Once Frederick Miller arrived from Germany in 1855, he immediately began brewing beer. Brewery tours include historic brewing equipment in the Caves Museum, a segment of the original "cooler" where beer was stored.

Milwaukee Antique Center: The oldest antique center in the state has three floors of odd, offbeat, and interesting antiques.

Mitchell Park Domes: Three seven-story, curved glass spheres, covering extraordinary gardens. The Domes were constructed between 1959 and 1967, replacing the 1898 Old Conservatory and Sunken Gardens.

Pabst Mansion: Built between 1890 and 1893, this 37-room, 14-fireplace, Bavarian castle once was the home of the Captain Frederick Pabst family. The conservatory is so large it was once used to display Pabst brewery items. Tours.

Pfister Hotel: Elegant 1893 hotel near Lake Michigan is more than a lodging establishment—it has several well-known restaurants.

Three Brothers Restaurant: The 1897 building was once the pride and joy of the Schlitz brewery. This is where the famous brew was created, and the feeling of an Old World pub atmosphere is still here. Serbian food choices. Bayview.

HISTORICAL EVENTS AND FESTIVALS
Ethnic festivals abound in Milwaukee.
These are a few that are held at Henry Maier Festival Park:
African World Festival
Asian Moon Fest
Festa Italiana
Fiesta Mexicana
German Fest (the largest German festival in the U.S.).
Indian Summer Festival
Irish Fest
Polish Fest

CHAPTER 12

BEYOND MILWAUKEE

RE-CREATING THE PAST

The town of Hamilton has preserved numerous historic structures; the town has been named a National Historic District.

THE ITINERARY FOR this historical trek beyond the close-in suburbs of Milwaukee is nice in that it is very manageable in a weekend but offers a rich variety of things to see. For proximity's sake, visitors can stop first in the timeless old village of Cedarburg, a mere five miles north of Milwaukee County and three miles west of Interstate 43/Highways 32 and 57. After that, it's off to Port Washington, situated 12 miles northeast on Lake Michigan. Check out the port, then head west on Highway 33 for only 20 miles to West Bend. From there, Hartford is 16 miles southwest. After that, meander past Holy Hill and head south of I-94 to Eagle and Old World Wisconsin. Despite the multiple destinations, travelers will end up less than an hour southwest of the heart of Milwaukee. It's all an easy two-day drive.

CEDARBURG

In the early 1840s, once German immigrants were drawn to the power-producing potential of Cedar Creek, life along its banks was never the same again. For history buffs, Cedarburg, 20 miles north of Milwaukee, is a must-see place where they can soak up the atmosphere of an historical gem.

To understand the origin of this charming settlement, you have to know a bit about rocks, water, and Germans. In 1844, Frederick Hilgen and William Schroeder, two immigrants looking for a place to settle, followed their instincts north. They walked the 20 miles from Milwaukee to the village of Hamilton.

Dissatisfied, they cleared trees and cut a road northwest. When they heard the sound of falling, crashing water, their instincts paid off. Frugal as they were, they recognized a source of free energy when they saw it. Soon, they were owners of streamside land, where they constructed an enormous gristmill. A store and a smattering of log shanties followed, the early beginnings of a new community called Cedarburg, built along the banks of Cedar Creek.

In 1864, with the Civil War was in full force and wool was in fierce demand, an imposing structure known as the Wittenberg Mill was built. Today, the five-story mill, with walls 32 inches thick, is one of the town's predominant landmarks. The massive structure was built entirely by hand from stones quarried from the nearby creek bed.

What stones these were. To understand why this historic town looks different from other preserved communities, you have to understand the origin of its building materials. Many of the 104 buildings in the National Historic District were constructed with an unusual limestone called Niagara dolomite. This craggy, blue-gray stone is unique to the area—it is found in the great divide region west of Lake Michigan, and where the Great Lakes and the Mississippi River spin off.

In the late 1880s, when the mill business began to grow, so did news about the creekside storybook village. Travelers journeyed to the town by horse and buggy from up and down the Lake Michigan shoreline, from nearby Milwaukee, and as far away as Chicago. What they came for was rest and recuperation from the hectic life they left behind.

Visitors today seek the same sort of respite and diversion. But the transition from late 1880s to the 21st century did not happen automatically. After many flourishing decades, the era of the mills came to a close, and at this point the community could have folded. The opposite happened.

Cedarburg planners realized visitors were interested in making the drive north of Milwaukee so they could get a close look at an old stone village seemingly lost in time. Holding onto the time-warp identity, the resurgence of Cedarburg began. A frenetic restoration began in the late 1960s. By then, many of Milwaukee's historical buildings had gone the way of the wrecking ball. But it would not happen in Cedarburg—fiercely stubborn residents were determined to save the local structures. Not content to save downtown buildings alone, residents worked to salvage historical buildings in the surrounding area.

Iowa may have the bridges of Madison County, but Cedarburg can claim its own picturesque covered bridge. Three miles north on Washington Avenue, at Highways 60 and 143, is Covered Bridge Park, which encompasses 12 acres along Cedar Creek. The centerpiece is the 1876 bridge, believed to be the last original covered bridge in Wisconsin. Originally called the Red Bridge, the enclosed pathway that crosses Cedar Creek near Cedarburg was one of about 40 covered bridges in the state. Now it is the only one that remains.

Farmers petitioned the town of Cedarburg back in 1876 to replace the bridge that was continuously becoming washed out, a chronic problem for local commuters. The farmers won their case, and the project began with pine logs, cut and milled in the Baraboo area, then transported to Cedar Creek. The style of construction, now considered rare, is called lattice truss. The intricate workmanship of three-by-10-inch planks was interlaced and secured by two-inch wooden pins. The bridge, which is now in semiretirement—a modern road was set next to it to accommodate traffic—can still be walked. Nearby is a pleasant picnic area that includes grills and tables.

If you can't get to Cedarburg during other times of the year, schedule a visit the first weekend in December. For more than two decades, the town has offered a juried arts-and-crafts show that showcases work by some of most talented artisans in the state. You will find jewelry, paintings, home accessories, wearable art, and many other exquisite finds.

Be prepared: This is not Cedarburg at its most quiet time of the year (not that there are many of those—the town averages around 30,000 visitors a month). Because of the spell of the historic village, dressed up for the holidays and combined with the high quality arts and crafts show, expect throngs of curious shoppers. Even so, it is a treat to step back in time when the town is adorned in holiday gear.

To most visitors, the impression left by a restored Cedarburg is that it feels like home—like the hometown they came from or longed to have been from. In Remembering Main Street: An American Album, a book celebrating small-town life of a bygone era, Pat Ross describes Cedarburg as one of 10 U.S. communities with a thriving downtown that still reminds visitors of its vigorous past.

The town that revived itself never lost its Old World identity. Downtown buildings along Washington Avenue, the city's main street, have been transformed into interesting shops and innovative arts. Cedarburg has gone from sleepy to prosperous. Most are drawn to the artisan and antique shops for several blocks on each side of the street. Serious shoppers love Cedarburg because of the number of antique shops specializing in specific collectibles such as rare jewelry and lamps.

Probably the best place to begin your exploration of the town is the Cedarburg General Store Museum. In a tin-ceilinged old building, this is an escape route to the past. Opened in July 1999, the museum, in the newly restored circa 1860 building, holds a marvelous collection of antique advertis-

The Cedarburg River.

ing art, such as old lard cans, Nicolet rolled oats, Oscar Mayer packaging, and Depression-era treasures. Another reason to head to this landmark is that it houses the Cedarburg Visitors Center and Chamber of Commerce.

For more information, contact the Chamber of Commerce and Visitors Center, W61 N480 Washington Avenue, P.O. Box 104, Cedarburg, 53012, (800) CDR-BURG; the website is www.Cedarburg.org.

One of the many interiors in the Cedarburg area that capture the spirit of nineteenth-century Wisconsin.

OTHER SITES AND ATTRACTIONS

Cedar Creek Winery, first stoplight at Bridge Road and Washington Avenue, N70 W6340 Bridge Road, (262) 377-8020. In the Cedar Creek Settlement, this regional winery is a good place to discover award-winning Wisconsin wines. Tour the cellars, taste fine whites and rich reds, or shop the gift shop. A nice selection of wine-related items, as well as other interesting gift choices.

Covered Bridge Park. Take Washington Avenue north of Cedarburg to five corners, then go north on Covered Bridge Road. Walk the last original covered bridge in the state or picnic along the banks of Cedar Creek.

The Family Farm, 328 Port Washington Road (County W), Grafton, (262) 377-6161. As the name implies, there is something for every family member here. The century-old restored farm on 46 acres has been transformed into an entertainment mecca. A farm zoo, draft horse-drawn rides, historic buildings, antique tools, gifts, deli, even winter bobsled rides.

Historic Hamilton. Take in the countryside and enjoy more history by driving a mile south of downtown Cedarburg. Hamilton, an 1840 community on the National Register of Historic Places (also a State of Wisconsin Historic Site), has lovely old stone buildings and mills.

Pioneer Village, 4880 County I, Saukville, (262) 377-4510 (the Ozaukee County Historical Society). A living museum of 17 buildings dating from 1840 to 1907. Antiques galore outfit the homes, outbuildings, barn, and railroad depot. Open Memorial Day to late October. Usually open Wednesday, Saturday, and Sunday, but call. Admission charge.

LODGING

American Country Farm, 12112 N. Wauwatosa Road, Mequon, (262) 242-0194. Stay in a charming 1844 stone cottage four miles from Cedarburg, overlooking an ancient apple orchard. Amenities include up-to-date kitchen, TV, and air conditioning. Continental breakfast.

Stagecoach Inn Bed & Breakfast and Weber House Annex, W61 N520 Washington Avenue, (888) 375-0208 or (262) 375-0208; Web site: www. stagecoach-inn-wi.com. A favorite 1800s stopover with the stagecoach trade traveling between Green Bay and Milwaukee, this is a great example of how to transform a historical building into a memorable bed-and-breakfast inn without losing its integrity. Beautifully restored, the 1853 atmosphere permeates the stone structure. There are 12 guest rooms, nine in the main stone house and three in the 1846 Weber Haus across the street. The rooms, some with fireplaces, are guaranteed to give a flavor of the past. Amenities such as whirlpools bring visitors out of their time warp.

Washington House Inn, W62 N573 Washington Avenue (Washington at Center), (800) 554-4717 or (262) 375-3550; website: www.washingtonhouse-inn.com. This cream stone building with the red brick path has plenty of history. The inn dates from 1846 when Conrad Horneffer, a German immigrant, built the Washington House as Cedarburg's first saddle shop. Over the years the inn was used as the town's first hotel, then in the 1920s, as offices and apartments.

In 1983, businessman James Pape began restoring and transforming the building. The following year, the Washington House Inn, filled with antiques including some original to the property, opened as a bed-and-breakfast inn. Inside, fresh flowers, a corner fireplace, and comfy furniture beckon. Accommodations include guest rooms in the elegant Victorian area or charming country rooms with exposed beams and modern amenities, including large whirlpools, in the country wing.

DINING

Barth's At The Bridge, N58 W6194 Columbia Road, (262) 377-0660. Art and antiques galore. Soup, salads, sandwiches. Popular entrees include prime rib, seafood, meat loaf, roast duck, soups, salads, and German dishes. Open for lunch, dinner, and Sunday brunch.

Beerntsen's Candy, in the Stagecoach Inn, (262) 377-9512. Not really a meal, but these hand-dipped chocolates and other goodies are to die for.

C. Wiesler's Saloon & Eatery, W61 N493 Washington Avenue, (262) 377-8833. Dine in or out (weather permitting) at this landmark eatery. The early 1900s bar is a beauty, lending atmosphere to this lively tin-ceilinged spot. Savory soups, hearty sandwich concoctions, seafood, grilled items.

The spirit of nineteenth-century Wisconsin life is recaptured at Old World Wisconsin.

Settlers Inn Restaurant, W63 N657 Washington Avenue, (262) 377-4466. You can't leave Cedarburg without making at least one stop here to absorb the 1800s flavor. Featured in *Midwest Living* and called the best pie place around by readers of *Milwaukee* magazine, this casual dining spot offers super sandwiches, vegetarian dishes, specialties from the grill, and as you already know, exceptional pies.

Tomaso's Italian American Restaurant, W63 N688 Washington Avenue, (262) 377-7630. Pizza lovers take note: *Milwaukee* magazine readers have anointed Tomasco's as having the best pizza in the area. In addition to the wildly popular Italian dish, the menu includes sandwiches and dinner items. Open for lunch and dinner. Next door to the easy-to-find general store.

SHOPPING

There are dozens of terrific shops in town, many of which specialize in items like elegant old lamps and antique jewelry. Here are a few places to whet your appetite.

Armbruster Jewelers, W62 N620 Washington Avenue, (262) 377-0480. An old-fashioned jewelry store serving the community since 1884. Fine jewelry, old jewelry, jewelry restoration, repair.

Cedar Creek Settlement, N70 W6340 Bridge Road, (262) 377-8020 or (800) 827-8020; website: www.cedarcreeksettlement.com. Listed on the National Register of Historic Places. Nestled on the shores of Cedar Creek, this 1864 restored woolen mill houses more than 30 shops.

Heritage Lighting, W62 N572 Washington Avenue, (262) 377-9033. If you love old lights, you will have a field day at this shop, said to have one of the best selections of antique lighting fixtures in the Midwest.

PORT WASHINGTON

This is the irresistible lakeside city that earned a reputation for playing hardball during the Civil War. Anti–Civil War rioters stormed the courthouse and were so intent on aggressively demonstrating their concerns, the Army was brought in to quell the rampage.

In addition to being a carefully restored antebellum town of note (Queen Anne houses abound), Port Washington also has plenty of nautical treasures, including a large marina (fishing charters are prevalent) plus a lighthouse with art deco styling. From Upper City Park, on the side of a bluff just north of the downtown area, you can get panoramic views of Lake Michigan and environs.

The best place to find out about the city's past is the Port Washington Historical Society Museum, 311 Johnson Street; it's usually open weekends in summer.

LODGING

Port Washington Inn, 308 W. Washington Street, (262) 284-5583, www.Port-Washington-Inn.com. About 10 minutes from Cedarburg, this serene 1903 Victorian bed and breakfast, in a quiet neighborhood, is a short stroll from Lake Michigan. Breakfast lovers are provided with a full breakfast and freshly baked treats during the day.

DINING

Port Washington has plenty of good restaurants. In fact, you could come back weekend after weekend and it would take some doing before running out of places to try. These two are among some of the popular dining out gathering places. The city is an especially good place to enjoy a wide range of fish fries.

Port Hotel, 101 E. Main Street, (262) 284-9473. Good selections including prime rib, steaks, frog legs.

The Wilson House, 200 N. Franklin Street, (262) 284-6669. Popular, good food, friendly staff.

WEST BEND

Midway between Milwaukee and Fond du Lac, not far from the Northern Unit of the Kettle Moraine State Forest and 15 minutes northeast of Hartford, West Bend is known worldwide for the production of home appliances. The city has become a cultural center of note during the last few decades, and during the 1990s it was one of the three fastest growing areas in Wisconsin.

Growth has long characterized West Bend. The Potawatomi and Menominee Indians were the first inhabitants. Then, around 1845, settlers began converging on this site because of proximity to the Milwaukee River. The river's rapids were used to harness energy and power for local sawmills and gristmills. The first sawmill was built in 1846, and in 1850 the city became the Washington County seat.

When the railroad arrived in 1873, the city's population doubled. Now boasting 28,000 residents, West Bend has been diligent about preserving its roots. Many fine old buildings representing 19th-century cream city brick, Italianate, Greek Revival, and Queen Anne styles are identifiable along Main Street, East Decorah Road (the home at 906 East Decorah was built in 1851 and is one of the oldest in town), North Sixth Avenue, Monroe Street, and Fond du Lac Avenue.

For more information, contact the West Bend Area Chamber of Commerce by dialing (262) 338-2666.

OTHER SITES AND ATTRACTIONS

Washington County Historical Museum, 320 S. 5th Avenue, (262) 335-4678. Once the 1889 Washington County Courthouse and jail, the museum houses a selection of exhibits, including an old jail cell. Free admission. Call for hours.

West Bend Art Museum, 300 S. 6th Avenue, (262) 334-9638. Founded in 1961, the museum has the world's largest collection of work by 19th-century Milwaukee and Munich artist Carl von Marr. A wide collection of art dating from the 1850s. Many special exhibits, workshops for adults and children. Free admission. Open daily. Call for hours.

DINING

Timmer's, 5151 Timmer Bay Road, (262) 338-8666. A must when you are in the area. To get here you have to drive a bit out of town to Big Cedar Lake,

Wisconsin has long been an attraction for a variey of waterfowl.

but this spot, listed on the National Registry of Historic places, is a treasure. Fish fries, Sunday brunch, supper club fare. The old-time ambiance is here, as it might well be, since the building was constructed in 1864. Open daily. Call for hours.

HARTFORD

Forty miles northwest of Milwaukee, Hartford is worth a side trip primarily because of the Wisconsin Automotive Museum. The facility houses several old Kissels, which were manufactured in Hartford for nearly three decades, and about 80 other antique vehicles. The Kissel Motor Car Company once was Wisconsin's second largest automaker. It started producing the Kissels in 1906 and continued until 1931, when it was the largest manufacturer in the city. The museum is located at 147 N. Rural Street, (262) 673-7999.

The city was settled in 1843 but didn't begin to grow until 1855, when the railroad reached Hartford. Once the rail line was in, several industries sprang up. Hartford once had three tanneries (the oldest tannery in Wisconsin is here), a brewery, and a farm-equipment manufacturer, which was the forerunner of the Kissel company.

Architectural attractions of note include the Otto Kissel House at 134 South Street, a 1905 structure now listed on the National Register of Historic Places that was built by Otto for his bride. If you're interested in seeing the original Kissel home, go to 402 Sumner Street and look over the 1880 landmark.

One of the town's recent achievements is the restoration of the old Chandelier Ballroom at 700 S. Main Street. The Hartford area Rotary Club spent $500,000 to restore the building so it can be used as a community dining, dancing, and recreational center.

LODGING

Jordan House Bed & Breakfast, 81 S. Main Street, (262) 673-5643. A lovely Victorian loaded with period antiques. This four-bedroom beauty is a conveniently short walk to downtown antique shops and restaurants.

EAGLE

The drive from Hartford to Eagle is short but engaging as you head west out of Hartford on Highway 60, then turn left (south) on Highway 67. Motor through Oconomowoc and over I-94, deep into the Southern Unit of the Kettle Moraine State Forest. Here lies the village of Eagle and, on its southern edge, Old World Wisconsin, the largest outdoor museum of immigrant history in the country. From Hartford, it is 40 miles and at least a century away.

The first time I took my three children here, it was a hard sell. "Who wants to go out in the country and see old buildings?" they wondered. The surprise, to them, was that they loved Old World Wisconsin, begging to return time and again. We've traipsed through the 19th-century log houses, barns, farm buildings, schools, and churches so many times I often thought I could fill in for the costumed guides.

The Koepsel House, a replica of a German farmstead in Wisconsin, is one of 10 such ethnic re-creations at Old World Wisconsin.

Each time there is something new to see, and each time visitors can interact with the guides doing household tasks like stirring stews and, in character, talking about what their family would eat that night. Or, there is the schoolmarm at the one-room schoolhouse who strictly disciplines the children who don't know the answers to the blackboard questions by relegating them to standing in the corner. Or, travelers can take in the attributes of the sauna at the Finnish farmstead.

Old World Wisconsin, run by the State Historical Society, is a living, breathing outdoor facility stretched over 576 acres on the eastern edge of the Kettle Moraine State Forest. The place is so big it is best to get around via the trams that make continuous circuits of the property. However, plan on doing some walking, even if you take the tram, which costs $2 per person. If you walk to the each of the settlements, the circuit encompasses two and one-half miles.

Old World Wisconsin holds historical interest for all members of the family. It interprets farm and village life of 10 farmsteads, representing ethnic and cultural lifestyles of various groups of people who came to Wisconsin to build new lives.

Visitors wonder at the origin of the 19th-century buildings, representing about 16 different immigrant structures. The buildings were found in all corners of the state, then brought to the site and adapted for use in the settlements. Many of the buildings, particularly the barns, are simply marvelous architectural creations—breathtaking buildings, most seen only in history books. This is a fascinating spot and an integral part of Wisconsin's history.

It's open 10 a.m. to 5 p.m., early May through October, and there is an admission fee. Call (262) 594-6300 for special events, like the 1876 Independence Day celebration, or postseason events such as sleigh rides and "Christmas Through the Years."

Old World Wisconsin is a continuously evolving project. In 1998 it added Pleasant Ridge, a replica of an African-American community founded by freed slaves in Wisconsin. The original Pleasant Ridge was located in Grant County, five miles southwest of Lancaster in the southwestern part of the state.

African-American families began putting down stakes in Pleasant Ridge in 1850 when the Shepard family, slaves from Virginia, arrived. After a few years, and the Shepards became landowners, the first African-American family in the area to do so. They purchased farms for $1.50 an acre.

As Pleasant Ridge grew it consisted of more than 50 African-Americans, as well as German, Irish, and English farmers. A strong sense of community bonded the farmers. Together they built a log schoolhouse in 1873 and the United Brethren Church in 1884. The site offers insight into the unique partnership among Wisconsin farmers who worked together to develop and shape a community.

Visitors to the settlement, the first African-American exhibit at the site, can see a replica of the Pleasant Ridge United Brethren Church, and the restored chapel overlooking 18 memorial gravestones. The town cemetery can still be viewed in its original surroundings near Lancaster.

LODGING

Eagle Centre House, W370 S9590 Highway 67, (262) 363-4700. Relax at a five-bedroom, 1846 Greek Revival manor house, once a stagecoach inn. Set on 20 acres, this historical getaway has been featured in Country Living and Recommended Country Inns.

Novel's Country Inn and Coach House, 229 E. Main Street, (262) 594-3729. Why stay in an inn when you can stay in a historic coach house? This 1890s home features a sun parlor, library, and plenty of comfortable antique furnishings. Stay in the inn, which comes with breakfast, or, if you choose the coach house, you will be on your own for breakfast. The coach house has whirlpools, fireplaces, and an abundance of historical atmosphere.

DINING

Clausing Barn Restaurant. At Old World Wisconsin, this octagonal 1897 barn features cafeteria-style food with an emphasis on ethnic specials and a popular fish fry that runs 5 p.m. to 9 p.m. Friday nights. Hours may vary—typically open 11 a.m. to 5 p.m. Monday through Friday and weekends July and August.

Beyond Milwaukee at a Glance

MUSEUMS

Old World Wisconsin: Run by the State Historical Society, it's the largest outdoor museum of immigrant history in the country. A living, breathing outdoor museum stretched over 576 acres on the eastern edge of the Kettle Moraine State Forest's Southern Unit. Sixteen different immigrant structures. Historical interest for all members of the family. Eagle.

Port Washington Historical Society Museum: A wide range of historical information and exhibits.

Washington County Historical Museum: Once the 1889 Washington County Courthouse and jail, the museum houses a selection of exhibits, including an old jail cell. West Bend.

West Bend Art Museum: The world's largest collection of work by 19th-century Milwaukee and Munich artist Carl von Marr.

HISTORICAL SITES AND ATTRACTIONS

Covered Bridge Park: Twelve acres along Cedar Creek. The centerpiece of the park is the 1876 bridge, believed to be the last original covered bridge in Wisconsin.

Downtown Cedarburg: There are 104 buildings included in the National Historic District. Many of those along Washington Avenue, the city's main street, have been transformed into shops and restaurants.

Wittenburg Mill: The city's famous gristmill. Cedarburg.

OTHER HISTORICAL STOPS

Armbruster Jewelers: An old-fashioned jewelry store serving the community since 1884. Cedarburg.

Cedar Creek Settlement: Nestled on the shores of Cedar Creek, this 1864 restored woolen mill houses more than 30 shops. Cedarburg.

Historic Hamilton: This 1840 community is on the National Register of Historic Places and is also a State of Wisconsin historic site.

Pioneer Village: A living museum of 17 buildings dating from 1840 to 1907. Saukville.

Port Washington Inn: 1903 bed and breakfast is just a short stroll from Lake Michigan. Port Washington.

Settlers Inn Restaurant: A popular dining spot with 1800s atmosphere. Cedarburg.

Stagecoach Inn Bed & Breakfast: This 1853 inn, once a stagecoach stop between Green Bay and Milwaukee, has been beautifully restored. Stagecoach Inn visitors are also accommodated in the inn's 1846 Weber Haus establishment across the street. Cedarburg.

Timmer's: Listed on the National Registry of Historic Places, the site of this popular supper club was constructed in 1864. On Big Cedar Lake, near West Bend.

Washington House Inn: Built in 1846, it was the town's first saddle shop. Charming stone building in the midst of town now is an elegant bed and breakfast establishment. Cedarburg.

HISTORICAL EVENTS AND FESTIVALS

APRIL

Lang's Delafield Antiques Show, Delafield.
Heart of the Park Antique Show, West Allis.

MAY

Civil War Days, Brookfield.
Historic Preservation Week, Waukesha.
Crossroads Rendezvous, Saukville (Ozaukee County).

JUNE

Stone and Century House Tour, Cedarburg.
French and Indian Encampment, Saukville.

JULY

Old Farm Days, Saukville (Ozaukee County).

AUGUST

Summer Children's Day, Old World Wisconsin, Eagle.

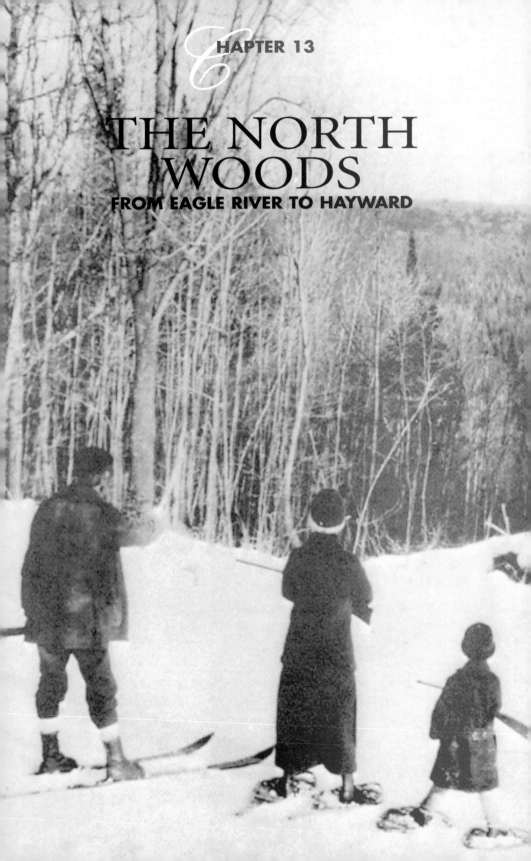

CHAPTER 13

THE NORTH WOODS
FROM EAGLE RIVER TO HAYWARD

A North Woods logging crew sits down for a midday dinner around 1905.

THE STATE OF Wisconsin can easily deceive travelers, no matter whether they are visitors or residents. The southern half, from east to west, seems to entail a reasonable driving distance and is, in fact, only about 180 driving miles wide. All that changes up north—travelers who motor west from Marinette on Lake Michigan to Hudson will find at least 270 miles on their odometer.

Before going further, we should decide where the "real" area known as the North Woods begins. A number of writers, tourists, and natives consider anything north of Highway 8 to be the "real" North Woods. The area includes towns like Rice Lake, Spooner, and Rhinelander but excludes Amery, Tomahawk, Wausau, and Marinette.

There is, however, a more accurate and surprising way to define the area, one that uses botanical designations. The Sierra Club Naturalist's Guide, The North Woods, indicates that the true North Woods lies above a line separating species of plants. Northern plants are generally found north of a line running roughly from Polk County southeast to Marshfield, then east to Green Bay, then sharply southeastward as far as Ozaukee County just north of Milwaukee! Nevertheless, for weekend historic purposes, we'll consider Vilas and Sawyer Counties representative of the North Woods.

The first inhabitants of the region were Native Americans, who arrived here as the glaciers were retreating. They left few clues as to how their daily lives were lived, most likely because everything they used has decayed and decomposed. French explorers arrived in the 17th century to find the natives supporting themselves with a mix of hunting, gathering, and agriculture.

The early white settlers established scattered outposts as they trapped voraciously. Several species of furbearing animals, such as the beaver, were virtually wiped out. In the 1830s, the land up here began to take on a different look, as the almost all the original-growth timber was cut down and used for the building boom that the young country was experiencing. Farmers further cleared the land but found the soil and climate unfriendly.

Tourists followed. They came from Chicago, Milwaukee, and other Midwest cities, especially in the summer to avoid the sweltering heat. Fishing, hunting, and other forms of recreation became popular pastimes in the region. In the winter, snowmobiles and cross-country skis opened up more of the wilderness to weekenders.

In terms of natural history, much of northern Wisconsin lies atop the great Canadian Shield. This is a solid piece of rock that runs from this area westnorthwest across half of North America. Because glaciers passed back and forth across it, the shield harbors a lot of water, above and below ground level. In fact, nearly 40 percent of the surface of Vilas County is comprised of water, in the form of lakes and streams.

Some species of the flora and fauna of the North Woods have changed dramatically over the years. The original growth timber, mainly white pines that grew to heights of more than one hundred feet and thus made wonderful building material, have nearly disappeared. This is because it's been estimated that about 60 percent of the wood framing used in American homes came from the North Woods. The Nicolet National Forest and Northern Highland American Legion State Forest show few original trees.

THE VAST NORTH WOODS

The area's woods and water are big magnets for year-round visitors, with large crowds descending upon the area in summer. No matter what the time of year, the 137-mile stretch between Eagle River in Vilas County and Hayward in Sawyer County will give visitors an accurate picture of the vast North Woods and a glimpse into the area's rich history. We suggest starting out in Eagle River and proceeding on Highway 70 to Fifield. Head north on Highway 13 to a point just past the village of Glidden, then turn left or west onto Highway 77 (Great Divide National Highway) to reach Hayward. Eagle River is 275 miles northeast of Minneapolis-St. Paul, 330 miles north of Chicago, 241 miles north of Milwaukee, and 216 miles north of Madison.

The Eagle River–Hayward drive will take you through three large segments of national or state forest and in or near a pair of Native American reservations. The Lac du Flambeau Chippewa make their home in western Vilas County, while the Lac Courte Oreilles live in Sawyer County, just south of Hayward.

VILAS COUNTY

Travelers interested in the early history of the area's Native Americans will want to visit WaSwaGoning, the Lac du Flambeau Chippewa reservation 36 miles west of Eagle River. The reservation, which has been a permanent community since 1745, is an authentic Ojibwa village on beautiful Moving Cloud Lake. Visitors are shown historically significant displays of Indian culture. Here, too, is the George W. Brown Jr. Museum and Cultural Center. Those with the time can sign up for a workshop in weaving baskets, creating moccasins, or making beaded items. It is all well worth it to spend some time examining this historically interesting site showcasing Indian life. Call (715) 588-3303 or (715) 588-9052.

The Vilas County Historical Museum in Sayner presents a historical perspective on the area that vividly contrasts with the one portrayed by the Chippewa. It is a must-see for anyone interested in the European version of North Woods pioneer history. The museum has expanded several times since its inception in 1959, resulting in an extensive collection of historic exhibits and memorabilia from the 19th century. Sayner is located about 20 miles northwest of Eagle River on Highway 155. It's open daily Memorial Day through mid-October and there is no admission charge. Call (715) 542-3388 for more information.

For a glimpse into what life was like for North Woods settlers in the late 19th century, be sure to visit the Dr. Kate Museum, 923 2nd Avenue, in Woodruff. Dr. Kate, the "Angel on Snowshoes," as she was called, was the area's pioneer doctor who often visited patients by traveling on snowshoes. She was highlighted on a popular television show, "This is Your Life," in 1954 for getting a hospital built in tiny Woodruff. Schoolchildren also got behind the cause and collected a million pennies to help the hospital building fund. Learn how the million pennies became a $20 million bequest. The museum is affiliated with the State Historical Society of Wisconsin. It's open mid-June through Labor Day. Call (715) 356-9421 or (715) 356-5562.

OTHER SITES AND ATTRACTIONS

Carl's Wood Art Museum, Eagle River, (715) 479-1883. Carl Schels migrated to the North Woods from Bavaria in 1920 and began carving up a

A crew tackles the dangerous job of breaking a logjam on the Peshtigo River in 1907.

North Woods loggers relaxing and getting warm in the early 1900s.

storm. The shop and museum have amazing sculptures made from trees, most created with chain saws. Open Memorial Day through mid-October. Just west of McDonald's.

Northwoods Children's Museum, 346 W. Division Street, Eagle River, (715) 479-4623. A hands-on museum which adults will enjoy as much as children. The new museum (it opened in 1998) features life in the North Woods through a variety of exhibits such as a mini–log cabin. There is even a fishing pond. Call for hours. Admission charge.

Three Lakes Winery, Highways 45/32 and County A, Three Lakes, (800) 944-5434. For more than 25 years, the McCain family has been producing cranberry wine as well as a range of other fruit and berry wines. Fruits and berries used in the operation include cranberries, blackberries, strawberries, apricots, and rhubarb. Tours, complimentary wine tasting, and gift shop. Free tours in summer and fall. Call for hours. In the old railroad depot.

Trees for Tomorrow, Eagle River, (715) 479-6456. Nature programs, weekend ski packages, and a chance to learn about preserving and growing trees at this nonprofit center and school in association with the U.S. Forest Service. Near the Nicolet National and Northern Highland–American Legion forests (dorms with private baths).

EVENTS

World Championship Snowmobile Derby, Eagle River, (715) 479-2764. Huge crowds congregate at the derby pavilion to see snowmobiles typically reach speeds of one hundred mph. This is often referred to as the "best little racetrack in the world." Mid-January. Call for dates and times.

LODGING

There is no other area of the state that has more diverse accommodations than the North Woods, particularly around the Minocqua and Eagle River areas. The following represents a fraction of lodging establishments that have either been part of North Woods history for some time or are special in their own right. The majority of the require a minimum two-night stay during the peak summer season, mid-June through Labor Day.

The Braywood, Highway 45 at Catfish Lake Road, Eagle River, (715) 479-6494. A North Woods landmark since 1949 when Billy Bray and Frances Woods, dancers who performed with Lawrence Welk and others, built the lakeshore lodge. One of its claims to fame was that it was the first waterside inn in the state with private baths. Travelers can rent motel units, suites, and cottages in addition to the main lodge. Restaurant on site serves a mean Brayburger.

East Highland School Bed & Breakfast, W 4342 County D, Phillips, (715) 339-3492. Here is a fun place to stay for travelers who have yet to sleep overnight in a school building. This turn-of-the-century school has four bedrooms, a library, lots of country charm, and abundant space to spread out on the surrounding property. Bring a fishing pole, because you will find a trout pond and covered bridge here.

Inn at Pinewood, 1820 Silver Forest Lane, Eagle River, (715) 477-2377. A splendid inn on Carpenter Lake. Elegance in a wondrous setting deep in the forest at the end of a winding road. Eight bedrooms, whirlpools, fireplaces, lakeside views, two miles from Nicolet National Forest. The pampering continues with a full breakfast, including freshly baked pastries.

Pap-Qua Estates on Trout Lake, 3552 Rocky Reef Road, Boulder Junction, (715) 356-5352. An enchanting estate, more than one hundred years old, features 300-year-old virgin pines on the property. Private island and excellent spot for fishing in the spring-fed lake. For rent: three restored vacation homes, with plenty of amenities like TV and free firewood. Visitors receive fresh flowers and an assortment of goodies when they arrive.

Pine-Aire Resort, Highway 45 at Chain of Lakes Road, Eagle River, (715) 479-9208 or (800) 597-6777. Back in the 1920s, the property was a children's camp. The compound still caters to families by offering many activities, including entertainment in the Logging Camp Kitchen and Still, outdoor sing-alongs, child performers, and bonfires. Weekly scheduled events are open to the public. Campgrounds and cottages. Boat rentals on the shore side boat dock.

Tamarack Lodge Bed & Breakfast, 7950 Bo-di-Lac Drive, Minocqua, (715) 356-7124. This is no historic lodge, but it holds plenty of historic treasures. For starters, the lodge (it has two guest bedrooms) was built with gargantuan 150-year-old logs. Breakfast, in this terrific wooded setting, is cooked on a 19th-century woodburning cookstove. The old and the new blends here, in a rustic, peaceful setting on Squirrel Lake.

White Birch Village, (715) 385-2182. Lakeside setting in Northern Highland State Forest features 12 vacation homes, many with fireplaces. The original lodge was built in the 1920s and for decades was known as Wilsie's White Birch Lodge. Back then, guests stayed in the main lodge and took their meals in the same building. Now, visitors can rent a home away from home, tucked into niches of this wondrous wooded setting. Dazzling nighttime drama via lit walkways around ponds and footbridge. Swimming beach, boating, fishing, children's play area, indoor whirlpool spa.

Whitehaven Bed & Breakfast, 1077 County F, Minocqua, (715) 356-9097. A grand home in the pines, built as a summer residence in 1922. An interesting configuration upstairs features a great room with stone fireplace and tall ceilings. Overlooking Whitefish Lake, this is a peaceful spot for sitting on the screen porch, enjoying the call of the loons and the beauty of the setting.

DINING

The North Woods has an abundance of eating establishments, from simple fare to haute cuisine, amid whispering pines and lakeside views. The following restaurants represent some of the North Woods institutions, as well as a sprinkling of historical spots with a few stories to tell. In case a visitor has never traveled in these parts, he or she soon realizes it is supper club territory—a remnant from the early- to mid-20th century. Up north, supper clubs are alive and well.

It took a good-sized cook staff to keep early lumberjacks well fed.

Black Forest Pub & Grill, Three Lakes, (715) 546-3400. It's been a landmark dining establishment for more than 60 years. Nice menu selection—a good place to come for a Friday night fish fry. Game room and bar. Open for lunch and dinner.

Bosacki's Boat House, Highway 51 at the bridge, Minocqua, (715) 356-5292. One of the more interesting restaurant stories in the north belongs to Bosacki's. The restaurant opened with a splash (pardon the pun) in 1917 in a waterside 1896 building. On July 22, 1972, a boat exploded by the gas dock and the original building was destroyed. So, did the restaurant rebuild? Not at first, but when petitions to rebuild circulated around the globe (the menu states cries to rebuild came even from Russia), the Bosackis took up the challenge. The new digs has a marina, a water-ski business, a bait and tackle shop, and a fine restaurant with a 1903 hand-carved bar. Entrees include tenderloin, steak, walleye pike sandwich, and very good burgers. After all these years, this is still a family-run place. Expect crowds, particularly on Friday nights in summer. Open for lunch and dinner.

The Chanticleer Inn & Resort, 1458 Dollar Lake Road, Eagle River, (715) 479-4486. Since 1922, the resort, with splendid waterside views of a chain of lakes, has been serving up carefully prepared entrees such as swordfish, prime rib, and chicken. Open to the public for dinner; breakfasts on weekends.

The Copper Kettle, 207 E. Wall Street, Eagle River, (715) 479-4049. Here is where it all started: the all-you-can-eat Pancake Hall of Fame. There are testimonials to the fact that crazy, brave, or famished (or maybe all of the above) diners have downed a considerable number of pancakes at one sitting (the tradition started with a 15-year-old in 1977, who stopped at 10 gargantuan pancakes). There is more here than griddle cakes: good soups, sandwiches, and entrees. Open for breakfast, lunch, and dinner.

The Guides Inn, 5421 Park Street (County M), Boulder Junction, (715) 385-2233. This is where to go for choice cuisine served in a stylish dining atmosphere. The restaurant was named for the many North Woods guides who frequented it, most notably Porter Dean, a guide famous in these parts for bringing in trophy muskie and other fish and wildlife. Beef Wellington and other specialties, like walleye (big in the Boulder Junction area), are worthy of the restaurant's reputation. Open for dinner.

Jacobi's of Hazelhurst, 9820 Cedar Falls Road (south of Minocqua, west off Highway 51), (715) 356-5591. Expect a fairy tale-like setting, complete with wooded forest, flower garden, and a whimsically painted building, decorated in splashy pinks and purples. The gourmet house specialties include the superb garlic-stuffed beef tenderloin with cognac mustard sauce. Call for hours; no reservations.

Little Bohemia Lodge, Highway 51, south of Manitowish Waters, (715) 543-8433. Plenty of history here, mainly revolving around one event in 1934. That is when the FBI received at tip that John Dillinger and Baby Face Nelson were staying in one of the lodge's cabins. When the FBI arrived, gunfire ensued, but Dillinger and Nelson escaped. Today, the landmark is a museum of sorts (the hideout cabin is on Star Lake), but the main draw is a chance to eat dinner or lunch (in summer) where the gangsters used to hang out.

Logging Camp Kitchen, 4443 Chain O' Lakes Road (at Pine-Aire Resort), (715) 479-9208 or (800) 597-6777. Hearty breakfasts, pizza, sandwiches, fine wines, and nice selection of culinary choices for dinner. Served in an 1890s logging camp atmosphere. Open for breakfast on weekends and for dinner.

Winter of 1886 in northeastern Wisconsin's snowbound pinery.

Ma Bailey's, 8591 Woodruff Road, Minocqua, (715) 358-6830. A restaurant with a distinctive past. This spot once was a house of ill repute, a favorite stop with 1920s Chicago mobsters. Today, it keeps the legend rolling with menu selections with names like the Happy Hooker. A lively atmosphere you should see at least once on your trail of historical weekend getaways. Open for dinner.

The cook was king in the dining area, and talking at the table was not permitted.

Norwood Pines Supper Club, Highway 70, Minocqua, (715) 356-3666. Discriminating dining starts with interesting appetizers. Choose from Nor-wood Pine Cones (ask your server to describe, or be surprised by these novel creations), artichoke scampi, grilled portabella mushrooms, and others. Entrees include a honey-mustard chicken breast, coquilles St. Jacques, and succulent prime rib. Popular place for a Friday night fish fry—cod and perch baked and fried every which way. Screened porch, open in summer. Open for dinner.

Paul Bunyan's Northwoods Cook Shanty, Highway 51 between Minocqua and Woodruff, (715) 356-6270. OK, so it isn't historical, but they have been running a fun operation since the 1960s. Those who have seen every conceivable replica of a logging cook shanty will still enjoy this cheery place where families go to enjoy potato pancakes, poor man's lobster, camp-style chicken, and other fare surrounded by logging memorabilia. Open mid-May through September. Large gift shop, bakery, and tavern. Open for breakfast, lunch, and dinner.

The Plantation, Highway 51/70, Arbor Vitae, (715) 356-9000. This is one of those places whose reputation proceeds it. Now known for exceptional food, it also has a wild and rich history starting in 1938. Gambling of every conceivable notion went on here during the early years. The notoriety continued after a night watchman was killed during a robbery. In 1974, a fire left it a total loss. A high-spirited place that draws crowds for its chicken, ribs, seafood, and homemade soups. Entrees include orange roughy, lobster tails, barbecued ribs, and Plantation felt. Open Tuesday through Sunday for dinner.

T. Murtaugh's Pub & Eatery, downtown Minocqua, (715) 356-7712. This pub has really moved up in the world. In 1905, the owner of the brick building decided to move it a few blocks up the street, using a team of horses. Since then, the building has been used for many purposes, including pool hall, pharmacy, and tavern. It has had a full spectrum of names over the years, but in the early 1990s the name was changed to reflect the building's original owner. Full grill, appetizers, deli sandwiches, cocktails, beer.

The Thirsty Whale, 453 Park Street, Minocqua, (715) 356-7108. This is one of those places where people gravitate when the temperature rises (or falls, as the case may be, since it is equally popular with the snowmobile crowd). The century-old building has a good and popular Friday night fish fry.

The Whitetail Inn, 9038 County C, St. Germain, (715) 542-2541. Not a historic place, but constructed from enormous pine logs, the ambiance is lovely to behold. Steaks and seafood, including grilled salmon. Open for lunch and dinner.

HAYWARD

The Hayward area is a good place to drop anchor for a weekend in the North Woods. Once settled in, visitors can explore areas known primarily for their natural beauty, but also rich in historical significance. Ever since the area's first resort was built on Spider Lake in 1885, visitors—mostly city dwellers—have been drawn here because of the abundance of lakes and streams, rolling hills, and hardwood forests. Even before that time, lumber was king, and Hayward was a center of the local timber industry—so much so that the town was named for one of the area's pioneer lumbermen,

Eons before the loggers arrived and even before the French discovered the area as a rich source of furbearing animals, the Lac Courte Oreilles tribe of Ojibwa Nation took up residence near Hayward. LCO Indians are purported to be the first humans to occupy the area. Archaeological research dates their presence back to 5000 B.C.

For history lovers, Hayward offers plenty of romance, legend, and lore about old-time logging industries that were prevalent in these parts. Equally distinctive is the fact that this is fishing country—as in fishing for large and aggressive fish. To get a flavor for what the area was like 50 or more years ago, schedule a stay at one of the area's many old fishing lodges. It will give a fascinating insight into the idyllic pleasures of long ago.

Another opportunity to glimpse the past, albeit the fairly recent past, is presented by the Hideout (Al Capone's North Woods Retreat & Museum of the Roaring '20s), about 17 miles southeast of Hayward near Couderay, (715) 945-2746. This 400-acre former gangster compound really was a hideout for Al and his gangster friends in the 1920s. Step inside a notorious world that reveals mobsters lives amid the pines. Tours include a look at the retreat's personal furnishings in the main house, bunkhouse, jail, and gun tower. Definitely worth a look. A curiosity that also features an exceptional restaurant and ice cream parlor and, of course, the expected gift shops. The eight-car garage, where Capone used to house his limos is now the dining room and bar.

For more information, contact the Hayward Lakes Resort Association: (715) 634-4801 or (800) 724-2992.

OTHER SITES AND ATTRACTIONS

Historyland, County B, one mile east of Hayward, (715) 634-2579. Logging museum and newly created version of a logging camp. There are also an Old Freight Depot and Blacksmith Shop, cook shanty, and paddleboat rides.

National Freshwater Fishing Hall of Fame, Highway 27 and County B, Hayward, (715) 634-4440. Four and a half stories high, that is how big the muskie is in this parklike area. Walk through the giant fish and delight in all the fun; the museum is where serious fishing recognition takes place. This non-profit organization is the only place of its kind in the country that collects and exhibits memorabilia related to the sport of fishing. Then there is the World Record Gallery, where photos tell the stories of fresh water fishing. Open daily, mid-April through October. Admission fee.

LODGING

Garmisch USA, eight miles from Cable on County M, (715) 794-2204 or (800) 794-2204. This resort on Lake Namakagon has a Swiss-style ambiance. Two housekeeping homes with fireplaces, as well as lodge rooms with fireplaces. The property has a tennis court.

Lumberman's Mansion Inn, 15844 E. 4th Street, Hayward, (715) 634-3012. A visit to this impeccably restored 1887 Victorian is akin to staying in a small European hotel. Five bedrooms with rich detail linking visitors to the graciousness of the past. Convenient for jumping off to area sights and attractions. Three spacious rooms and two suites, complete with sitting rooms.

Clearing a hardwood forest near Butternut in 1895.

Loggers sitting on the "deacon's seat" in a camp near Cable in 1895.

Northland Lodge, 9181 W. Brandt Road, Hayward, (715) 462-3379. Three generations have preserved the beauty of the original 1921 hand-wrought cedar log cabins. The resort, on 175 acres, is adjacent to two class "A" muskie lakes and nature trails. Canoe, hike, bike, or swim along a sandy beach with water slide.

Ross's Teal Lake Lodge, Highway 77, Ross Road, Hayward, (715) 462-3631. Set deep in the Chequamegon National Forest, the log lodges were built in 1908. Many log buildings have been added to the retreat over the years. This family-run business offers vacation homes, cabins, a golf course, and old-fashioned lakeside serenity. Interestingly, when the property was purchased in 1908 from the Weyerhauser Lumber Company, it contained more than 30 acres of virgin hemlock and yellow birch trees. These massive trees still stand and can be seen on the golf course. Located on Teal Lake, one of Wisconsin's "quiet lakes," called that since it is illegal to cruise at speeds of more than 10 mph on the water.

Spider Lake Lodge Bed & Breakfast Inn, Hayward, (715) 462-3793 or (800) OLD-WISC. Ted Moody, said to be Al Capone's auto mechanic in Chicago, built this lodge in 1923 as a fishing retreat. Lumbermen here built it from native logs from the surrounding forest. Notice the chinking (wood pieces that fit perfectly between the grooves of the logs) in the great room and dining room. A magnificent lodge on the Spider Lake Chain, a class "A" muskie lake. Huge stone fireplace, screened porch overlooking the lake. Woodsmoke from fireplace, waves lapping shore, loons calling from lake. Seven guest rooms, rustic decor. Ask owners Min Grossi and Barb Grossi for more history about the lodge and the area. They have many stories to tell. Swimming, boating, fishing. A few miles down Murphy Boulevard.

DINING

The Beach Club, 7377 N Highland Shores Land (County K), Hayward, (715) 634-3090. Not a historic place, but worth the trip to Lac Court Oreilles to splurge in a tropical (odd, but it works) atmosphere amid the pine trees. Creole and Jamaican cooking, plus entrees such as chicken and steaks, that bring you back to North Woods reality. Open for dinner.

Diamond Dave's BBQ Shack and Resort, Big Round Lake, Hayward, (715) 462-3352. Hickory-smoked BBQ and all the trimmings, in a fun log lodge.

Garmisch USA, County M, Cable, (715) 794-2204 or (800) 794-2204. Rustic Swiss lodge resembles a Bavarian estate. Fine German cuisine on the shore of Lake Namakagon. Open daily for breakfast, lunch and dinner. Dinner reservations recommended.

Historyland Cook Shanty, County B, Hayward, (715) 634-2579. This is where to gravitate if you've been working as a lumberjack all day. It has all-you-can-eat meals with a different menu every day of the week. Sample Sunday selections: Roast chicken, homestyle ham, potatoes, potato pancakes, corn fritters, plus trimmings like baked beans, potato bread (potatoes are big here), pie, and beverages. One price for all the fixings. Open for breakfast, lunch, and dinner. One mile east of Hayward.

Sawmill Saloon, Highway 63, Hayward, (715) 634-5660. A museumlike place right off the path of the Berkie Trail. Diners won't be bored waiting for their food—there is a lot to look at, most of it donated by patrons. Mandolins on the ceiling, for instance, and old advertising paraphernalia, plus paintings of historical figures. The logging mill atmosphere is fun (country and rock bands sometimes perform) and the hearty pub fare is fine. Open for breakfast, lunch, and dinner.

SHOPPING

Nelson Bay Antiques, Nelson Bay Road, north of Hayward off Highway 63, (715) 634-2177. Since the mid-1970s, the same family has been combing the landscape for interesting antiques. Look for lamps, art, primitives, collectibles, and more. Open daily; call for hours.

The North Woods at a Glance
MUSEUMS

Carl's Wood Art Museum: Carl Schels migrated to the North Woods from Bavaria in 1920 and began carving up a storm. The shop and museum have amazing sculptures, most created with a chain saw. Eagle River.

Dr. Kate Museum: Learn about "Dr. Kate: Angel on Snowshoes." The museum tells what life was like in the North Woods in the late 19th century, from a physician's point of view. Dr. Kate was a pioneer doctor who often visited patients by traveling on snowshoes. The museum is affiliated with the State Historical Society of Wisconsin. Woodruff.

National Freshwater Fishing Hall of Fame: Walk through the giant muskie, over four stories tall. Then visit the world's largest fishing museum. It's the only place of its kind in the country that collects and exhibits memorabilia related to the sport of fishing. Hayward.

Northwoods Chidren's Museum: A hands-on museum which adults will enjoy as much as children. A variety of exhibits include a mini–log cabin and fishing pond. Three Lakes.

Railroad Memories Museum: The old OMAHA/CNW depot houses a fascinating look at Spooner's railroad heritage. Eight rooms of old railroad items, including track inspection and vehicle inspection books. N8425 Island

Lake Road (715) 635-3325, (715) 635-2752, Spooner.

Vilas County Historical Museum: North Woods pioneer history. Extensive collection of historic exhibits and memorabilia from the 19th century. Local history displays include the world's first snowmobile. Sayner.

HISTORICAL SITES AND ATTRACTIONS

WaSwaGoning: An authentic Ojibwa village, on beautiful Moving Cloud Lake. Visitors learn about Indian culture and early tribal life on this reservation which has been a permanent community since 1745. Lac du Flambeau.

OTHER HISTORICAL STOPS

Bosacki's Boat House: One of the more interesting North Woods restaurant stories belongs to Bosacki's. This popular place opened in 1917, but was destroyed when a boat exploded while refueling at Bosacki's docks. By popular demand—legend says petitions to reopen were circulated around the globe—the restaurant, still family run, was rebuilt. Minocqua.

The Braywood: A North Woods landmark lodge since 1926. Eagle River.

The Chanticleer Inn & Resort: Since 1922, the resort, with splendid views of a chain of lakes, has been serving up carefully prepared food. Open to the public for dinner, breakfasts on weekends. Eagle River.

John Heisman commemorative statue and gravesite: John Heisman, for whom the Heisman football trophy is named, died in New York, October 3, 1936, and was buried in Rhinelander, in the family plot of his second wife. Heisman was the originator and twice president of the American Football Coaches Association. After 37 years of coaching, from 1892 to 1928, he became athletic director of the Downtown Athletic Club of New York City in 1930. In 1935, the club decided to award a trophy to the country's most outstanding college football player. Heisman's statue can be seen at the Rhinelander-Oneida County Airport terminal building. His gravesite is at Forest Home Cemetery. Rhinelander.

The Hideout: This 400-acre former gangster compound really was a hideout for Al Capone and his gangster friends in the 1920s. Tours include a look at personal furnishings, main house, bunkhouse, jail, and gun tower. The eight-car garage, where Capone used to house his limos, is now the dining room and bar. Six miles north of Couderay.

Pine-Aire Resort: A camp compound since the 1920s, it caters to families by offering many activities including outdoor sing-alongs and bonfires. Eagle River.

Ross Teal Lake Lodge: Set deep in the Chequamegon National Forest, the log lodges were built in 1908. More than 30 acres of virgin hemlock and yellow birch trees still stand on the property. Hayward.

Spider Lake Lodge: Log lodge on Spider Lake was built in 1923 as a fishing retreat by Ted Moody, said to be Al Capone's auto mechanic. Now the rustic inn is a bed-and-breakfast inn with seven guest rooms. Plenty of history of the lodge and the area here. Hayward.

HISTORICAL EVENTS AND FESTIVALS

JANUARY

American Birkebeiner: North America's largest cross-country ski race. Hayward.

World Championship Snowmobile Derby: In January, huge crowds congregate at the derby pavilion to see snowmobiles typically reach speeds of one hundred mph. Eagle River.

MAY

Spring Arts and Crafts Show, Minocqua.

Journey's Marathon, Boulder Junction to Eagle River.

Holiday Antique Show, Eagle River.

Classic Car Roundup, St. Germain.

JUNE

Muskie Festival: This June fishing contest and jamboree has been feted in Hayward since 1949. Hayward.

JULY

Indian Bowl Powwows: Ojibwa dancing, colorful costumes. July through early August. Usually held on Tuesday evenings. County D (715) 588-3333, Lac du Flambeau.

AUGUST

Wisconsin Concrete Park Celebration, featuring the folk artwork of Fred Smith, Phillips (Price County).

Lazy Days Craft Show, St. Germain.

National Championship Musky Open, Eagle River.

SEPTEMBER

Northwoods Decoy and Sporting Collectible Show and Sale, Lac du Flambeau.

Antique Show and Sale, Eagle River.

Railroad Heritage Days, Spooner.

Heritage Festival of the Arts, Lac du Flambeau.

INDEX

HISTORICAL WISCONSIN GETAWAYS

INDEX

INDEX

INDEX

PHOTO CREDITS